Hammer, house of horror

behind the screams

Howard Maxford

B.T. Batsford Ltd · London

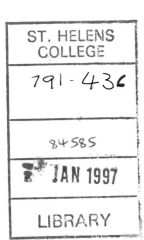
For Christopher, Peter and Terence...

For Denis Gifford, whose *Pictorial History of Horror Movies* was the first film book I ever bought...

And for my mate Lee Moone.
See, it can happen!

© Howard Maxford 1996
First published 1996
Printed in Great Britain by The Bath Press

for the publishers
B.T. Batsford Ltd
4 Fitzhardinge Street
London W1H 0AH

ISBN 0 7134 7768 7

A CIP catalogue record for this book is available from the British Library

contents

section one

behind
the screams

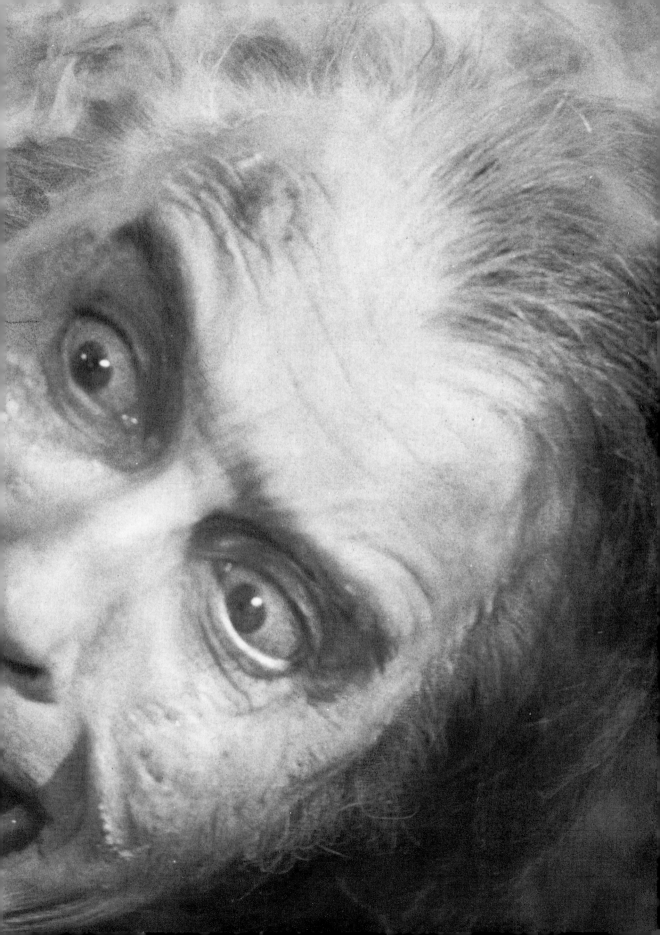

introduction

In its glory days, which roughly spanned the years 1955 to 1972, Hammer Films were regarded as Britain's leading purveyors of cinematic horror. During this period they produced a legacy of films which have remained in the public consciousness ever since. Count Dracula, Baron Frankenstein, The Mummy and Professor Quatermass are characters synonymous with the studio, thanks to such classics as *Dracula*, *The Curse of Frankenstein* and *The Quatermass Experiment*, all of which continue to be late night favourites on television around the world, while the advent of video, cable and satellite has introduced the studio's output to a whole new generation of fans and horror devotees.

The studio's penchant for all things Gothic made it a force to be reckoned with in the fifties and sixties, at a time when audiences were deserting the cinema in droves for the rather more accessible delights of television. Yet while other studios battled to survive the coming of the one-eyed monster, Hammer sailed through this period on the waves of profit and success, thanks to their proven formula. Indeed, they even picked up the Queen's Award to Industry in 1968 for bringing £1.5 million worth of American dollars into the country for three years running.

However, there was much more to Hammer than just horror: psychological thrillers, prehistoric epics, swashbucklers and comedies all played an important part in the studio's success story - in fact their 1971 TV spin-off *On The Buses* ironically proved to be their biggest

financial hit, pulling in an impressive £1 million in British receipts alone - and this during a time when the British film industry itself had all but collapsed.

During its heyday, Hammer's product was lapped up by audiences around the world, yet to the critical fraternity their output was sneered at and derided. The studio's landmark production of *Dracula* in 1958 was greeted with disdain by many reviewers of the day, yet the film is now cited as a classic and a model of its kind. Not all of Hammer's output is worthy of comparison with *Dracula*, of course, and a lot of their films fall below this high watermark - yet over the years, a number of their films have been re-assessed and given their due place in the horror film hall of fame.

With Peter Cushing and Christopher Lee, the studio found the perfect incarnations of Baron Frankenstein and Dracula, and successfully launched the two actors onto the international scene. Meanwhile, with Terence Fisher, Hammer had the perfect journeyman director to interpret their ghoulish delights with tact and, when the elements were right, style.

Naturally, like all studios, Hammer were in the business of film production to make a profit, and would return to proven formulas again and again to reap the financial benefits - though ultimately to diminishing effect, both commercially and artistically. And, as it would for most of the British film industry, the lack of finance in the seventies gradually took its toll on the studio, combined with an apparent inability to change with the times. The release of *The Exorcist* in 1973 re-defined the horror genre overnight, yet Hammer remained blinkered to the changes, preferring to produce yet further variations on the by now rather tired Dracula and Frankenstein legends, when instead they should have been exploring charnel houses new.

By the end of the seventies, big budget science fiction epics such as *Star Wars* and *Close Encounters* ruled at the box office, whilst the ever-growing number of smaller independent companies themselves continued to re-invent the horror genre via such modern day slices of Grand Guignol as the *Hallowe'en* and *Friday the 13th* series. Hammer, however, simply failed to adapt and, some undistinguished television productions and an ill-timed remake of *The Lady Vanishes* aside, were all but defunct by the early 1980s.

From time to time, rumours of a return to production appear in the trade papers, usually followed by long periods of silence, though a recent deal with Warner Bros, to remake a number of their horror and sci-fi classics, seems to bode well for the future. The phoenix could yet rise from the ashes. And not for the first time, either, for whilst many associate the Hammer name with the studio's successful double decade of horror, its history can in fact be traced back many decades more, to much humbler - not to mention less horrifying - beginnings...

in the beginning

Like Warner Bros and Universal, which were established by the Warner and Laemmle dynasties respectively, the founding of Hammer Films was very much a family business - or rather, the business of two families.

The most important of these was the Carreras family, headed by the Spanish-born Enrique Carreras, a would-be business tycoon who came to England at the turn of the century and involved himself in a number of small businesses with varying degrees of success, including a venture in toothpaste manufacturing which, somewhat ignominiously, led to his being declared bankrupt. The ambitions of the dapper-looking Carreras were not to be dampened, however, and by the time his brother Alphonse joined the determined young Enrique in Hammersmith, London, the family was ready for its first major brush with showbusiness.

This occurred in 1913 when the brothers acquired the first of what would grow to be a chain of London-based theatres which came to be known as the Blue Hall circuit, whose bills featured well-known variety and music hall acts of the day. The success of this venture confirmed to the Carreras brothers that their futures lay in some form of show business rather than precarious highstreet investments. Consequently, that same year, the ever-enterprising Enrique proved that showmanship was in his blood by hiring the Royal Albert Hall for a screening of the 1912 Italian epic *Quo Vadis?* An instant sell-out, the occasion was given the added esteem of being attended by the royal

family, pre-empting the first official Royal Film Performance, *A Matter of Life and Death* in 1946, by some 33 years.

The name of Carreras by now had a certain prestige, and over the next few years Blue Halls Ltd grew in size. So much so that in 1923 the company not only moved to larger offices, but had enough capital for Enrique to buy his first cinema - The Harrow Coliseum - in which he exhibited cheaply-acquired B-features and reissues. With the assistance of his general manager, Henry Lomax, further cinemas were acquired, and gradually an empire was born. Taking things a step further, Carreras then formed his own distribution company, Christened Exclusive Films, which acted as a distribution outlet for his own expanding circuit, which not only saved Carreras money, but meant a greater and more immediate return of profit.

Meanwhile, elsewhere in London, one William Hinds, whose family would also play a major role in the birth of Hammer as we now know it, was himself enjoying his first flirtations with showbusiness. Like Enrique Carreras, Hinds came to showbusiness via a circuitous route. Early business interests included a chain of bicycle shops (an off-shoot of his days as a record-holding cyclist), hairdressing salons and jewellers, whilst his financial acumen resulted in his being named chairman of a London-based building society.

But it was Hinds's love of the theatre which gradually forced his other interests into the

Paul Robeson (sitting left)
in *Song of Freedom*. Note
the crease in the back cloth.

shadows, for not only did he go on to form his own theatrical booking agency - which dealt primarily with music hall and variety acts - his own ambitions as a performer also saw him form (with a colleague) the comedy double-act Hammer and Smith. In fact, the name of the act had been hastily devised when the duo, about to make their debut in a talent contest, realised they had no stage name. They quickly decided on Hammer and Smith, after the borough in which they were appearing. For Hinds the name of Hammer stuck, even though the double-act quickly fizzled. So much so that, in 1934, when Hinds decided to form his own film company, it also took on the name of Hammer.

By this time Hinds's empire had grown to include four seaside theatres, which he owned outright, and three offices in Imperial House on Regent Street in London, which housed the fledgling Hammer Productions.

Despite the general depression it was a time of prosperity in showbusiness, and it was during this period that the fates of the two families merged, for Enrique Carreras and William Hinds met and, seeing that their ambitions lay in the same direction, decided to become distribution partners under the Exclusive banner, for which they purchased their first two films -Snowhounds and Spilt Salt - at the bargain basement price of just £100.

At this early stage, the Hammer company remained mostly in the care of Hinds and his associates, and between 1935 and 1937, Henry Fraser Passmore, one of the company's managing directors, would produce for them a total of five films - The Public Life of Henry the Ninth, The Mystery of the Mary Celeste (aka The Phantom Ship), Song of Freedom, Sporting Love and The Bank Messenger Mystery - all of which were introduced by a blacksmith hammering at an anvil, a distinctive trademark devised by Enrique

Carreras to help distinguish their product. (Noteworthy in itself, the trademark's blacksmith was played by Billy Wells, whose even greater claim to fame, aside from being a Britsh heavyweight title holder, was as the muscleman who banged the gong on the early Rank films.)

None of the films Hammer made during this period are particularly noteworthy, save for Song of Freedom (1936) which stars the great Paul Robeson as a black docker who, having become an opera singer, later uses his influence to help an African tribe, of which he discovers he is the long lost chief! The film was helmed by J. Elder Wills, a former set designer and one of Hammer's company directors, whose efforts here were described as 'distinguished but not above reproach' by Graham Greene in his column for The Spectator. The rest of the cast includes singer Elizabeth Welch, in one of her rare film appearances, and brief cameoes by William Hinds (billed as Will Hammer in his only ever screen appearance) as a pub potman, and George Mozart, another company director who, like Hinds, had appeared in variety.

Never quite able to resist the urge to perform, Mozart had previously appeared in Hammer's very first film, The Public Life of Henry the Ninth (1935), whose title cheekily alludes to the 1933 Charles Laughton Oscar winner The Private Life of Henry the Eighth, the American success of which had done much to open up the worldwide market for British films. Here, however, it is Leonard Henry who stars as a street busker who finally gets his big break in showbusiness after an impromtu performance in a local pub.

This was followed by The Mystery of the Mary Celeste (1936) which was not only Hammer's first brush with a horror subject (albeit of the melodramatic kind), but also stars one of the genre's biggest names, Bela Lugosi.

Unfortunately the film, which offers a solution to the famous seafaring mystery, turned out to be a rather dull affair, with Lugosi playing the role of Anton Lorenzen, a sailor who kills his fellow crew members as an act of revenge before jumping overboard and swimming ashore. George Mozart again pops up briefly during the proceedings, as does character actor Dennis Hoey, who went on to play Inspector Lestrade opposite Basil Rathbone's Sherlock Holmes in the popular Universal series. Otherwise, both the cast and Denison Clift's script and direction are of a strictly routine nature, lacking the over-the-top 'fie thee' hamminess of a Tod Slaughter vehicle, which at least would have made the film enjoyably bad.

After *Song of Freedom* came the comedy *Sporting Love* (1937), which top-lines the popular stage comedian Stanley Lupino (father of actress Ida Lupino). Stanley, with co-star Laddie Cliff, plays one of two stable owners who decide to kidnap their own prize horse in order to collect on the insurance and pay off their mortgage. Based on Lupino's own stage play, the film, directed by J. Elder Wills, also contains a few brief musical numbers, but is otherwise a fairly half-hearted effort. After this, Wills would direct just one more film, *Big Fella* (1937), again starring Paul Robeson and Elizabeth Welch. However, this was for British Lion rather than Hammer. Yet despite *Big Fella's* moderate success, Wills hung up his director's spurs and returned to art direction for the duration of his career.

Meanwhile, Hammer's following film, *The Bank Messenger Mystery* (1937), which again features the stage-struck George Mozart in a brief cameo, failed to gain a release until 1941, when it was distributed by Exclusive. For some reason, despite the by-now established ties between Carreras and Hinds, this was the only Hammer film to be distributed by Exclusive up until that point, the other four films having been distributed by the likes of British Lion, MGM and GFD, the latter of which even gained a US release for *The Mystery of the Mary Celeste* (under the title of *The Phantom Ship*), where *Variety* described it as 'Very strong stuff for those who like tragic entertainment.' No doubt helped by the marquee value of Lugosi's name, the film did moderately well as a second feature, which makes one wonder why Hammer didn't import more internationally know stars to give their films a shot at a US release. This, after all, was where the real money was, as Alexander Korda had already discovered with the huge success of *The Private Life of Henry The Eighth*.

The reason for the hold up in the release of *The Bank Messenger Mystery*, however, was simple: a sudden slump in the British film industry combined with the imminent threat of war had forced the company into liquidation. Exclusive Films, which at this point operated independently from Hammer, continued on quite successfully throughout the war years, re-issueing such Korda product as *Q-Planes* and Michael Powell's *The Spy in Black*. For the time being, though, Hammer, was dead. However, as it frequently was for Count Dracula, resurrection was not far away...

the exclusive years

The revification of Hammer came about primarily through an infusion of new blood into the company in the form of Enrique Carreras's son James and William Hinds's son Anthony, both of whom ensured that Hammer 'stayed in the family' for a second generation.

Anthony Hinds had in fact joined Exclusive briefly in 1939 before serving in the RAF during the war, after which he returned to them in 1946. James Carreras, meanwhile, served with the HAC for the duration and was made an MBE in 1944. By the time he joined his father at Exclusive, after being demobbed in 1946, he had risen to the rank of Lieutenant Colonel. With his natural skills at PR and showmanship (he was the man behind the 'Salute a Soldier' parade in London in 1944), he was ideally equipped for the role of movie mogul.

As they had continued to do throughout the war, Exclusive carried on distributing other people's films during the next two years - mostly 'quota quickies' and reissues. By this time, however, the company had a certain degree of influence over the product they presented, in as much as the young Hinds kept an active eye over the programmers being produced on their behalf by others. This would prove to be valuable experience, for upon the resurrection of Hammer Films in 1946, not only would Anthony Hinds be one of the company's directors (along with Enrique Carreras, his son Michael and William Hinds), he would also go on to produce personally much of Hammer's initial output.

The much-mentioned 'quota quickie' had been a staple of the British film industry since 1927, when the Cinematograph Act stipulated that 25 percent of features and 30 percent of supporting films (or programmers as they were known) had to be British made. This was a bid not only to prevent Hollywood from dominating the market entirely, but also to nurture the ever-fragile British film industry.

Some filmmakers took advantage of this low budget training ground, such as Michael Powell who, in the early thirties, directed a number of 'quickies' before going on to helm such classics as *The Red Shoes* and *Black Narcissus*. But the industry in general simply saw the quota as a void to be filled by almost any means possible, in order to reap the benefits of the rather more lucrative Hollywood product. Consequently, rather than encouraging the British film industry, the quota system sunk it to new depths. And it was this void in the market that Hammer/Exclusive found themselves, by neccessity, catering for in their formative years.

Of course, it would be pleasant to believe that much of Hammer's early product was little more than a dress rehearsal for the greatness that followed - a gearing up of talent and ideas. However, given the sheer volume of their output and the general inadequacies of the results - both as art and entertainment - it is hard to be so charitable.

Encouraged by Jack Goodlatte, the bookings manager of the then ABC circuit, Exclusive geared itself up to enter the quota quickie market, which they did in 1946 with several documentary featurettes, now rarely seen, such as *Old Father Thames* (1946), *Cornish Holiday* (1946) and *We Do Believe in Ghosts* (1947). The subject matter of these short and now seemingly lost documentaries often prefigured themes for drama featurettes, so after two crime drama shorts in 1947 (*Crime Reporter* and *Death in High Heels*), Hammer returned to the Thames as the location for a slightly more ambitious forty-six minute featurette titled *River Patrol*, which was released (or possibly allowed to escape) in 1948. Co-produced by the newly formed Hammer Films Ltd and Knightsbridge Productions, the film was produced by Hal Wilson, directed by Ben R. Hart and stars John Blythe as a customs officer out to track down a gang of nylon smugglers (a hot topic in nylon-starved post-war Britain). Also featuring busy Cockney actor Wally Patch (who had appeared in Hammer's first film, *The Public Life of Henry the Ninth*, some thirteen years earlier), this location-filmed thriller seemed to fare well enough and prompted Hammer to go into production with their next featurette.

A mystery-thriller, this went by the title of *Who Killed Van Loon?* Like all of Hammer's early quickies, this was again filmed on location, simply because they couldn't afford to hire studio space, and stars Canadian actor Raymond Lovell in a possible bid to find an American release.

An adequate if unambitious time filler, *Who Killed Van Loon?* didn't seem get too many pulses racing and, at just forty-eight minutes in length, it wasn't likely to bring in huge profits for the fledgling company. Two more crime features quickly followed: *The Dark Road* (1948) and *The Jack of Diamonds* (1949), both weighing in at around 70 minutes. Compared with Hammer's thirties films, particularly *Song of Freedom*, the results were also fairly poor. What

Hammer needed was a money spinner with built-in audience appeal - all of which they found in a character called Dick Barton.

A fearless crimefighter and 'natural leader of men', Barton, played by Noel Johnson, was the star of BBC radio's first daily serial, and between 1946 and 1951 (after which he was displaced by *The Archers!*) Barton regularly attracted an audience of fifteen million, who thrilled to his cliffhanging adventures. Accompanied by a pulse-racing signature tune ('The Devil's Gallop' by Charles Williams) *Dick Barton - Special Agent* was little more than a comic strip for the airwaves, yet in the austerity of post-war Britain, his heroic escapades (more often than not involving thickly-accented foreign agents) proved to be a welcome distraction to radio listeners. If Hammer could acquire the film rights to this series, which also pulled in an average of 2000 fan letters a week, surely they'd be onto a winner? Consequently, *Dick Barton - Special Agent* (aka *Dick Barton -Detective*) went into production in 1948, with a budget of less than £20,000. As the rate of purchase for a second feature on the circuits was £25,000, the film was already £5000 in profit before it was even screened to the public, thanks to the ruthless trimming of its production costs.

Produced by Henry Halsted and helmed by the American director Alfred Goulding (whose previous credits include Laurel and Hardy's *A Chump at Oxford*, which briefly features a twenty-six-year-old actor called Peter Cushing), the film stars Don Stannard as Barton (leaving it to Noel Johnson to continue playing him on the radio). Supported by George Ford and Jack Shaw as his sidekicks Snowey White and Jock Anderson, the film's plot revolves round Barton's attempts to prevent foreign agents from planting germ bombs in Britain's reservoirs. Hard to sit through today, the results - no doubt helped by the

(Opposite) A selection of Hammer posters.

built-in familiarity of the Barton character - nevertheless proved popular enough at the time, with audiences keen to see instead of just hear their hero's exploits.

It appeared that Hammer had happened upon a succesful formula. Indeed, so buoyed were they by the film's success that they immediately put into production two more Barton adventures. But not before raiding the radio archives for further ideas, the first of which was derived from Wilfred Burr's series *Dr Morelle*. Called *Dr Morelle - The Case of the Missing Heiress* for cinema release, the film was co-scripted by Ambrose Grayson and *Desert Island Discs* creator Roy Plomely, and stars the velvet-voiced Valentine Dyall as the crime-solving doctor of the title.

An unremarkable mystery thriller which has dated rather badly, the film was nevertheless important to the company for the introduction of several key players to Hammer/Exclusive's growing family. Among these were director Godfrey Grayson (who would helm another six films for Hammer before moving to the equally poverty-stricken Danziger studio), cinematographer Cedric Williams and composers Frank Spencer and Rupert Grayson. The film was also the first to be fully produced by Anthony Hinds, who was assisted by James Carreras's son Michael, perhaps the most important player in the overall history of Hammer.

The young Michael Carreras had in fact worked in various departments for Exclusive (including publicity, where he posted off stills and posters to the cinemas) between 1943 and 1946, after which he did his National Service in the Grenadier Guards. When he came out in 1948 he returned to Exclusive where, after an initial period in sales and distribution, he not only became one of the company's casting directors, but was also made Assistant to the Producer, despite his almost complete lack of

knowledge in the ways of production. The experience he gained here would quickly prove invaluable.

Meanwhile, hot on the heels of *Dr Morelle*, Hammer turned their attention to their second Dick Barton adventure, *Dick Barton Strikes Back* (billed on the posters as 'The picture that puts showmanship back into show business'), in which our hero tracks down a gang who have stolen some vital atomic apparatus. There was also another radio-inspired thriller, *Celia*, which centres round the exposing of a poisoner. It also proved to be the first of nine films helmed for Hammer by their other regular director, Francis Searle.

These two films were in turn followed by *The Adventures of PC 49*, another popular radio character who, between 1943 and 1953, starred in over 100 crime-fighting episodes, as well as being featured in books, advertisements and cartoon strips in the *Eagle*, not to mention a board game called *Burglars* and a jigsaw puzzle which went by the title *PC 49 and the Organ-Grinder's Monkey*! Like the Dick Barton films, no matter how bad it was (and it is pretty dreadful), *The Adventures of PC 49* couldn't fail, thanks to its built-in appeal.

Though played by Brian Reece on the radio, it was Hugh Lattimer who was chosen to star in the hour-long second feature, in which our hero (full name Archibald Berkeley-Willoughby) disguises himself as a villain in order to infiltrate a gang of dastardly thieves. Though hard to tolerate for long today, the film nevertheless proved popular enough and provoked a sequel, *A Case for PC 49*, in which the brave Bobby is this time played by his radio counterpart Brian Reece, who finds himself averting a model's plans to murder a millionaire. At 79 minutes, the film was more than most people could bear, even in 1949, and mercifully no more sequels followed.

NO-ONE WHO SAW IT
LIVED TO DESCRIBE IT!

THE CURSE OF FRANKENSTEIN

CERT X   EASTMAN COLOUR

PETER CUSHING   HAZEL COURT   ROBERT URQUHART
CHRISTOPHER LEE AS THE CREATURE   A HAMMER FILM PRODUCTION

WOULD YOU TRUST THE NANNY... OR THE BOY?

BETTE DAVIS

THE NANNY

WENDY CRAIG · JILL BENNETT · JAMES VILLIERS · WILLIAM DIX · PAMELA FRANKLIN

EMI FILM PRODUCTIONS LIMITED
presents
A HAMMER PRODUCTION

BLOOD FROM THE MUMMY'S TOMB

Starring
ANDREW KEIR
VALERIE LEON
JAMES VILLIERS

Also Starring
HUGH BURDEN
GEORGE COULOURIS

TECHNICOLOR ®

Screenplay by CHRISTOPHER WICKING
Produced by HOWARD BRANDY
Directed by SETH HOLT
Distributed by ANGLO-EMI Film Distributors Limited.

The TERRIFYING Lover –
who died – yet lived !

Universal-International presents A Hammer Film Production

PETER CUSHING in

DRACULA

(Cert. X) Adults only

also starring MICHAEL GOUGH
and MELISSA STRIBLING
with CHRISTOPHER LEE as Dracula

In Eastman Colour processed by Technicolor

Screenplay by JIMMY SANGSTER   Associate Producer ANTHONY NELSON-KEYS
Produced by ANTHONY HINDS   Directed by TERENCE FISHER
Executive Producer MICHAEL CARRERAS

Distributed by Rank Film Distributors Ltd.

DON'T DARE SEE IT ALONE!

JOAN FONTAINE

THE WITCHES

KAY WALSH · ALEC McCOWEN · DUNCAN LAMONT · GWEN FFRANGCON-DAVIES

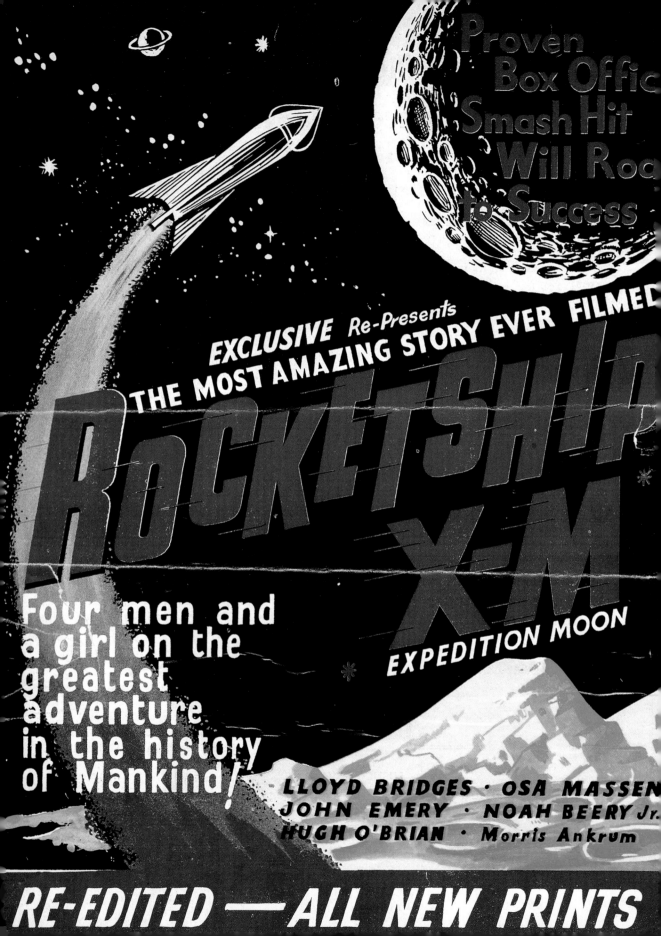

By 1950, Hammer/Exclusive were in full production, and a definite trend had developed, for a good many of their films were derived from radio plays or series, including *The Man in Black* (a murder melodrama, again with Valentine Dyal), *Meet Simon Cherry* (which features a crime-solving clergyman) and *Room to Let* (a variation on *The Lodger*), all of which were shot on four to five week schedules. One of the few exceptions was *Someone at the Door*, which was a remake of a 1935 thriller, itself based on a successful stage play about an apparently haunted house. Better than most of Exclusive's output during this period, it remains of interest chiefly for its title sequence, in which the cast pass through a mansion door, which is subsequently removed by two stage hands who reveal it to be a piece of scenery in a field, behind which the crew are lurking.

A third Dick Barton adventure, *Dick Barton at Bay*, also appeared in 1950, this time involving a missing scientist and the death ray he has invented. However, plans for a fourth Barton film were scuppered when star Don Stannard was killed in a car crash.

Nineteen Fifty also saw the unexpected death of Exclusive's founder Enrique Carreras, whose place on the board of directors was consequently filled by his grandson Michael who, in 1951, finally gained his first producer credit with *The Dark Light*, a badly-made programme filler about a group of lighthouse workmen who fall foul of a gang of thieves. Over the next few years further producer credits would follow, though at this stage the young Carreras mainly oversaw the company's casting duties, for which he received credit on many of their films.

Meanwhile, 1950 was rounded out with *The Lady Craved Excitement*, another radio-inspired thriller involving the uncovering of an art smuggling racket by two cabaret artists. Barely

watchable by today's standards (and probably not much more tolerable at the time), it nevertheless remains of passing interest for its cast, which includes Michael Medwin, Sid James and Andrew Keir, all of them then in the early stages of what would prove to be lengthy and successful careers.

As well as the Carreras-produced *The Dark Light*, early 1951 saw the release of *The Rossiter Case* (a by-numbers murder mystery) and *To Have and to Hold* (a stiff upper lip romantic melodrama). Hammer also finally acquired their own full-time 'studio', having previously rented space in a number of large country houses and clubs when the need arose (such as Dial Close and Gilston Park in Essex), a further example of their attempts to keep production costs low.

Consequently, a small country estate called Down Place in Bray, near Windsor (previously used by Hammer in 1950 for *The Lady Craved Excitement*), became Hammer's base. The house itself acted as both office space, studio floor and outdoor location, with further studio space later being built in the grounds.

Filming 'on location' at Dial Close, one of Hammer's early country house 'studios'. Note the sound recordist in the back of the van.

(Opposite) Artwork for Exclusive's release of Robert Lippert's *Rocketship X-M*.

Neighbouring houses, such as the chateau-like Oakley Court, which appears in many of Hammer's later gothic horrors, such as *The Curse of Frankenstein* and *The Brides of Dracula*, were also made good use of, often belying the low budgets of the films set around them.

Now that the studio itself was established at Bray, James Carreras ensconced himself in Wardour Street in London (the business heart of the British film industry), from whence he became the driving force behind the company, even though never involving himself directly in the day-to-day making of the films themselves. And it was from here that Carreras used his considerable charm and skills as a diplomat to part financiers from their money - usually over a lavish, all expenses-paid meal. Sales meetings and annual conferences for cinema-owners also became a fixture, some of which were even held in the luxurious surroundings of the impressive-looking Oakley Court, all of which helped to build up an image of confidence and prosperity, even though the company's product was still struggling to achieve the distinction of being merely third rate.

Nevertheless, things were certainly looking good for Hammer/Exclusive at this time, for not only had their turnover doubled, James Carreras had also instigated a distribution deal with Robert Lippert, an American theatre owner, producer and distributor (via Screen Guild Pictures) who himself had a long-standing arrangement with Twentieth Century Fox to provide them with cheap second features, all of which gave Hammer a much-needed foot-hold in the all-important American market. As a consequence, Hammer gradually began to veer away from the radio-inspired fillers they had been making and began to look at stories which would appeal to more than just a homegrown audience. The US deal also meant that Exclusive acquired the UK

distribution rights to such Lippert-produced movies as *Rocketship XM*, *Loan Shark* and *Lost Continent*, as well as such low budget clunkers as *Robot Monster* and the hilariously inept *Cat-Women of the Moon* (aka *Rocket to the Moon*).

The Lippert deal aside, attempts had already been made by Hammer/Exclusive to break into the international market. In 1951, American star Robert Preston, whose career was then in the doldrums, was brought over to star in *Cloudburst*, which did actually manage an American release through United Artists (who cut the film's running time from ninety-two minutes down to eighty-three). The story of a code expert who avenges himself against the criminals who ran down his wife during a getaway, it was described on the posters as 'The torment of a man's split mind', though in truth it is pretty standard second feature stuff, despite the presence of Preston.

The first film to be shot at Bray, *Cloudburst* was hampered by the cramped and primitive conditions in which it was made. The lack of studio gantries meant that the film had to be lit and photographed by the best means possible, whilst the lack of soundproofing on the main stage - a converted ballroom - produced problems of its own. As Michael Carreras later recalled, 'You couldn't flush a toilet if they were shooting below!'. Nevertheless, over the next couple of years, conditions gradually improved - especially when the first sound stage proper was erected outside the mansion's entrance, followed by extra space for the editing suites and workshops for the plasterers and carpenters.

Soon, Bray was in full swing with such films as *The Black Widow* (another radio-inspired murder mystery), *A Case for PC 49* and *Death of an Angel* (which centres round the murder of a doctor's wife).

Meanwhile, Richard Carlson proved to be the next American import to cross the Pond for the expanding company, this time for *Whispering Smith Hits London*, which found release in the States through RKO under the title *Whispering Smith vs. Scotland Yard* (where it was also trimmed down from eighty-two minutes to a more manageable seventy-seven). One of Hammer's better efforts, the film is a sequel of sorts to Paramount's 1948 detective western *Whispering Smith*, which had starred Alan Ladd as a government agent out to clear his best friend (played by previous Hammer import Robert Preston) who has been implicated in a series of robberies. Ladd's asking price was too high for Hammer to bring him back for the follow up, hence the presence of the less appealing but more affordable Carlson. The first film's use of Technicolor was also jettisoned in favour of standard black and white.

For British audiences at least, compensations could be found in the film's better than aver-age supporting cast, which includes Greta Gynt, Herbert Lom (future star of Hammer's *Phantom of the Opera*), Reginald Beckwith, Dora Bryan (later to feature in *Hands of the Ripper*) and Rona Anderson (wife of Gordon Jackson), though the plot was still pretty routine: Smith's investigation of an apparent suicide leads him to believe it was murder. But at least Hammer's board of directors could take comfort in the fact that their product was getting seen by a much larger audience, even if it still lacked the required panache to distinguish it from other low budget second feature fare.

The first of Hammer's associations with Robert Lippert came next on the production schedule. Titled *The Last Page*, it was another so-so second feature thriller, this time set in a small book shop which becomes the focus of blackmail and murder. Based on the play by James Hadley Chase and scripted by *Dial M for Murder* author Frederick Knott, it was still a run-of-the-mill

Exclusive launch their latest picture, *Cloudburst*. James Carreras and the film's star, Robert Preston, can be seen centre left, while Michael Carreras (end of table) wonders why he can't sit near the star too. Note the lavish spread: smoked salmon, wine, cigars, flowers - Exclusive could have financed another film with what this lot cost!

Michael Carreras (pointing) on location with the crew during the filming of *Never Look Back*.

Fisher finally became a fully-fledged editor in 1935 on the classic World War One drama *Brown on Resolution* (aka *Born for Glory/Forever England*), which stars the young John Mills as a seaman who dies a hero. Following this, Fisher quickly established himself as a fast and reliable editor, and went on to work on a variety of projects, from Will Hay comedies to bodice rippers such as *The Wicked Lady* (1945). Then, in 1947, after editing his last film, *The Master of Bankdam*, Fisher enrolled as a trainee director with the Rank Organization. His first credit was *Colonel Bogey* in 1948, which was followed in the same year by *Portrait from Life*, *A Song for Tomorrow* and a short, *To the Public Danger*.

Nineteen forty-nine brought *Marry Me* and *The Astonished Heart*, the latter of which was a disappointing association with Noel Coward, which he co-directed with Anthony Darnborough. This in turn was followed in 1950 by the much-mentioned *So Long at the Fair* (co-directed with Anthony Darnborough again), a popular if somewhat uninspired little thriller revolving round the mysterious disappearance of a young woman's brother during the 1889 Paris exposition. By no means a great film, it nevertheless proved that Fisher was capable of better things if given the right material.

effort. Yet despite its routine nature, the film remains noteworthy for being the first Hammer film to be directed by Terence Fisher, another key player in the studio's later success in the horror genre. Fisher would ultimately direct a record thirty films for Hammer, including a good percentage of their horror classics, though it must be said that his early output gave no indication whatsoever of the great things that were to follow.

Born in London in 1904, Fisher joined the Merchant Navy at an early age and seemed for a while destined for a career at sea. The romantic appeal of this waned after three years, however, and after a stint at London's John Lewis department store, where he became assistant display manager, Fisher joined the film industry at the relatively late age of twenty-eight. Beginning as a clapper boy at the Lime Grove studios in London, where his first film was the Jack Buchanan comedy *Falling For You*, Fisher literally worked his way up from the bottom, first to third assistant, then to assistant editor.

Sadly, it would be another six years before he got to display his true worth with *The Curse of Frankenstein* in 1956, the interim being filled by a series of unadventurous second features, a good number of them for Hammer. The first of these, *The Last Page*, nevertheless got an all-important US release care of Robert Lippert in 1952 under the title *Man Bait*, which certainly did Fisher's standing no harm, and remains of passing interest for its cast, which includes George Brent, Diana Dors and Raymond Huntley who, back in the late twenties, had played Dracula on stage in the original London production.

Meanwhile, 1952 continued to be a busy year for Hammer/Exclusive, for as well as producing *Death of an Angel*, *Whispering Smith Hits London* and *The Last Page*, they churned out another five co-features: *Wings of Danger*, a smuggling thriller with Zachary Scott, *Lady in the Fog* (aka *Scotland Yard Inspector*), a mystery with Cesar Romero, *Mantrap* (aka *A Man in Hiding*), a Paul Henried vehicle involving the escape of a mental patient accused of murder, *Stolen Face* (Henreid again) and *Never Look Back*, another thriller involving a false alibi - and the only one to fail to achieve a US release, no doubt because it lacked the required American 'star'.

Out of these films, *Stolen Face* perhaps remains the most interesting, thanks to a story that involves a plastic surgeon's attempts to alter a female convict's face so that it resembles that of the girl he loves but cannot have. A tolerable if ultimately rather silly melodrama, it contains vestiges of yet-to-come *Vertigo*, and even echoes of *Frankenstein*, with the surgeon's creation ulti- mately turning against him. Helped along by a solid cast (Paul Henried as the surgeon, Lizabeth Scott excellent as both the scarred convict and the beautiful pianist the surgeon has fallen for), it was director Terence Fisher's most polished film up to that point, and actual- ly did quite well at the box office. (But gaffe spotters should note the reflection of the cam- era crew in the windscreen of a car as it pulls up outside Henried's surgery early on in the film.)

1953 saw another five co-features go into pro- duction, including two more brushes with the sci-fi/horror genre in the form of *Four-Sided Triangle*, in which, like *Stolen Face*, a scientist (Stephen Murray) attempts to clone the girl who has rejected him only to discover that the duplicate has the same preferences, and *Spaceways*, in which another scientist (Howard Duff) stands accused of stowing away the corpse of his dead wife in a space rocket! As

directed by Terence Fisher, both films were slightly (but not much) better than the Hammer norm, with *Spaceways* ballyhooed in the trade press as being 'Even greater than *Rocketship XM*,' the Lippert- produced film which Exclusive had success-fully distributed back in 1950. Today, however, it must be said that the plots of both films make them sound more interesting than they actually are, whilst their low budgets are obvious, to say the least. So much so that Michael Carreras later said of *Spaceways*, 'The budget was the same as it would have been had it been about two people in bed!'.

Meanwhile, the studio maintained its policy of importing downward-sliding American stars to top-line their films during this period (Tom Conway, Paulette Goddard, Dan Duryea, Don Taylor, Lloyd Bridges, Dane Clark, Barbara Payton and Louis Hayward among them). This approach continued to secure US releases for Hammer care of Robert Lippert and a new association with Astor Distribution, all of which displayed the company's determination to keep their foothold in the States. They even entered into an agreement with RKO to make a Saint thriller, *The Saint's Return* (aka *The Saint's Girl Friday*) with the series' original star Louis Hayward. However, if a new series was intended it never materialised.

The year's production schedule was finally rounded out with *The Gambler and the Lady*, a gang warfare thriller with Dane Clark, and *The Flannagan Boy* (aka *Bad Blonde*), a boxing drama with Tony Wright and Barbara Payton.

A further nine films were churned out by Hammer in 1954, including *Face The Music* (aka *The Black Glove*), *Blood Orange* (aka *Three Steps to Murder*), *The House Across the Lake* (aka *Heat Wave*), *Five Days* (aka *Paid to Kill*), *Thirty-Six Hours* (aka *Terror Street*) and *Mask of Dust* (aka *A Race for Life*). Most of these stuck to the proven formula of the low budget thriller, such as *The Stranger Came Home* (aka *The Unholy Four*), the first film to be scripted by Michael Carreras, which involves an amnesiac (William Sylvester) being accused of murder.

One of the exceptions was the comedy *Life with the Lyons* (aka *Family Affair*), which stars the American husband and wife duo Ben Lyon and Bebe Daniels. Long resident in Britain, Lyon and Daniels came over in 1935 after having both enjoyed successful movie careers in Tinseltown, where they were known as 'Hollywood's happiest married couple.' In Britain they became just as popular in such films as *Hi,Gang* and several successful radio series, which included *Life with the Lyons*, a family sit-com which also featured their real-life children, Barbara and Richard.

Not wanting to miss the chance of making yet another film with built-in audience appeal, Hammer secured the movie rights from the BBC. The result was a cheap but cheerful romp centred around confusion over a tenants' lease, all of which proved successful enough to provoke a sequel, *The Lyons in Paris*, which appeared the following year. However, though energetically performed by the Lyons family, the real star of the piece was co-writer and director Val Guest who, in the following few years, would help to take Hammer into the big time.

One of the British cinema's most prolific writer-producer-directors, Valmond Guest began his career in the movies as a supporting actor during the silent period, then turned to journalism when the parts dried up. For this he travelled to America where he contributed to the likes of *Variety*, *The Los Angeles Examiner* and *The Hollywood Reporter*, all of which proved valuable experience when, in 1935, he returned to Britain to become a script writer for Gainsborough/Gaumont British. There he became a valuable comedy writer and

Behind the scenes on *Never Look Back*. Michael Carreras (bottom left) can be seen sitting in director Francis Searle's chair. Searle (in the glasses) is watching the action from behind the camera. Note the dolly track and the top of the set.

co-scripted some of Will Hay's best vehicles, including *Good Morning, Boys*, *Ask A Policeman*, *Oh, Mr Porter* and *Convict 99*. He also wrote for Arthur Askey (*Charley's Aunt*, *The Ghost Train*) and The Crazy Gang (*Alf's Button Afloat*, *The Frozen Limits*).

Guest eventually turned to direction in 1943 with the Arthur Askey comedy *Miss London Ltd*, which he also co-scripted and wrote the lyrics for. A busy career followed, mostly in the comedy genre, including several with his American- born wife Yolande Donlan. However, Guest's lengthy association with Hammer would help to change that, thanks to the success of 1955's *The Quatermass Experiment*, which led to a number of taut thrillers and sci-fi classics, including *Jigsaw* and *The Day the Earth Caught Fire*, both for British Lion.

Before embarking on the sequel to the successful *Life With The Lyons*, Guest directed *Men of Sherwood Forest* for Hammer, a Robin Hood adventure which is notable for two reasons: it confirmed the studio's continued wish to diversify, and was also their first feature to be shot in colour, a medium Guest had previously had experience with on both *Penny Princess* and *Dance, Little Lady*.

22

Starring American import Don Taylor (better known these days as the director of *Damien: Omen II* and *The Final Countdown*), *Men of Sherwood Forest* revolves around Robin's attempts to help return King Richard to the throne after his return from the Crusades. A popular enough success, it was easily one of Hammer's better efforts, and a sequel, *Friar Tuck*, was quickly announced, along with a further swashbuckler, *King Charles and the Roundheads*. Neither of these were produced, though, for an even more lucrative formula was just around the corner...

In the meantime, 1955 saw Hammer continue to churn out yet more undistinguished crime thrillers, including *Murder by Proxy* (aka *Blackout*), *Third Party Risk* (aka *Deadly Game/ Big Deadly Game*), *Break in the Circle* and *The Glass Cage* (aka *The Glass Tomb*). They also made *Cyril Stapleton and the Show Band* in 1955, the first of a number of thirty-minute musical programmers, all of which were directed by Michael Carreras and shot in both Eastmancolor and Cinemascope.

Of course, wide lenses like those used in the Cinemascope process had been around for a considerable time, yet their use had been restricted until the advent of television, when they proved to be another gimmick with which to entice dwindling audiences away from their TV screens, even though some filmmakers expressed their disdain at the process ('A formula for funerals and snakes, but not for human beings' said director Fritz Lang).

The Robe (1953) had been the first film to be shot in Cinemascope, the success of which helped to open the floodgates. Not wanting to be left behind, Hammer thus jumped onto the bandwagon with the likes of *The Eric Winstone Band Show*, *Just For You* (with Cyril Stapleton again), *Parade of the Bands* and *Eric Winstone's Stagecoach*. Photographed by the young Geoffrey Unsworth (later to win Oscars for both *Cabaret* and *Tess*), these musical featurettes were mostly shot at the ABPC Studios at Borehamwood, the 'studio' at Bray not yet being up to the task of the stereo recording which was part of the Cinemascope process.

The experience gained with this wide screen process would later prove handy when Hammer chose to shoot some of their bigger features in Scope. In fact they even produced their own version of Cinemascope, called 'Hammerscope', which they first tested in 1956 on *Dick Turpin - Highwayman*, a half-hour featurette which still stands up quite well when seen today.

Meanwhile, 1955 saw the end of Hammer's useful association with Robert Lippert, *Murder by Proxy* (aka *Blackout*) being the last film to be distributed by him in the States. Hammer had by now established other distribution outlets in America, but the end of this contract and the general unrest in the film industry caused them pause for thought. Consequently, while the company figured out a new way forward, they shut down production on everything but their shorts (which now included mini travelogues such as *Copenhagen* and half-hour dramas like *Man on the Beach*) and their musical featurettes. Little did they know, but they had already completed the film which would re-shape their destiny. Called *The Quatermass Experiment*, it had been made in late 1954 and was simply waiting to be released. The horror was about to begin.

the quatermass interim

Just as they had done with their radio adaptations, Hammer were playing it safe again when they acquired the rights to Nigel Kneale's TV sensation *The Quatermass Experiment.* Originally aired by the BBC in 1953 in six thirty-minute episodes, the series revolves round the (fictional) first manned space flight. The one surviving astronaut begins to mutate upon returning to earth. Pre-empting the Apollo moonshot by some sixteen years, the series was basically an intelligent variation on the old monster-on-the-rampage theme, yet such was its vision and originality that its broadcasts cleared the streets and pubs on the successive Wednesday evenings it was transmitted.

Central to the plot is Professor Quatermass himself, of course, here played by Reginald Tate. The man behind the space programme, his blind, Frankenstein-like ambition ultimately results in his having to destroy the product of his experiments, the mutating astronaut, who is eventually cornered and electrocuted in Westminster Abbey.

Conceived and scripted by Manx writer Nigel Kneale (who found the name of his title character in the telephone book!), the series was commissioned by the BBC simply to fill a gap in their summer schedule, the first episode actually being transmitted before Kneale had finished work on the final two. However, as directed by the Austrian-born Rudolph Cartier (a former UFA staff writer), the series was very much a television event, despite the rush in which it was executed. Consequently,

Hammer producer Anthony Hinds, who had seen all of the programmes and been greatly impressed by them, suggested to James Carreras that they buy the rights for a film version. Seeing the potential, Carreras agreed and a deal was struck with the BBC - with whom Hammer had an excellent relationship, given their many previous film adaptations of BBC radio plays and serials. As a result, Hammer agreed to split any profits engendered by a film version down the middle with the television company.

In acquiring the rights, Hammer no doubt felt that they were on to a winner, though other studios balked at the idea. Films inspired by TV originals were pretty thin on the ground in 1955 (the Oscar-winning *Marty* being a rare exception), the general consensus being that audiences would not want to pay to see something at the cinema which they had already seen for free on the box. Television was also looked down upon by the film industry as an inferior cousin. However, Hammer pressed ahead, pre-empting the fashion for big screen adaptations of small screen hits by some twenty years. It was a formula they would later successfully revive in the seventies with their big screen versions of *On The Buses*, *Man About the House* and others.

The Quatermass Experiment was basically seen by Carreras as yet another low budget item whose public familiarity could successfully be exploited, and consequently the production was assigned a meagre budget of just £45,000, though more consideration than usual seems

Victor Caroon (Richard Wordsworth) reveals what he's been hiding under his raincoat in *The Quatermass Experiment*.

to have been given to the casting of actors and technicians, all of which augered well for the film's ultimate impact. To direct the film, Anthony Hinds chose Val Guest, to whom he gave a copy of the BBC script to read just before he left for a two week holiday in Tangiers. Guest originally dismissed the idea of directing the film, not having seen the series. But a reading of the script at the request of his wife quickly changed his mind, and upon returning to England Guest contacted Hinds and agreed to direct it. A wise decision, as it altered the course of his career.

Now regarded as among the most important films of its kind, *The Quatermass Experiment* was by no means the first space-themed science fiction film to be made in the fifties. The trend had started back in 1950 with George Pal's Technicolor adventure *Destination Moon*, though this was actually beaten into the cinemas by the Robert Lippert-produced quickie *Rocketship X-M*, a low budgeter about a moon-bound

rocket which veers off course and lands on Mars. A dull and somewhat naive affair (certainly by today's standards), *Rocketship X-M* nevertheless benefitted financially from being the first of its modern day kind (unlike the *Flash Gordon* serials of the thirties, which were pure hokum) and was, as has been noted, distributed in Britain by Exclusive through their existing deal with Lippert. Not everyone swallowed whole the film's predictions about space travel, though, particularly the critics. Said the *New York Times* of the film: 'If things are really as dull out there in the stratosphere as [the director] would have us believe, science is in for a big surprise.' Luckily, *The Quatermass Experiment* proved to be a different kettle of fish entirely.

Upon his return from Tangiers, Guest began working on the film adaptation of Kneale's television script, paring the three hour running time down to a more manageable length. However, the American financiers Hammer had managed to interest in the project insisted

Professor Quatermass (Brian Donlevy) wonders what could have happened to the two other astronauts in *The Quatermass Experiment*.

that Guest co-write the script with an American, Richard Landau (who had co-written *Stolen Face*), so that the film would contain 'appeal' for US audiences. With this in mind, they also insisted on an American star to play Bernard Quatermass. Of course, Hammer were by now used to importing American stars to beef up their productions, which explains how the role of an obssessed British polymath came to be played by Brian Donlevey, an Irish-born Hollywood B-actor whose finest moment had been as the sadistic sergeant in the 1939 version of *Beau Geste*. Yet Donlevy invested the role with a certain intensity and determination, even if he did fail to win over Nigel Kneale, who referred to his interpretation of Quatermass as 'a wet raincoat looking for somewhere to drip.'

Like the television serial, the film follows the misfortunes of astronaut Victor Caroon (Richard Wordsworth), the only surviving member of a three-man team sent into space by Professor Quatermass (though how Quatermass financed the mission and got the rocket built is never referred to). Save for a jelly-like substance discovered in the rocket ship, there is no trace of Caroon's companions upon the mission's return. This leads Quatermass to ponder what could have happened to them, given that the rocket remained sealed throughout the journey. Could the answer perhaps lie with Caroon himself? Medical examinations follow, yet little headway is made with the astronaut, who has remained in a trance-like state since his return.

However, what Quatermass fails to notice during these examinations is Caroon's curious attraction to plant life, which ultimately compels him to smash his fist into a potted cactus. After this incident, Caroon gradually begins to change - unnoticed at first by those around him. First to go is his arm, which begins to mutate, taking on the prickly qualities of a cactus, a blow from which proves deadly, as a number of concerned on-lookers discover!

Inadvertently helped to escape from the hospital by his wife (Margia Dean), who simply wants him back home, Caroon subsequently goes on the rampage, encountering along the way all manner of characters, including a lonely little girl (Jane Asher) playing with her dollies by the disused barge he has just spent the night in. Unafraid of the astronaut, whose arm is now wrapped up in a trench coat, the girl asks Caroon to join in her game, recalling Boris Karloff's similar encounter with an equally unafraid little girl by a lake in the 1931 classic *Frankenstein* (though this time the child remains unharmed).

By now, the police - in the inevitable guise of longtime film and TV copper Jack Warner (he of *The Blue Lamp* and *Dixon of Dock Green* fame) - are in pursuit of Caroon, who isn't above attacking zoo animals during the dead of night for sustenance. When the hapless astronaut fully mutates, it isn't long before the police are able to track down his slimy trail to Westminster Abbey, where he is electrocuted during a television programme on church architecture! Quatermass is undeterred by all of this though, and the film closes with the launch of the Professor's next rocket, leaving the pathway open for further adventures...

Despite its obviously low budget, *The Quatermass Experiment* stands up very well for its age, thanks to Guest's brisk, cinema verite-style direction, good character work from a reliable cast and a plethora of incident. As Caroon, Richard Wordsworth (whose first film this was) certainly makes the greatest impact. Like the best movie monsters, he retains audience sympathy throughout the film, even during the climax when, while being frazzled to death care of Battersea Power Station, a human scream emanates from the blob-like monster he has become.

As Quatermass (which, for some reason, he pronounces Quatermuss), Donlevy is suitably intense and single-minded, and certainly unworthy of Kneale's scorn, while Jack Warner's copper, Lomax, brings a touch of warmth to the proceedings. Also of note are Thora Hird's comic cameo as a drunken derelict unable to believe that - unlike the pink elephants she usually sees - the monster is for real, and Gordon Jackson as a TV producer whose help Quatermass engages in destroying Caroon.

The film is also packed with memorable incidents, including the crash landing at the top of the picture - even if the rocket itself looks as if it's made of cardboard (it was actually built against a tree for support). Equally effective are the medical examination sequences at the hospital, an encounter with a hapless chemist, and of course the electrifying finale amid the cloistered hush of Westminster Abbey, the setting helping to give the proceedings an extra dimension.

Photographed by long-time Hammer cinematographer Jimmy Harvey, designed by former director J. Elder Wills (remember *Song of Freedom?*) and edited by James Needs, the film has pace, an air of urgency and workmanlike style a-plenty. So much so that one can even forgive the fact that Les Bowie's effects - produced on a shoestring - don't always convince, though make-up man Phil Leakey manages to create a more than convincing 'cactus arm'.

In the cold light of day, Les Bowie's effects for *The Quatermass Experiment* don't look too convincing. Sooty looks suitably unimpressed.

Most importantly, though, the movie marked the film debut of composer James Bernard, who took over from John Hotchkiss (who had previously provided Hammer with scores for their shorts *Copenhagen* and *Man on the Beach*), when he became ill at the last moment and had to drop out.

A close friend of Hammer's in-house musical director John Hollingsworth, Bernard had trained at the Royal College of music and met Hollingsworth while both were serving in the RAF during the war. After this, Bernard began working for the BBC scoring radio dramas, and it was one of these, *The Duchess of Malfi*, (which Hollingsworth had actually conducted) that led to his being hired by Hammer for *The Quatermass Experiment*.

Hollingsworth played the tape of the *Malfi* music to Anthony Hinds, who was suitably impressed and agreed that Bernard was the

man for the job. Little did he know it, but Bernard would go on to write a total of 23 scores for Hammer (more if one counts TV contributions), including impressive work for *The Curse of Frankenstein*, *Dracula* and *The Devil Rides Out*.

Written exclusively for strings and percussion, Bernard's stark-sounding score for *The Quatermass Experiment* helps to heighten the film's effect, adding immeasurably to its atmosphere and tension (particularly during those scenes accompanied simply by an incessantly beating kettle drum).

By this time, the Hammer executives realised that - intended or not - they had something special on their hands, and so began to exploit the picture for all it was worth. For the British release, James Carreras came up with the idea of emphasising the film's X certificate by spelling the title phonetically. Hence,

The Quatermass Experiment became the rather more eerie-sounding The Quatermass Xperiment.

Since the creation of the X Certificate by the British Board of Film Censors in 1951, to denote a film's stronger than usual content of sex, violence and/or horror (over 16 only, until 1970, when it became over 18 only), there had in fact been few instances of the category being used. The X rating had usually spelt death at the box office, which could have spelled disaster for Hammer. However, James Carreras's instinct that times were changing paid off, and when the film finally opened at The London Pavillion on Friday 26th August 1955, the lines stretched around the block.

Paired with Hammer's musical featurette Eric Winstone's Band Show, The Quatermass Experiment went on to break the Pavillion's house record and, paired with the Jules Dassin crime thriller Rififi (a rather odd double bill) for its national release, also did very well up and down the country.

United Artists quickly acquired the US distribution rights, and though they changed the title to The Creeping Unknown and cut the running time down from eighty-two minutes to seventy-eight, the film nevertheless proved to be Hammer's biggest Stateside release to date when shown there in 1956.

In advertising the film's British release, James Carreras came up with even more gimmicks, the kind even William Castle would have been proud of. Midnight showings were arranged for brave customers to watch on their own ('If properly exploited, this stunt could be of great value and cause much controversy,' ran the suggestion to cinema managers), whilst seats with dummies chained to them were displayed outside some theatres, accompanied by a card which read, 'What is the strange force that will keep you chained to your seat whilst seeing The Quatermass Xperiment?' Meanwhile, trade ads pumped up the ballyhoo further with such promises as, 'X is not an unknown quantity - make sure your public know about The Quatermass Xperiment.'

Cheap gimmicks, surely, but in 1955 they paid dividends. But all this posed a dilemma for Hammer: where to next for the burgeoning studio? A return to low budget crime thrillers now seemed unthinkable in light of their new found (not to mention long awaited) success. The question was, how could they top The Quatermass Experiment?

frankenstein unbound

The first thing Hammer did following the success of *The Quatermass Experiment* was to scrap their planned production schedule, which had included the proposed *Friar Tuck, Stand and Deliver* and *King Charles and the Roundheads* projects. Instead, they aimed to cash in on the unexpected success of the Quatermass film by producing another X-orientated production, this one to be titled *X - The Unknown*.

Though now considered little more than a footnote in the company's history, *X - The Unknown* remains of interest primarily for two reasons: first, it firmly established Hammer's transition from B-movie thrillers to out-and-out horror/science fiction, and secondly, it was the first feature to be scripted by Jimmy Sangster, who would not only go on to write the studio's most important genre entries over the next couple of years - *The Curse of Frankenstein, Dracula, The Mummy*, etc. - but who would also later turn to producing and directing for Hammer.

Sangster had actually joined Hammer back in 1948 after serving in the RAF during the war, his first post being third assistant director. Gradually, he worked his way up the hierarchy, becoming a second assistant director, a first assistant director, production manager and, finally, in 1954, assistant to the executive producer (Michael Carreras). In 1955 the ever-ambitious Sangster wrote his first screenplay for the featurette *A Man on the Beach*. Based on the novel by Victor Canning, it was directed by Joseph Losey - then resident in Britain after

having left America in the wake of the McCarthy witch hunts.

A Man on the Beach was followed in 1956 by Sangster's first original feature-length screenplay, *X - The Unknown*. A low budget effort, it centres round a curious radioactive mud-like creature with the ability to kill a man on contact. Accidentally unearthed by the army during training exercises on the Scottish moors (a disused quarry in Beaconsfield, actually), the 'creature' is soon running (slithering?) amok, at which point the army call in the Quatermass-like Dr Adam Royster, played by the Brian Donlevy-like import Dean Jagger (perhaps best remembered for his Oscar-winning role in *Twelve O' Clock High*) in an attempt to destroy the creature.

This was all directed with competence if not flair by Ealing veteran Leslie Norman (father of film critic Barry Norman), who took over from one Joseph Walton when he had to withdraw from the project because of illness. In reality, Walton was a pseudonym for Joseph Losey who, at the request of the star, Dean Jagger, was booted off the film because of his alleged Communist sympathies.

The film also suffers from an over-padded plot and poor effects work (care of Les Bowie) which make the monster look no more threatening than a giant helping of chocolate pudding ('How do you kill mud?' asks someone at one stage). Yet despite these deficiencies, the film did reasonably well at the box office and even garnered praise from *Variety* (who referred

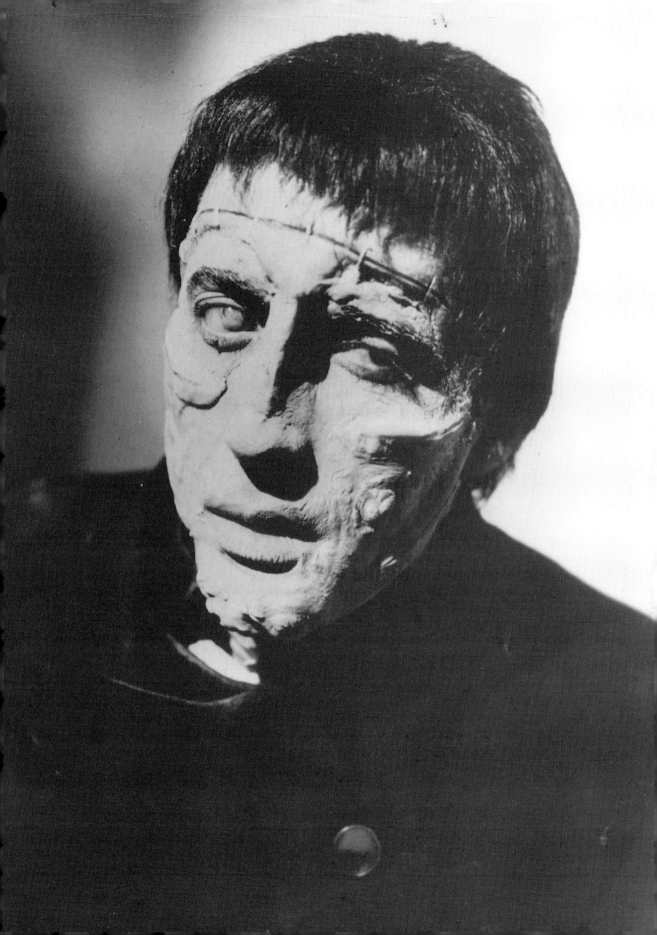

to it as 'highly imaginative and fanciful') when Warner Bros released it in America, though the film by no means approached the success of *The Quatermass Experiment*. With that in mind, Hammer decided to bring back the originator of this success with a sequel, *Quatermass II* (aka *Enemy From Space*).

Based on Nigel Kneale's own 1955 TV follow-up to *The Quatermass Experiment* (again directed by Rudolph Cartier, though this time with John Robinson in the lead), the script was adapted by Kneale himself and director Val Guest, the need to use an American writer to insure US 'appeal' apparently no longer a concern after the first film's success.

The theme again is alien invasion, this time in the form of a substance able to take over humans (pre-empting the similarly-themed *Invasion of the Body Snatchers* by a year). Acclimatizing to the earth's atmosphere in a giant industrial plant allegedly making synthetic food, the substance, which again has the look of a giant chocolate pudding, presumably left over from *X - The Unknown*, is ultimately destroyed when oxygen is pumped into its containers (echoes of *War of the Worlds* in which the aliens were destroyed by bacteria), though not before it has zombified most of the local population and half the British government (nothing new there, then!).

An incident-packed adventure, most notable for its themes of corruption in high places, the film again stars Brian Donlevy as Quatermass and re-united much of the crew responsible for the first film, including editor James Needs, composer James Bernard and effects man Les Bowie, who apparently had shares in blancmange.

Though the film did fairly well when released, it was obvious that Hammer could not continue plundering what was basically the same idea indefinitely. So Jack Goodlatte, now the managing director of the ABC circuit (who'd previously encouraged Hammer to go into production back in 1948) came to the rescue again, this time by suggesting that Hammer remake the Frankenstein story. Hammer needed no more encouragement ('It was like receiving word from God' said Michael Carreras later), and immediately plans were set in motion by James and Michael Carreras.

The proposed film was to be called *Frankenstein and the Monster*, a low budget affair to be shot in black and white within the breakneck time of just three weeks. Hastily scripted by Milton Subotsky, an American writer who would later become a successful producer of low budget horror compendiums (*Vault of Horror*, *Tales From the Crypt*, *The Monster Club* etc.), this all implied a brisk if somewhat uninspired re-tread of the Frankenstein story as movie audiences already knew it. Which is why Universal stepped in at the last minute, threatening legal action. For whilst Mary Shelley's novel was in the public domain, the make-up designed by Jack P. Pierce for Boris Karloff's appearance in the 1931 classic was not. Neither were certain of the plot developments Universal had imbued the Shelley story with. Consequently, Hammer found themselves having to tread very carefully.

As a result, the Subotsky script was scrapped and Jimmy Sangster was given the task of coming up with a new one which contained no reference, either verbal or visual, to the Karloff film. Thus, the 'monster' became the 'creature', and the emphasis of the story was shifted from the exploits of the 'creature' to the Baron's single-minded quest to play God. These revisions consequently led to changes in the production schedule, which was extended to four weeks, and the budget, which was upped to £70,000. Most important, however, was the decision to shoot in colour, which

(Opposite above) Christopher Lee as the Creature in *The Curse of Frankenstein*. Note that for the still, his eyebrows, eyelashes and scars have been touched up.

(Opposite below) Italian artwork for *The Curse of Frankenstein* (literal translation: *The Mask of Frankenstein*).

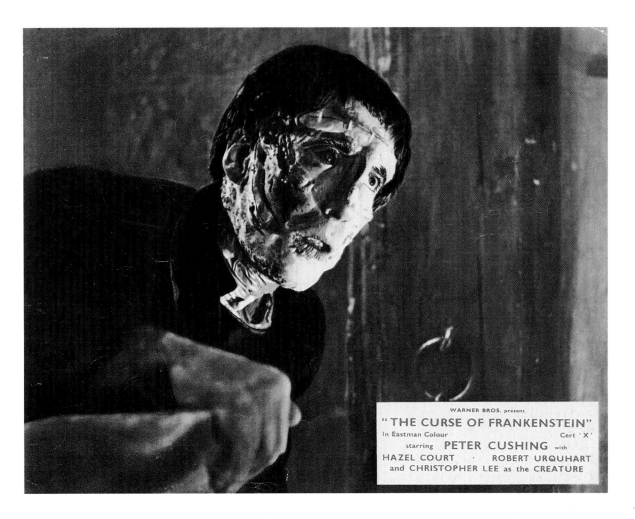

LA MASCHERA DI FRANKENSTEIN

WarnerColor · PETER CUSHING · HAZEL COURT · ROBERT URQUHART · CHRISTOPHER LEE
Sceneggiatura di JIMMY SANGSTER · Regia di TERENCE FISHER · Produttore Esecutivo MICHAEL CARRERAS

made *The Curse of Frankenstein*, as it was now known, not only the first colour Frankenstein, but the first British colour horror film - all of which would help its box office potential immeasurably.

As they had done for the Quatermass films and their previous B-thrillers, Hammer's American backers (this time Eliot Hyman and David Stillman, through whom Milton Subotsky had been connected with the project) suggested that an American star play the lead in the film to guarantee its release in the US market. Yet for the first time Hammer dithered over this proviso, ultimately opting for an actor unknown in the States but already very well known in Britain: Peter Cushing. Nevertheless, despite this refusal to honour his suggestion, Hyman invested 50 percent of the film's budget (for a 50 percent return of profits), the other half coming from the likes of ABPC (which owned the ABC cinema circuit) and Hammer themselves.

Future Frankenstein star Peter Cushing had shown an interest in puppetry and amateur dramatics from an early age, yet was dissuaded from pursuing this as a career by his parents. However, after a brief interlude as a surveyor's assistant, his passion for acting got the better of him and he joined the Worthing Repertory Company, which began four years of rep work up and down the country, culminating in a one-way ticket to Hollywood (paid for by his father) in an attempt to break into the movies.

This Cushing did with variable success, acting as Louis Hayward's stand-in double in *The Man In The Iron Mask* (1939) and as a stooge to Laurel and Hardy in their last great comedy *A Chump at Oxford* (1940). He returned to Britain in 1942 after bit parts in four more films and, failing to get into the armed services, joined ENSA for the duration. In the late forties, he hooked up with the Old Vic Company and played Osric

opposite Olivier's indecisive Dane in the touring production of *Hamlet*, a role he repeated in the acclaimed film version of 1948.

Further stage work followed, but it was in the world of live television drama that Cushing ultimately made a name for himself in the early fifties. Work here included Dr John Rollason in Nigel Kneale's *The Creature* (1954), a part he would later revive when Hammer filmed the play as *The Abominable Snowman* in 1957, and Winston Smith in an acclaimed adaptation of George Orwell's *1984*, for which he received the National Television Award and The Guild of Television Producers and Directors Best Performance Award - all of which brought him to the attention of Hammer, who saw a movie star in the making. Thus, Cushing signed to play Frankenstein on 26 October 1956, a role which would not only make him an international star, but which he would revive a further five times.
The rest of the cast, meanwhile, was being fleshed out slowly but surely, though there was still one important role to fill; that of the 'creature'. For a while it looked like future *Carry On* star Bernard Bresslaw had won the role, but ultimately it went to an unknown actor called Christopher Lee, who just happened to have the same agent as Peter Cushing.

Lee had in fact briefly appeared in the film version of *Hamlet* in 1948, though not in the same scenes as Cushing. His career, which had been faltering, badly needed a kick start. Having decided to become an actor after finishing voluntary service during the war, Lee managed to secure himself a seven year contract with the Rank Organization, and had played a number of minor parts in relatively big films, such as *Moulin Rouge* (which again featured Cushing) and *Private's Progress*. But he had apparently been restricted from progressing up the star ladder by his height - which ironically proved to be his eventual ticket to fame and fortune.

By the time Lee had been signed, the rest of the cast and crew had fallen into place. To direct, Hammer chose Terence Fisher, simply because he was still owed a film on the short contract he was then under with the company (making one wonder what Francis Searle or Godfrey Grayson would have made of the film had they been assigned it). The editing chores went, as they usually did, to James Needs, whilst James Bernard, working on his fourth Hammer film, was brought in to score the picture. To photograph it, colour expert Jack Asher was added to the crew, whose work was greatly enhanced by the ravishing production design of Bernard Robinson.

By the time Sangster had finished reworking the script, the story had been suitably redefined to avoid comparison with Universal's *Frankenstein* - which is why director Fisher refused to see the original, lest it influence him in any way. In Hammer's new version, the Baron recounts his story in flashback to a priest (Alex Gallier), whilst awaiting execution by guillotine for the crimes he has committed in the names of Science and Medicine.

Begining in his teenage years just after the funeral of his father, the story initially follows the education of the young Victor Frankenstein (here played by Melvyn Hayes) by his new tutor Paul Krempe (Robert Urquhart). The Baron's thirst for knowledge is unquenchable, and it isn't long before tutor and pupil are on an equal footing. At this point, their scientific experiments turn to life itself, and they successfully revive a dead puppy. Though pleased with the results of this experiment, Victor reveals to Paul that his ambitions stretch further, his ultimate goal being to create a human being from dead tissue.

Appalled by the idea at first, Paul grudgingly agrees to help Victor in his quest, their first task being to find a suitable body with which

to begin their work. Victor, in fact, has already discovered one: a recently hanged highwayman, whose body they cut from its roadside gibbet once night has fallen. Far from being a perfect specimen, the highwayman's eyes have been pecked out by birds, so Victor begins the search for replacements, along with the other various anatomical bits and pieces required to complete his creation, including a new pair of hands and, of course, a brain.

The latter unfortunately eludes the Baron, but so driven is he by this point that he determines on murdering a brilliant professor (Paul Hardtmuth), whom he invites to his castle, so that his creature will be born with 'a lifetime's knowledge'. A quarrel between Paul and Victor follows when Paul discovers the origin of the brain and the means by which it has been procured. In the subsequent struggle, the jar in which the brain has been placed gets smashed. Undeterred, Victor picks out the shards of glass from the organ, determined to carry on. But, as we later discover, the damage is extensive.

From here on in, things take a distinctly ghoulish turn as the Baron, having been abandoned by Paul, strives to complete the task at hand on his own. Paul, meanwhile, stays on at the castle to protect Elizabeth, the Baron's cousin and intended, who has come to stay, but who remains ignorant of her fiance's experiments.

Finally, after various setbacks, Victor succeeds in animating his creature, but the damaged brain means that it is not only an imbecile, but a psychotic one, attempting to strangle the Baron on sight. As to be expected, the creature escapes and goes on the rampage in the local woods where it kills a blind woodman and his grandson. It is eventually caught, after having half his face blown away by Paul's gun, and buried in the woods.

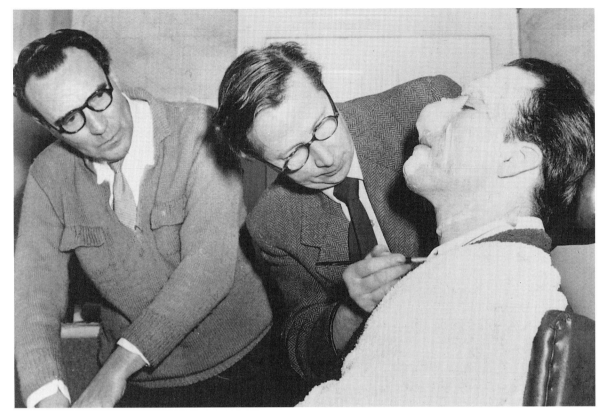

The Baron isn't above grave-robbing, though, and once Paul has left the castle (sure that Frankenstein will now abandon his experiemnts), he digs up the creature's body so that he can continue working on it. At this stage, Justine the maid (Valerie Gaunt) attempts to blackmail Victor into marrying her by threatening to disclose his work to the authorities, a situation Victor quickly remedies by locking Justine up in the same room as the creature, with the expected results.

Things finally come to a head on the eve of Victor and Elizabeth's wedding when Paul returns to take part in the celebrations. Victor shows him the crude advances he has made with the creature, which compels Paul to tell the authorities what the Baron has been up to in his laboratory. While they argue outside Elizabeth's curiosity finally gets the better of

her, and she decides to sneak a peek at her intended's workplace, only to discover the creature.

Running to protect his beloved, Victor races to the roof where he battles it out with the creature who, after being set alight with an oil lamp, is pushed through a sky light into a convenient vat of acid where all trace of him disappears. All of this leaves the Baron with the task of explaining who committed the murders, especially as Paul and Elizabeth deny all knowledge of the creature. The picture ends with the Baron, now a raving wreck, being led away to the guillotine...

The first Frankenstein movie since Universal wound down their own series in 1948 with *Abbot and Costello meet Frankenstein*, and the first official re-telling of the story since that series

Christopher Lee has his make-up applied for *The Curse of Frankenstein*.

began back in 1931 with the original *Frankenstein*, this new Hammer version, though no more faithful to the Shelley novel than all the other variations, at least has the courage of its penny dreadful convictions. From the opening titles, set against a blood red background, this is very much a colour production which also, for the first time, shows in close-up those elements which had previously been shied away from. Cadavers, severed hands, eye-balls and brains are displayed in all their gory glory, all of which delighted audiences in the fifties.

Certainly, when viewed today, these elements seems fairly tame when compared to current offerings in the horror genre, yet their impact at the time was astonishing - comparable, in fact, to the effect *The Exorcist* would have on seventies audiences and *The Silence of the Lambs* on nineties moviegoers. So one can perhaps forgive the film today if its editing in some sequences seems on the slow side and the camera set-ups for the most part unadventurous. However, while assessing the film in the context in which it was made, it remains something of a genre milestone.

Sangster's script moves at a commendable clip while Fisher's direction, if occasionally a little clumsy, makes the most of the situations at hand. The first appearance of the creature is particularly well handled - a quick dolly into his face as he pulls away his bandages - as is the sequence in the woods when Paul shoots the creature, its face exploding in a spurt of vivid red (though where the creature got his clothes from and how he managed to dress himself in order to make his escape is never explained, given his mental deficiencies). Bernard Robinson's sets, though obviously limited, are certainly eye-catching, whilst James Bernard's score has plenty of drive and atmosphere (though parts of it do seem a little relentless, it must be said).

Lee's make-up, meanwhile, is suitably horrific. Created by Phil Leakey, who'd successfully mutated Victor Caroon in *The Quatermass Experiment*, the creature has the look of a road accident victim, his facial tissue looking suitably waterlogged after spending months in a holding tank. Contructed from undertaker's wax, cotton wool and glue, Lee's mask took several hours to apply each morning and, once on, severely restricted his facial movements. So much so that he could only eat soup and mashed potatoes at lunch for fear of cracking the laboriously applied effect. The results were worth the trouble, though.

Yet despite the creature's horrific appearance, Lee's wordless performance still manages to invoke a certain degree of sympathy, particularly in the scene in which he is forced to perform simple tricks by the Baron, such as standing and sitting, which he does with the clumsiness of a spastic child.

Once completed, Anthony Hinds, James Carreras and Michael Carreras took the film to America themselves in early 1957 in search of a distributor, feeling that this time they had something special. They had, and Warner Bros (the distributors of *X - The Unknown*) quickly snapped up the film, agreeing to distribute it worldwide. Warners would also give *Frankenstein* the kind of promotional campaign Hammer could only dream of affording. Consequently, when the film opened at the Warner Bros theatre in London's West End on May 2nd 1957, the lines stretched round the block, despite an almost universally hostile reaction from the press. The *Observer's* C. A. Lejeune summed up the general consensus when she reported that, 'Without hesitation I should rank *The Curse of Frankenstein* among the half-dozen most repulsive films I have encountered.' *Variety* proved to be one of the exceptions to this rule, finding much to admire in the direction, camera work and performances.

Terence Fisher, Hazel Court
and Peter Cushing
between scenes on *The
Curse of Frankenstein*.

The film certainly received its fair share of bal-lyhoo. The lobby of the Warner theatre was decked out to look like Frankenstein's laborato-ry, while the media reported on the huge crowds, who helped break the theatre's box office records, clocking up its biggest weekend take ever. These crowds actually increased in the second week of release and Hammer became a buzz-word practically over night.

Even the censor was kind to the picture. Despite its (no doubt desired) X certificate, the film suffered little interference, the only major cut being a shot of Frankenstein dropping the bird-pecked highwayman's head into a vat of acid. Otherwise, the close-ups of the severed hands and eye-balls remained intact. Indeed, the only cuts seemed to have been instigated by Hammer themselves, for the pressbook refers to Victor working from 'notes and formulas left by his father, the old Baron, who has been the creator of a former monster.' No such reference is made to the old Baron's activities in the film, and it now seems uncertain whether such a scene, in which his work was alluded to, was

actually shot. However, this does go part way to explaining the film's title. It also implies that the film is a sequel to rather than a remake of the 1931 version, another step, perhaps, to ensure that no writ was served for breach of copyright.

The film's 'monster business' at the British box office was nothing compared to the reception it received when it finally opened in America in June 1957. 'Full week's business in two days,' boasted the trade ads, whilst cinema managers were encouraged to go the whole hog in promoting the film. 'Feature the crea-ture and go!' exclaimed the pressbook, which went on to suggest 'Around-the-clock horror-a-thon shows, ambulances outside, smelling salt displays, money-back-if-you-faint tickets and nurses in attendance,' all of which paid dividends. Indeed, the film eventually grossed £2 million worldwide - not bad for a small independent British company who, up until recently, had barely been scraping by in the quota quickie market.

dracula has risen from the grave

Having presented the world with a new, full-blooded version the Frankenstein legend, it was perhaps inevitable that Hammer would next turn their attention to Dracula, the Bela Lugosi version of which had previously started the Universal horror cycle of the thirties and forties. However, while preparations were being made to bring the king of the undead to the silver screen, Hammer carried on with the day to day running of their studio, enabled by the success of *The Curse of Frankenstein* to turn out fewer but now slightly more prestigious productions.

The first of these was *The Steel Bayonet*, a wartime thriller starring Leo Genn, Kieron Moore and Michael Ripper (the latter of whom was already proving to be one of Hammer's most regular supporting players). Produced and directed by Michael Carreras, the film follows the exploits of a platoon of British soldiers who find themselves having to face the enemy at an isolated farm during the assault on Tunis. Shot in black and white and in 'Hammerscope', it's a gritty but straightforward production which served its purpose at the time.

A further selection of shorts, among the last Hammer would make, also followed, such as *Danger List* and *Clean Sweep*.

More ambitious and more in keeping with the studio's newfound horror label, though, was

The Abominable Snowman (aka *The Abominable Snowman of the Himalayas*), which was based on Nigel Kneale's successful 1955 TV play *The Creature*, starring Peter Cushing. Shot in black and white, and rather less aggressive in its determination to shock than *The Curse of Frankenstein*, the film nevertheless delivers a certain degree of tension, built up through atmosphere, and still stands up remarkably well today.

Directed with style by Val Guest and adapted by Kneale from his own tele-play (making this his first solo screenplay credit), the film revolves round a Himalayan expedition headed by an American entrepreneur (Forrest Tucker) and an English doctor (Peter Cushing), both out to find proof of the Yeti's existence. This they find, but not without the number of their party being diminished one by one.

Mostly shot on the backlot at Bray, with additional sequences filmed at Pinewood and on location in the Pyrenees, the film generally manages to convince one of its Himalayan setting thanks chiefly to Bernard Robinson's design work, which includes a draughty-looking Tibetan monastery presided over by a wise old Lhama (Arnold Marle), who seems to know more than he is prepared to divulge about the elusive Yeti.

The supporting cast, which includes the likes

of Richard Wattis and Maureen Connell, are also top notch (particularly Marle as the kindly Lhama), while Cushing and the usually stolid Tucker give their best.

The Yeti themselves, much to the disappointment of some audiences at the time, are glimpsed only briefly towards the end of the film. But as has already been noted, this was never intended as a monster on the loose shocker, more a cerebral thriller, and as such it succeeds admirably, with the Yeti presented as benign, super-intelligent creatures with telepathic abilities, determined only on concealing themselves from the destructive forces of man. By the film's end, Cushing's character - the only survivor - is happy to oblige...

A character driven piece with a more philosophical approach to its subject than might be expected, the film was nevertheless advertised with a horrific come-on in the States, where the posters exclaimed, 'We dare you to see it alone!'. Its uncommon restraint, however, earned it extra points with some critics. Said the *Sunday Times*: 'For once, an engaging monster is neither bombed, roasted nor electrocuted. For this welcome courtesy, as well as its thrills and nonsense, I salute *The Abominable Snowman*.' Certainly among Hammer's best films of the period, it remains sadly under-valued.

The Abominable Snowman was followed by another war film, the less than subtle *The Camp on Blood Island*. A sort of early *King Rat*, it was promoted as Hammer's fiftieth film, stars Andre Morell, Barbara Shelly, Michael Gwynne and Richard Wordsworth, and was directed and co-scripted by Val Guest. A brutal prisoner of war drama whose exploitative poster campaign boasted 'Jap war crimes exposed,' the film generated a certain degree of controversy at the time - which certainly didn't harm its box office potential, the total worldwide gross being in excess of $4 million.

A naval comedy titled *Up The Creek* came next, which features a veritable army of British comedy talent, including David Tomlinson, Peter Sellers, Lionel Jeffries and Wilfred Hyde White. Scripted and directed by the constantly busy Val Guest, its story centres round the black market activities of a run down shore establishment, and proved popular enough to engender a hasty sequel, *Further Up The Creek*, which appeared a few months later towards the end of the year.

However, the studio's main player of 1958 proved to be their production of *Dracula* (aka *The Horror of Dracula*), the success of which not only confirmed Hammer as the world's leading purveyors of horror, but made them a bucketload of money to boot. That it was also their most sleek and sophisticated production to date didn't harm their growing prestige, either.

The success of *The Curse of Frankenstein* had provoked a certain degree of interest in Hammer from Hollywood, so that by the time they came to make *Dracula* and the films which immediately followed it, they had financial backing from a number of American sources, including Columbia, Universal and United Artists. These companies also distributed Hammer's product in the US and throughout the world, which eliminated the need for Hammer's own distribution arm Exclusive - which was gradually wound down.

In fact it was Universal, who'd previously threatened Hammer with legal action over *The Curse of Frankenstein*, who would distribute *Dracula* in America. However, like *The Curse of Frankenstein* before it, the new colour production of *Dracula* would bear little relation to the original 1930 version, which had been based on the creaky stage play by Hamilton Deane and John L. Balderston rather than the Bram Stoker novel itself. Consequently, despite an atmospheric opening reel in Transylvania, the Lugosi

Christopher Lee's Dracula
faces the power of the crucifix in the 1958 movie.

version (directed by Tod Browning) is a somewhat static affair, with much of the vital action,
including the staking of Dracula, discreetly
taking place off-screen.

For their version, Hammer went back to the
original Stoker novel, though as usual, budgetary
limitations meant that the flavour of the book
would be the object of the exercise rather than
the exact letter of Stoker's epic *tour de force*.

To make the film, much of the cast and crew of
The Curse of Frankenstein was re-united in the hope
that lightning would strike twice. This included
scriptwriter Jimmy Sangster, who began working on the screenplay in the summer of 1957,
having read the Stoker novel, which he suitably
condensed. Gone was Dracula's trip to Whitby
and Renfield's scenes in the insane asylum.
Instead, the film was wholly set in and around
Dracula's castle, with the Holmwood's home
not more than a few miles away.

The film thus opens on a suitably ominous
note as Jonathan Harker (John Van Eyssen)
makes his way to Castle Dracula to take up his
new post as a librarian. Despite it being a
bright and cheerful day, as he approaches the
Castle he notes that no birds are singing...

Having crossed the bridge to the castle forecourt
(the energetically splashing river was provided
by the local fire brigade, who can also be seen in
the first Quatermass film), Harker enters the castle's baronial hall, only to find the place deserted
and a note from his employer apologising for his
absence. Soon after, Harker encounters a curious
woman in white (Valerie Gaunt) who begs him
to take her away from the castle. However, her
pleadings are cut short and she quickly disappears. The reason for this? The arrival of Dracula
himself at the top of the stairway!

Silhouetted at first, we are led to expect the
worst. Cliche is quickly turned on its head,

though, as Dracula (Christopher Lee) briskly
descends the stairway and greets Harker in the
most urbane manner imaginable. Escorting
him to his room, Dracula exchanges pleas-
antries with Harker, explaining that he won't
be available the next day, upon which he leaves
Harker for the night, locking his bedroom
door as he does so. It is shortly after this that it
is revealed that Harker has come not to tend
the Count's library, but to destroy him, being
in the employ of vampire hunter extraordinaire, Professor Van Helsing (Peter Cushing).

Later that night, Harker finds that his door has
been unlocked, and so goes to investigate,
meeting in the hall the mysterious woman in
white who again pleads with him to take her
away from the castle. She soon reveals her true
colours, however, by baring her fangs and
attempting to sink them into Harker's neck,
but is prevented from doing so by Dracula
himself who, eyes red, fangs bloody and
bared, rushes across the hallway and attacks
Harker himself.

After this encounter, the story moves to the
following day when Harker, despite having
been infected by the vampiric attack, sets out
to destroy Dracula and his 'bride'.
Unfortunately, he manages only to destroy the
woman - who dishevels into an old hag when
staked through the heart - before the sun
inconveniently sets and Dracula rises from his
coffin to extract a bloody revenge.

At this point, Sangster's script introduces
Professor Van Helsing, who takes it upon
himself to investigate Harker's disappearance,
which inevitably leads him to Castle Dracula.
Here he not only discovers that Harker is now
himself a vampire, but that Dracula has
apparently disappeared, taking with him the
photograph of Harker's fiancée Lucy Holmwood
(Carol Marsh), his plan, as we soon learn,
being to replace his dead 'bride' with Lucy.

Despatching Harker with a stake, Van Helsing thus gives chase to Dracula, who has since exited somewhat dramatically atop a horse-drawn hearse.

But Van Helsing arrives too late at the Holmwood residence. Lucy's brother Arthur (Michael Gough) informs Van Helsing that she is sick, though a closer inspection by the Professor reveals that she has already been given the bite by Dracula. Van Helsing attemps to stress the severity of the danger Lucy is in, but as to be expected, his advice is mostly unheeded and Lucy, welcoming the Count into her bedroom later that night, is found dead the next morning.

Unable to come to terms with what has happened, Arthur remains skeptical about what Van Helsing has told him. It is only when Lucy rises from her grave and Arthur sees her for himself that he begins to believe the Professor's claims. Consequently, Lucy is staked and Van Helsing continues his pursuit of the elusive Count.

Dracula next sets his sights on Arthur's wife Mina (Melissa Stribling), whom Arthur and Van Helsing attempt to protect, without realising that the Count has actually secreted his coffin in the Holmwood cellar, thus giving him easy access to the household! He thus kidnaps Mina and takes her back to his castle. Van Helsing again gives chase, this time catching the Count and destroying him by exposing him to sunlight in a battle to the death.

Reducing the Stoker novel to its bare bones like this, Sangster's adaptation certainly moves at a fair old clip and leaves audiences with little time to catch their collective breaths between the thrilling highlights. Indeed, as Sangster later said, the reason so much of the novel was left out was simply because, 'There was no room for it', though discarded elements did

appear in the numerous sequels that followed. For budgetary reasons, Dracula also lost his ability to turn into a bat or a wolf, though he did, for the first time on screen, bear fangs.

Filmed on a budget of £83,000 in just 25 days on Hammer's new sound stage, *Dracula* is a model of its gothic kind. Production designer Bernard Robinson truly excelled himself on this film, his hallway set in Dracula's castle making the very most of the limited space (71 ft by 36 ft) available, using the powers of forced perspective to make things look much more expansive than they actually are, while his Holmwood and Van Helsing interiors have a suitably fussy Victorian feel to them.

Composer James Bernard, meanwhile, produced not only one of his most intense and dramatic scores for the film, but one of the horror genre's most identifiable themes. His Dracula motif, based around the three syllables of the Count's name, became synonymous with Hammer - almost their theme tune - and was later revived (like Dracula himself) for several of the sequels and spin-offs.

James Needs and Bill Lenny's editing is also spot on, ensuring that none of the scenes outlast their narrative usefulness, all of which keeps the running time down to a brisk and economical 82 minutes.

Hero of the piece, though, is director Terence Fisher. If ever a man realised the directorial gift he'd been given, then Fisher did here. Undoubtedly assisted by the efforts of the film's other technicians, particularly cinematographer Jack Asher who here surpasses himself, Fisher makes the very most of the opportunities at hand. Directorial flourishes abound, most notably Dracula's first entrance, as has been mentioned, and the climax, in which Van Helsing and the Count do battle across a giant refectory table, ending with Van

Helsing running its length, leaping and ripping down the drapes to expose Dracula to a fatal dose of sunlight. The idea for this last bit of action came from Peter Cushing himself, who felt the film needed 'some sort of Douglas Fairbanks scene.' This, combined with his idea of using two candlesticks crossed to form a makeshift crucifix to finish off Dracula, was inspiration indeed, perfectly visualised by Fisher and helped immeasurably by Phil Leakey's make-up and Sydney Pearson's special effects, which show the Count disintegrate before our very eyes.

Also of note is the scene in which Dracula comes to pay a midnight visit on Lucy. Her window open, the autumn leaves gently rustling on the patio in the breeze outside as she anxiously awaits the arrival of her caller, this is a scene of lingering tension and persua-siveness, perfectly complemented by James Bernard's seductive music. Lee's Count also has, for the first time, a certain sexual magnetism, as verified by Lucy's willingness to succumb to his advances. This had only been hinted at in Lugosi's heavily-accented comic book interpre-tation of the role. Here it is a statement of fact, with the Count's carnal lust serving to arouse and satisfy his blood lust, and vice-versa.

To alleviate the tension, the film isn't without its humorous scenes. Van Helsing is introduced to the audience dictating notes into a primitive dictaphone, much to the bemusement of his servant (Geoffrey Bayldon), while the pursuit of Dracula back to his castle towards the climax of the film is interspersed with comic business involving an irate frontier official (George Benson), whose barrier gets smashed in the chase before he can raise it. Best of all, though, is Miles Malleson's turn as a jovial undertaker, not adverse to relating jocular anecdotes about his clients as Van Helsing and Arthur Holmwood search his cellar for Dracula's coffin.

Performance-wise, the film confirmed Peter Cushing and Christopher Lee as the genre's top stars, having inherited the crowns of Boris Karloff and Bela Lugosi. Cushing's Van Helsing proved to be the definitive interpretation of the role, despite being nothing like Stoker's description of the character, while Lee would forever be identified with the role of Dracula, so perfectly was he cast. Michael Gough, it must be said, makes a rather dreary Arthur Holmwood, though the rest of the supporting cast helps to disguise his apparent lack of interest in the role.

As had been hoped, the film was another box office smash for Hammer when it was finally released in 1958, even surpassing the box office take of *The Curse of Frankenstein*. Some of the critics were even slightly more disposed to praise this time round, with *Film Bulletin* refer-ring to the film as a 'Technicolored nightmare, directed by Terence Fisher with immense flair for the blood-curdling shot.'

By now, the name of Hammer was synony-mous with horror. All they had to do now was to keep up the flow of product and reap the benefits - which they did with a vengeance.

gory, glory days

Hammer returned to crime for their next outing with *The Snorkel*, which stars theGerman-born Peter Van Eyck (perhaps best remembered for *The Wages of Fear*) as a husband out to drown his wife, aided by the snorkel of the title. But his perfect crime proves to be less than flawless, as his observant step-daughter (Mandy Miller) picks up a number of clues, all of which point the finger of suspicion at her step-father.

A tolerable potboiler which could have made more of its ingenious central plot gimmick, it was directed by former cinematographer Guy Green (an Oscar winner for *Great Expectations* back in 1945) and lensed in black and white by Jack Asher. Yet despite its general competence, the film is little revived today, perhaps because it was surrounded by so many of Hammer's classic horror films, the next of which proved to be *The Revenge of Frankenstein*.

After the success of *The Curse of Frankenstein*, it was inevitable that Hammer would return to the Baron, just as they had done to Professor Quatermass (and Dick Barton and PC 49). But what of the story? The creature had been destroyed in a vat of acid at the end of *Curse*.

After some deliberation, it was decided that, unlike the Universal films, Baron Frankenstein himself would be the focus of the series rather than his monster. Even so, this still created a problem, for *Curse* had concluded with the Baron being escorted out to the guillotine. Said Sir James Carreras at the time when questioned about the new film: 'Oh, we just sew his head back on. It's fascinating!'. Scriptwriter Jimmy

Sangster's actual solution proved to be rather more ingenious; he simply arranged to have the priest who had read the Baron his last rites executed in his stead, the executioner and his hunchbacked assistant (Oscar Quitak) being Frankenstein's paid accomplices.

Produced for Columbia Pictures, the film was originally announced in the trades as *The Blood of Frankenstein*, while *Curse* was still enjoying its successful box office run. And with the exception of composer James Bernard (who was here replaced by Leonard Salzedo, who'd previously written the scores for *The Steel Bayonet* and three of Hammer's crime programmers), the production crew remained the same as on *Curse* and *Dracula*.

In this episode, set in 1860, some three years after *Curse*, the Baron, now safely rescued from the blade of the guillotine and known as Dr Stein, has a thriving practice in Carlsbruck, catering to the whims of weathly hypochondriacs. He has also set himself up at a hospital for the poor. It isn't compassion that has led him to care for the needy, though; rather the access the post gives him to harvest from their bodies the limbs and organs required to create a new creature.

Helped in this task by his hunchbacked assistant Karl (Oscar Quitak) and Dr Hans Kleve (Francis Matthews), a young surgeon eager to learn the Baron's secrets, Frankenstein determines on transplanting Karl's brain into his newly created body, an operation the hunchback is all too willing to undergo. Surprisingly, the operation goes well and Karl (now played by Michael Gwynn) turns out to be both intelligent and articulate - just as in the Mary Shelley novel. Unfortunately, a violent encounter with a brutish nightwatchman (George Woodbridge) damages the creature's brain, and as a result he begins to contort into the crippled state of Karl's former body.

The creature naturally goes on the rampage after this and is tracked down by the police in the expected manner. The Baron, meanwhile, is beaten to death by the patients he has so recklessly exploited for his experimental means. Luckily for him he has conveniently had the foresight to assemble a second creature, into which Dr Kleve now transplants the Baron's brain, making Frankenstein both creator and created. The film concludes with the Baron resuming his practice in London's Harley street, now under the name of Dr Franck.

Viewed today, the film has its points of interest, most notably Bernard Robinson's plush design work and Cushing's performance, now less manically driven. Taken as a whole, however, the film, though quite entertaining on the surface, is not without its faults: Terence Fisher's direction is too stately, Jack Asher's phototography (though beautifully lit) too unadventurous in its movement, and the monster less than horrific (he even dies off screen). The plot, meanwhile, has more holes than a Swiss cheese.

The film starts off well, with a shot of the guillotine to which Frankenstein is being led for execution. However, not only is there no sign of Paul and Elizabeth (seen at the jail at the end of *Curse*) there are also no officials to oversee the execution, thus making it conveniently easy for the Baron to bribe the executioner and his hunchbacked assistant into beheading the priest instead of his good self (this isn't even shown, just alluded to with sound effects). The film also contains some rather unfortunate

comic business, primarily with two grave-diggers (Michael Ripper and Lionel Jeffries) and a hospital orderly (Richard Wordsworth), along with some lapses in both narrative and continuity (the Baron not only keeps his equipment locked up in a wine cellar, but Karl his assistant with it!). The film's suggestion that the monster has become a cannibal is also so subtly referred to as to be almost undetectable, while the creature into which the Baron's brain is transplanted at the end just happens to look and sound exactly like Peter Cushing! Yet despite its faults, the film did well at the box office, successfully riding on the coat tails of both *Curse* and *Dracula*.

While *Revenge* was being filmed in 1957, there was also interest from Columbia in producing a television series based round the Frankenstein character. To be called *The Tales of Frankenstein*, it was to feature the Baron in a number of stories involving voodoo, black magic and transplants, synopses for which were written by Jimmy Sangster at the request of Michael Carreras. A pilot episode, sponsored by Hammer and financed by Columbia, was even filmed in America. Titled *The Face in the Tombstone Mirror*, it stars Anton Diffring as Frankenstein and Don Megowan as the monster, and was written and directed by Curt Siodmak, whose previous screenplay credits include Universal's *Frankenstein Meets the Wolf Man* and *Son of Dracula*. Sadly, the results were deemed less than satisfactory and the proposed series was scrapped and the pilot never shown.

Plans for an immediate sequel to *Dracula*, to be titled *The Revenge of Dracula*, were also shelved when Christopher Lee expressed concern at being typecast as the Count. Consequently, Hammer's next production proved to be a comedy, *I Only Arsked*, based on the popular TV sit-com *The Army Game*, which had made stars of Bernard Bresslaw, Alfie Bass and Bill Fraser (the latter two as Bootsie and Snudge). This meant the studio's next genre outing was their adaptation of Conan Doyle's *The Hound of the Baskervilles*.

By no means the first Sherlock Holmes film nor the first version of *Baskervilles*, the celebrated Baker Street sleuth had in fact made his screen debut as early as 1900 in *Sherlock Holmes Baffled* (copyrighted 1903), while the first version of *Baskervilles* had appeared in Germany in 1915 under the title *Der Hund Von Baskervilles*. Many famous actors had already portrayed Holmes, including John Barrymore, Clive Brook, Raymond Massey and Reginald Owen, though it was Basil Rathbone's interpretation of the role, beginning with the 1939 version of *The Hound of the Baskervilles* and followed by a further thirteen adventures, which came to be recognized as the definitive incarnation.

The last of these, *Dressed to Kill* (aka *Sherlock Holmes and the Secret Code*) appeared back in 1946. Thus, like Frankenstein and Dracula, the character was ready for a Technicolor revival ('It's ten times the terror in Technicolor!' exclaimed the poster).

The film begins with a sprightly prologue set in the seventeenth century, explaining the Baskerville curse. 'May the hounds of hell take care of me if I can't hunt her down' exclaims Sir Hugo Baskerville to his drunken cronies one night as he sets off to track down a servant girl who has proved unwilling to respond to his sexual advances. However, he is only to be savaged to death by what appears to be a giant hound after he has completed his grisly deed.

The story then cuts to the Victorian era and to Sherlock Holmes' Baker Street apartments, where Dr Mortimer, the Baskerville family physician, is telling Holmes and Dr Watson of the recent death of Sir Charles Baskerville, allegedly brought on by the sight of the supposed 'hound from hell'. Dr Mortimer then implores Holmes to help protect the new heir to the Baskerville estate, Sir Henry, when he arrives from Canada. Reluctantly, Holmes agrees to do so, and the game is afoot in a generally faithful rendition of the well-known story.

Adventures on fog-wreathed Dartmoor (mostly Chobham Common in Surrey), an escaped convict, encounters in the ruins of an abbey, mysterious signals at night, a disused mine, disguise, deceit, a poisonous spider and the ever-present threat of Grimpen Mire all combine to produce the definitive version of this much-filmed Conan Doyle book, smoothly adapted by screenwriter Peter Bryan. The work of director Terence Fisher, photographer Jack Asher and designer Bernard Robinson is likewise top-notch after the comparative disappointment of *The Revenge of Frankenstein*, while James Bernard's score adds immeasurably to the film's brooding atmosphere.

The film's ace, however, is Peter Cushing's interpretation of Holmes, his steely approach to the case proving to be as single-minded as Van Helsing's determination to destroy Dracula. Cushing thus became the definitive Holmes to a new generation of movie-goers, returning to the role for a BBC series in 1967 and a TV movie, *The Masks of Death*, in 1984. Indeed, it wasn't until Jeremy Brett re-defined the role again for the celebrated Granada series that began in late 1984 that Cushing stopped being so closely identified with it.

In the *Baskervilles* film, Cushing is also very ably supported by Andre Morell, who makes an excellent Watson, mercifully jettisoning the comic buffoonery that made Nigel Bruce's Watson little more than an imbecile side-kick to Rathbone's Holmes ('A man of Holmes' intelligence would never have suffered such a clot around him', said Fisher of Bruce's Watson), while Christopher Lee's performance

as Sir Henry Baskerville carries the required
nobility and authority. Indeed, Lee proved to
be the only actor to play Sir Henry Baskerville,
Holmes himself (in the German film *Sherlock
Holmes and the Deadly Necklace*, directed in 1962 by
Terence Fisher) and Sherlock's older brother
Mycroft, in Billy Wilder's *The Private Life of
Sherlock Holmes* (1970).

The film's supporting cast is also top notch,
including Francis de Wolff's stern-looking Dr
Mortimer, Miles Malleson's comic turn as
Bishop Frankland and Maria Landi's hot-blood-
ed Cecile, the perpetrator of the dastardly
attacks on Sir Henry. In fact, the only let-down
proves to be the hound itself, all too clearly a
Great Dane (called Colonel) wearing a badly
made papier mache mask. But such are the
film's compensations this hardly seems to
matter.

Rather less could be said of Hammer's next
few cinematic outings, however, the least
involving of which is *Ten Seconds to Hell*, the story
of a bomb disposal unit (headed by Jack
Palance and Jeff Chandler) operating in Berlin
just after the end of World War Two. Directed
by Robert Aldrich from a script by Aldrich and
Teddi Sherman, it is far from being in the
same league as Michael Powell's similarly
themed *The Small Back Room*, and is effectively
scuppered from the first frame thanks to a
hilarious introductory narration.

Much better is *The Ugly Duckling*, a comic variation on *Dr Jekyll and Mr Hyde* (Hammer's first
contact with the Stevenson classic) which stars
Bernard Bresslaw as the dim-witted Henry
Jekyll, who finds himself transformed into the
with-it Teddy Hyde after partaking of his
ancestor's notorious potion. Directed by Lance
Comfort from a story by Sid Colin (who had
co-scripted *I Only Arsked* for Bresslaw), the
results are an adequate time filler.
This was followed by another featurette, a doc-

Bernard Bresslaw concocts
the potion that will transform him into Teddy Hyde
in *The Ugly Duckling*.

umentary titled *Operation Universe*, and yet another war film, *Yesterday's Enemy*, based on a TV play
by Peter R. Newman (who also scripted the
film). Directed by Val Guest and starring
Stanley Baker, Guy Rolfe and Leo McKern, it is
set in 1942 and involves the taking of a
Burmese village by a British unit. Also featuring Gordon Jackson, Richard Pasco and Bryan
Forbes, it is one of Hammer's better wartime
thrillers, and though by no means a classic, it
nevertheless displayed the studio's continued
willingness to be as diverse as possible, even
though, already, they were chiefly known for
their horror output. On which count, they certainly didn't disappoint their growing army of
fans with their next horror film, *The Mummy*,
another one of their genuine classics.

Much more than a straight remake of the classic Boris Karloff version of 1932, the film in
fact bears more of a resemblance to Universal's
1940 sequel *The Mummy's Hand*, in which a
mummy is revived to kill off the members of
an archaeological expedition. The script was
also influenced by the celebrated 1923
Tutankhamun expedition led by Lord

Caenarvon and Howard Carter, which ended with Caenarvon's own mysterious death.

In the Hammer film, written by Jimmy Sangster and again photographed in 'Terrifying Technicolor', Peter Cushing plays John Banning, the leader of an expedition which discovers the long lost tomb of Queen Ananka. Thanks to a broken leg, Banning is prevented from seeing the inside of the tomb himself, leaving it to his father Stephen (Felix Aylmer) to unearth the various artefacts. However, by reading aloud the words on an ancient scroll

The Mummy (Christopher Lee) vents its anger on Mehemet (George Pastell) in *The Mummy*.

he has come across, Banning's father unwittingly revives Ananka's protector, the high priest Kharis (Christopher Lee), who was buried alive with his beloved queen 4000 years earlier for attempting to bring her back to life with the very same scroll.

Driven to insanity by the sight of the Mummy, Banning senior is left a quivering wreck, leaving it to a modern day high priest, Mehemet (George Pastell), to steal the scroll and vow to destroy the desecrators. Thus the scene is set for the Mummy to be secretly transported back to England by Mehemet in order to murder all those connected with the expedition.

One of Hammer's most visual productions, the film contains many impressive moments, including the revification of Kharis in the dusty tomb, and his later emergence from a quagmire, where the crate in which he was being transported has sunk, thanks to the inefficiency of two frightened removal men. Called forth by Mehemet, who again reads the scroll, Kharis lumbers forth from the mud and slime, ready to do the priest's bidding!

A series of set pieces follow in which the Mummy carries out his murderous tasks, which include breaking into the mental home where Stephen Banning has now been placed. Naturally, when Banning tries to alert the doctors that a marauding mummy is on its way to kill him, they pay him no heed, leaving the path clear for Kharis to smash his way into Banning's fortified room and strangle him single-handedly.

The flashback sequence - which shows how Kharis came to be buried alive with his queen - also has its visual delights thanks to Bernard Robinson's plush sets, complete with all manner of Egyptian artefacts, while the cutting out of Kharis's tongue in an elaborate ceremony provides the film with its only moment of true Hammer-style gore (the scene as shot was originally so strong it was trimmed by the censor).

The attack against John Banning in the quiet of his library - with Kharis crashing through the French windows - is also a highlight. Banning fights off the apparently indestructible intruder with all manner of weapons, including a shot gun and a spear (which he plunges right through the mummy), only to have it stopped by a call from his wife Isobel (Yvonne Furneaux) who, somewhat conveniently, just happens to look like Queen Ananka!

With Isobel now in his arms, Kharis heads back to the quagmire to find eternal peace with his beloved queen, only to have her rescued at the last possible moment, leaving Kharis alone to sink into the murky depths, taking the life-giv-ing scroll with him.

As Banning, Cushing gives a customarily solid performance, though it is Lee's speechless turn as the Mummy that steals the film, for despite being bandaged from head to foot (care of make-up man Roy Ashton), he nevertheless manages to relay the pain and anguish of Kharis through mime and the power of his eyes. Also of note is George Pastell's perfor-mance as the dignified Mehemet, while the rest of the cast is rounded out satisfactorily with Michael Ripper (as per usual), Harold Goodwin and Raymond Huntley.

The film's production values are also top notch (the budget was around £100 000), with cam-eraman Jack Asher doing possibly his best work (the use of colour in the swamp sequences is quite breath-taking), while Terence Fisher's direction is brisk and to the point (the film runs a pacy eighty-eight minutes). Frank Reizenstein's excellent music, with its sepul-chral choral work, also adds immeasurably to the film's ultimate impact, the result being one

of Hammer's most impressive productions.

With *The Mummy* safely in the can, Hammer next turned to comedy again with *Don't Panic, Chaps!*, a wartime romp about British and German units both serving on the same Adriatic island, with both sides agreeing to a friendly cease-fire so as to sit out the war in comfort and safety. A promising idea, it is nevertheless poorly served by Jack Davies' screenplay, which leaves its cast (which includes Dennis Price, George Cole and Thorley Walters) with little to do.

The decade thus came to a close with *The Man Who Could Cheat Death* which, despite re-uniting Sangster, Fisher and Asher, proved to be one of Hammer's weakest ever horror entries. A re-working of the Barre Lyndon play *The Man in Half Moon Street*, which had previously been filmed in 1944, the story revolves around one Dr George Bonner (Anton Diffring, the man who would be Frankenstein in *The Tales of Frankenstein*) who has discovered the secret of eternal life, achieved through periodic gland operations. The doctor naturally gets his come-uppance when his physician refuses to carry out any more operations, the result being that Bonner reverts back to his real age, 104, before being engulfed in a spectacular fire.

Spectacular the film isn't, though. Fisher's direction lacks pace and Asher's camera seems immobile, giving the film a stagey, from-the-stalls look. Diffring does his best with what is basically a cold and unsympathetic part, while the supporting cast (which includes Christopher Lee and Hammer regulars Hazel Court, Arnold Marle and Francis de Wolff) are notably under-used. With the sixties just around the corner, this was the studio's only blot on an otherwise honourable record in a genre they had now come to dominate.

welcome to the sixties

Hammer began the sixties (financially) secure in the knowledge that they were, at the very least, the leaders of their chosen field. However, their success had opened the horror floodgates, which meant that they were by now not the only people making low budget horror films.

Producers Monty Berman and Robert S. Baker had turned out the very Hammeresque *Blood of the Vampire* in 1958 with a script by Jimmy Sangster, who also wrote *The Trollenberg Terror* (aka *The Creeping Eye*), *Jack the Ripper* and *The Hellfire Club* for them. Thanks to the success of *The Curse of Frankenstein* and the other Hammer horrors he had worked on, Sangster's name was now an effective tool in the advertising of these films, and he was often referred to as Jimmy 'Frankenstein' Sangster on the posters. Berman and Baker even managed to persuade Frankenstein himself, Peter Cushing, to headline their Dr Knox thriller *The Flesh and the Fiends*.

Elsewhere, Boris Karloff appeared in *Grip of the Strangler* (aka *The Haunted Strangler*) and *Corridors of Blood* for producer John Croydon in 1958 (the latter also featuring Christopher Lee, Francis Matthews and Francis de Wolff), while Anglo Amalgamated produced *Horrors of the Black Museum* (with Michael Gough) and *Circus of Horrors* (with Anton Diffring). In America, low budget producer-director William Castle gave audiences *The House on Haunted Hill* and *The Tingler* (both with Vincent Price), while Roger Corman's celebrated Poe adaptations (*The Pit and the Pendulum*, *The House of Usher*, etc.) were just around the corner.

None of this seemed to daunt Hammer. Said James Carreras at the time: 'We've found a formula for spine chillers that never misses. All the other boys in the horror business are beating their brains out trying to think of new monstrosities to frighten their customers: things from outer space, two-headed men and faceless women. And what happens? The more horrible they make them, the more the fans yawn. That sort of thing doesn't make them shudder any longer. I try to make the films as believable as possible. None of those silly monster insects - you can always see the wires working. My Draculas and things are real. They have quality. That's why *The Curse of Frankenstein* did better business in the States than probably any other British film has ever done. Quality - that's what counts!'

For his pains, the British press dubbed him 'The King of Nausea'. With the money rolling in, it didn't bother Carreras in the slightest, though. 'They called me a damn fool when I decided to remake *Frankenstein*' he said. 'Now it's my turn to laugh.'

Indeed, Hammer's production programme continued apace, their first release in 1960 being *The Stranglers of Bombay* (aka *The Stranglers of Bengal*), which had been completed late in 1959.

Scripted by David S. Goodman, it was director Terence Fisher's first Hammer film since *The Curse of Frankenstein* without screenwriter Jimmy Sangster. Cinematographer Jack Asher was also replaced by Arthur Grant (shooting in black and white and Megascope), though Bernard

Marie Devereaux taunts Guy Rolfe's Captain Lewes in *The Stranglers of Bombay*, one of Hammer's more sadistic exercises.

Robinson remained to design the film, as did composer James Bernard and editor James Needs.

Set in British East India in 1824, the film concerns an English officer's discovery of the notorious Kali-worshipping Thuggee cult, whose activities include robbery and ritual strangulation. Similarly plotted to John Masters' novel *The Deceivers* (which was later filmed by director Nicholas Meyer for Merchant Ivory in 1988), the story subsequently follows the soldier's attempts to bring the cult's reign of terror to an end.

Starring Guy Rolfe as the soldier hero, the film deals with several interesting themes, including racism and the effects of colonialism, though on the whole it seems mostly out to shock, which it does with several scenes of torture, one of which involves the cutting out

of a renegade member's tongue (recalling the similar scene in *The Mummy*). On this count, the film came in for a certain degree of criticism (though it was only awarded an 'A' certificate by the censors), but it did well enough at the box office to provoke a sequel of sorts, *The Terror of the Tongs*, which appeared later in the year. Even so, it is very rarely revived on (British) television.

Val Guest returned to Hammer next, this time for the excellent docu-thriller *Hell is a City*, which stars Stanley Baker as a tough police inspector out to track down an escaped prisoner who has murdered a man. A grittily realistic film in the cinema verité manner, it benefits enormously from its Manchester locations, effectively filmed in black and white by Arthur Grant, and solid supporting performances from the likes of Billie Whitelaw and Donald Pleasence.

David Peel as Baron Meinster (complete with Teddy Boy quiff) in *The Brides of Dracula*. Is that a portrait of Vlad The Impaler in the background?

Like most Hammer films of this period, *Hell is a City* also caused some controversy, but only in Manchester, where locals eager to see their city on film turned it into something of a hit when it premiered at the cavernous Apollo Theatre. However, not wanting to offend or disillusion the city's inhabitants, the police insisted on a filmed statement to precede each screening, in which a real police inspector reassured Mancunian audiences that the film was in no way a true account of life in Manchester, nor intended as a reflection upon its inhabitants' own lives! Despite this minor upset, the reviews were generally positive, with the *Monthly Film Bulletin* going so far as to say the film had, 'A hectic pace... mobility of camera... and much rapid, loud, intense dialogue.'

Meanwhile, back with the horror genre, the studio was about to release one of its classiest productions, *The Brides of Dracula*, regarded by many as Hammer's best vampire film behind 1958's *Dracula*.

As is known, the studio had hoped that Christopher Lee would be tempted back to the role of Dracula for a sequel, tentatively titled *Dracula II*, for which Jimmy Sangster had written a script. When Lee declined the offer on the grounds that another Dracula film would typecast him (which eventually proved to be the case when he did revive the character), the existing script was re-worked by Peter Bryan and Edward Percy. And an excellent job they made of it, too, eschewing the Dracula character in favour of one of his disciples, the decadent Baron Meinster.

Kept prisoner in his own castle by his mother (Martita Hunt), who has him locked to a chain to prevent him from vampirising the local villagers, Baron Meinster (David Peel) is kept alive by a string of victims procured by the Baroness, one of whom, a teacher waylaid on her way to taking up a post at a nearby girls'

school, unwittingly lets the Baron free (though why he didn't escape by turning himself into a bat, as he does later in the film, is not mentioned!).

Taking care to avenge himself against his mother, whom he turns into a vampire, Meinster thus hot-foots it to the girls' school where he discovers victims aplenty. Unfortunately for him, Professor Van Helsing (Peter Cushing) is at hand to end his reign of terror, alerted by the pretty young teacher (Yvonne Monlaur), who has managed to escape both the castle and the Baron's fangs.

A Gothic tour de force with a real Brothers Grimm atmosphere to it, the film benefits from the best production values Hammer had to offer. Bernard Robinson excelled himself in creating the interior of the Baron's castle. Jack Asher's photography is also among his best, while director Terence Fisher, working with a healthy £120,000 budget, keeps the action moving at a clip.

The performances are also truly excellent. Unlike Christopher Lee, Peter Cushing had no qualms about resurrecting Van Helsing. His performance here established him as the definitive interpreter of the role (though it would not be until *Dracula AD 1972* that he would return to the part again). Martita Hunt (best remembered for playing Miss Havisham in David Lean's *Great Expectations*) meanwhile brings an air of dignity to the role of the Baroness, emotionally torn between love and fear of her son. Her best moment comes late in the film: when discovered to be a vampire by Van Helsing, she attempts to shield her fangs with a veil, socially ashamed of what she has become.

As Baron Meinster, the effete David Peel, complete with a blond Teddy Boy-style quiff, is perfectly cast, bringing a touch of sexual

Oliver Reed in his full Wolfman make-up for *The Curse of the Werewolf*. Note the wrinkles on his chest.

ambiguity to the role. A bit part actor with only a few films to his credit (such as *Escape to Danger*, *Gaiety George* and *The Hands of Orlac*), *The Brides of Dracula* proved to be his only starring role, after which he retired to work as an antiques dealer.

Also worthy of note is Freda Jackson's performance as the Baron's housekeeper Greta, memorable in a scene in which she coaxes one of the Baron's recent victims from her (somewhat shallow) grave. Ditto Andree Melly as one of the Baron's many female victims.

Filled with many memorable sequences, the film nevertheless reserves the very best until last, when Van Helsing (who himself is vampirised at one point in the film, but saves himself by searing his wound with a burning poker) faces Meinster for the final time in a burning windmill. When it seems that Meinster has managed to evade him again by jumping from the burning building, Van Helsing leaps onto the sails of the windmill, turning them to form the shadow of a cross on the ground where the Baron has landed - a finale that manages to out-do even *Dracula* for sheer excitement and invention. And for once, the critics seemed to agree, the *The People's* description of the film as, 'A well-made shocker,' being the prevalent consensus, with audiences flocking to see the results.

The studio's next release proved to be one of their few box office flops, however. Called *The Two Faces of Dr Jekyll* (aka *House of Fright/Jekyll's Inferno*), it was Hammer's second take on the Robert Louis Stevenson story, the first being the comedy *The Ugly Duckling*. Like *The Ugly Duckling*, this version is far from straight in its adaptation, presenting Dr Jekyll (Paul Massie) as a bearded, middle-aged scientist, while as Hyde he becomes a handsome young sadist, not adverse to pleasures of the flesh.

This variation on the old, old story held promise and, like Fisher's Dracula, presents the villain not as a slobbering monster, but as an attractive, normal-seeming man - at least at first. Unfortunately, the script by Wolf Mankowitz lacks pace, as does Fisher's direction, while Jack Asher's photography, though beautifully lit as usual, is encumbered by an unnecessary widescreen process (Megascope again). The film certainly looks plush and is not without its moments, such as the fiery finale. But compared with Hammer's other films of the period, the results are tame and rather pedestrian, with too many subplots to distract one from the main story, which itself fails to grip as much as it should have done. Still, the film is held in affection by some Hammer fans.

The Brides of Dracula and *The Two Faces of Dr Jekyll* were by no means Terence Fisher's only films in 1960. Ever busy, he also helmed *Sword of Sherwood Forest*, a rather unimaginative big screen version of the popular TV series *The Adventures of Robin Hood*, with Richard Greene reprising the role of Robin to Peter Cushing's Sheriff of Nottingham. Shot on location in Ireland as well as at Bray, the film centres round the Sheriff's attempts to assassinate the Archbishop, with Robin and his men riding to the rescue in the nick of time. Sadly, though the cast has its interest (Richard Pasco, Niall MacGinnis and Desmond Llewellyn - soon to be Q in the Bond films), the end results lack the required vivacity.

Fisher was on firmer turf with his next film, *The Curse of the Werewolf*, which proved to be one of Hammer's more elaborate productions. Like the Dr Jekyll film, however, it failed to ignite at the box office, but is certainly not without its interest.

The production came about in a curious way. Hammer had originally intended on making a

film set at the time of the Spanish Inquisition to be called *The Rape of Sabena* (aka *The Inquisitor*). John Gilling (who had co-scripted several of Exclusive's crime fillers) was signed to direct, Kieron Moore was set to star and a script by Peter R. Newman was prepared. Production designer Bernard Robinson even built a number of sets on the back lot at Bray, including an elaborate village square. Unfortunately, the film - which was to centre round a Spanish community split by the Inquisition - was scrapped when the Catholic church objected to the subject matter, declaring that their censoring arm - The Catholic Legion of Decency - would condemn the film outright if it went ahead, which would have reduced its box office potential considerably.

Stuck with a back lot full of sets and nothing to film on them, Hammer decided instead to go ahead with their version of Guy Endore's 1933 novel *The Werewolf of Paris*, which they simply adapted to the sets available.

Alotted £100,000 for the production, producer Anthony Hinds found himself without sufficient funds to commission a script as a good deal of the money had already been spent on acquiring the rights to Endore's novel. Consequently, Hinds decided to write the script himself - free of charge - under the pen name of John Elder, a pseudonym he would use again many times in the years to come when he did similar scripting chores on the likes of *The Phantom of the Opera*, *The Reptile* and, later for Tyburn, *Legend of the Werewolf* and *The Ghoul*. Curiously, the studio doesn't seem to have considered remaking Universal's 1940 classic *The Wolf Man*, which would have proved cheaper than acquiring the rights to Endore's novel, especially given their success with remaking the other Universal classics to which they now had access (Universal would also release the film for Hammer in America).

Set in the eighteenth century, *The Curse of the Werewolf* opens with a hungry beggar (Richard Wordsworth), whose quest for food leads him to Castillo Siniestro, where the Marquis (Anthony Dawson) is in the midst of celebrating his wedding. The beggar is thrown a few scraps from the Marquis's table, but his presence ultimately irritates the Marquis, who has the derelict thrown into the dungeons, where he remains forgotten by all but the jailer and his mute daughter (Yvonne Romain) over the following years.

By now the Marquis is old and decrepit, but this doesn't prevent him from attempting to have his way with the mute servant girl. When she rejects his advances, he has her thrown into the dungeon too, where she is raped by the beggar, who has become a slavering animal.

The result of this liaison is a baby boy, born on Christmas Day. However, owing to the nature of his conception, it gradually becomes clear that, as he grows up, the boy, named Leon, is no ordinary child, especially when he begins to have nightmares about being a wolf. When sheep from a nearby flock are later found mutilated, it quickly becomes apparent that Leon has in fact been turning into a wolf...

Love and care from his adoptive father (Clifford Evans) helps to keep such manifestations at bay until Leon grows older and falls in love with a wine merchant's daughter (Catherine Feller). Unfortunately, an incident at a brothel finally sees Leon transform into a fully-fledged wolfman, in which guise he murders a prostitute and two villagers, for which crimes he is thrown into the local jail. However, come the next full moon, Leon (now played by Oliver Reed) transforms again, escapes and is finally hunted down by torch-bearing locals as he attempts to get away across the roofs of the village.

Though now considered something of a classic, *The Curse of the Werewolf* is by no means the best example of Hammer's output during this period, though it is not without interest. Arthur Grant's lighting and photography and Bernard Robinson's production design work again give the film a look that belies its budget, while Roy Ashton's make-up effects for the wolf man, the decrepit Marquis and the ravening beggar are excellent indeed. However, Fisher's direction is too frequently stodgy and the script seems unnecessarily ponderous in places.

Still, moments stay in the mind. The roof-top finale is certainly well staged, as are the transformation scenes. There are also incidental pleasures. For example, at Leon's Christening, the face of a devil is seen to appear in the font, only to be revealed as the reflection of a gargoyle overhead. The script also attempts to convey Leon's inner turmoil as he tries to come to terms with his fate, which makes for a more character driven piece, though as a result the film seems to lack the expected amount of action, which no doubt helped doom it at the box office at the time.

The performances are all up to the mark, particularly Anthony Dawson as the lecherous Marquis (quite revolting in his old age make-up) and Richard Wordsworth as the unfortunate beggar. Without question, however, it is Oliver Reed who holds the film together.

Very much a jobbing actor in the late fifties, Reed had briefly appeared in a number of British films of the day, including the Norman Wisdom 'comedy' *The Bulldog Breed* (which also featured a blink-and-you'll-miss-him appearance by the then unknown Michael Caine) and *The League of Gentlemen* (in which he played an hilariously camp actor looking for a rehearsal room). More importantly, Reed had also worked on *The Two Faces of Dr Jekyll* (as a rowdy club patron) and *Sword of Sherwood Forest*, both of which had been directed by Terence Fisher - who now catapulted Reed to leading man status for *The Curse of the Werewolf*. He was just 22.

Yet despite an energetic ad campaign which showed Reed in all his werewolf glory, and copy that read 'His beast-blood demanded he kill... kill... kill!', the film was generally perceived as a disappointment, perhaps because it promised more than it delivered. Some critics praised it, though. 'Presented with intelligence and sympathy, not horror for its own sake,' said *The Hollywood Reporter*, though the *Hollywood Citizen News* held the prevailing consensus that the film was, 'Excessively dull, tediously paced.' As a consequence, *The Curse of the Werewolf* proved to be Hammer's only cinematic venture into the realms of lycanthropy.

Elsewhere, the studio's other offerings for 1960 included *Never Take Sweets From a Stranger*, the story of an elderly man accused of child molestation in a Canadian town. Based on the play *The Pony Cart* by Roger Garis, it was intended as a heart-felt drama. However, given Hammer's attachment to the project, it was misconceived as a rather nasty horrific come-on by most critics, who condemned the film outright for its subject matter.

The year thus came to end end with *Terror of the Tongs*, the semi-sequel to *The Stranglers of Bombay*. Set in 1910 Hong Kong this time, as opposed to India, the plot follows a merchant's attempts to avenge the death of his daughter by using the services of a secret sect led by an Oriental-looking Christopher Lee. Directed by Anthony Bushell from a script by Jimmy Sangster, it was promoted with the tag line: 'Drug-crazed assassins carrying out their hate-filled ritual murders!' Even so, audience reaction was mostly indifferent and, like its predecessor, the film is little revived today, despite such ripe dialogue as, 'Have you ever had your bones scraped?'.

new directions

If 1960 had proved to be a hit and miss year for Hammer, so too would 1961 and 1962, highlights being few and far between - as indeed were actual horror films!

1961 contained such variable efforts as *Visa to Canton* (aka *Passport to China*), an uninspired thriller involving an attempt to get a refugee out of Red China. Limply directed by Michael Carreras and starring American import Richard Basehart, it recalls the studio's Exclusive years rather than its more recent glories. Barely better is Val Guests's *The Full Treatment* (aka *Stop Me Before I Kill!*), a would-be psychological thriller in which a shrink attempts to convince one of his patients, a disturbed racing driver, into thinking that he has murdered his new wife. Based on the Ronald Scott Thorn novel, it is well enough directed but lacks real inspiration and again seemed like a step back for Hammer.

Hammer's attempts to diversify into comedy, as they had successfully done so with the Lyons films back in the fifties, were also met with a certain degree of indifference. The supposedly farcical *Watch it, Sailor!*, a sequel to the hilarious *Sailor, Beware*, centres round an about-to-be-married tar (Dennis Price) who finds himself slapped with a paternity suit while *Weekend With Lulu* stars Bob Monkhouse, Leslie Phillips, Irene Handl and Shirley Eaton in a breezy but insubstantial jaunt, helped along more by its cast of familiar faces (which also includes Sid James and Kenneth Connor) rather than the script. A routine production, it remains of note solely for the fact that it was directed by John Paddy Carstairs (real name

John Keys) who was the brother of Hammer's associate producer Anthony Nelson Keys.

It was thus left to *Taste of Fear* (aka *Scream of Fear*) to redress the box office balance. Based on one of the best scripts by Jimmy Sangster (who also made his debut as a producer with the film), this is the coiled-spring shocker par excellence, which takes as its inspiration the celebrated George Cluzot thriller *Les Diaboliques*.

Written some years earlier by Sangster, *Taste of Fear* was his attempt to escape the gothic horror mould in which he had reluctantly found himself trapped, thanks to the success of *The Curse of Frankenstein*, *Dracula* and *The Mummy*. At the time of its writing, Hammer proved uninterested in the project, so Sangster attempted to set the film up at another studio. This unfortunately fell through. However, by this time, Alfred Hitchcock's *Psycho* had hit cinema screens around the world and was breaking box office records, which made Hammer quickly revise their thoughts about *Taste of Fear*, which was quickly put into production.

Susan Strasberg (daughter of Method guru Lee Strasberg) stars as crippled schoolgirl Penny Appleby who, during the school break, travels to the French Riviera to visit her father, whom she hasn't seen for years. Unfortunately, when she gets there, she is informed by her new stepmother (Ann Todd) that he is away on business. However, while waiting for his return over the next few days, Penny comes to believe that she is going insane, for she keeps seeing her father's corpse in all manner of places. A seemingly sinister local doctor (Christopher Lee) is called to examine her, but the 'visions' persist, and Penny becomes convinced that her father has in fact been murdered and that her stepmother and the doctor might be responsible.

As it transpires, Penny's father has indeed been murdered, not by the stepmother and the doctor, but by the stepmother and the chauffeur (Ronald Lewis) - who are now trying to drive Penny insane in an attempt to wrest her inheritance from her. They even try to kill her by placing her in a runaway car, which careers over a cliff.

But things aren't quite what they seem. It transpires that Penny and the seemingly sinister doctor are in cahoots in an attempt to uncover the murder plot. Penny isn't killed in the car crash, either. She turns up the next day *sans* wheelchair and reveals that not only isn't she crippled but that she isn't Penny either, but her best friend. The real Penny committed suicide (shown briefly at the beginning of the film) some weeks before by drowing herself in a lake.

A convoluted plot certainly, yet it is handled so persuasively by director Seth Holt that this hardly seems to matter. A former editor whose only previous film as a director had been *Nowhere To Go* in 1958, Holt would go on to helm two more highly regarded films for Hammer in the coming years (*The Nanny* and *Blood From The Mummy's Tomb*), his technique, when in form, arguably as effective as Hitchcock's when it came to the intricacies of this particular genre. Helped immeasurably by Douglas Slocombe's crisp black and white photography and a strong central performance from Susan Strasberg (a photograph of whose screaming face made an enticing ad campaign), the film was an immediate hit.

For Sangster this box office success meant a

welcome (though not final) escape from gothic horror - only to be replaced by a demand for more of the same, the result being numerous variations on the *Taste of Fear* format, which included the likes of *Maniac*, *Paranoiac*, *Crescendo* and *Fear in the Night*.

These sequels, though often well done, never quite manage to equal the impact of the original, though even the critics came out firmly in favour of *Taste of Fear*. 'It plays its particular brand of the three-card trick with ingenuity and without scruple,' said *The Times*, while Penelope Houston added, 'All those creaking shutters, flickering candles, wavering shadows and pianos playing in empty rooms still yield a tiny frisson.'

Just as things were beginning to hot up at the box office, so they did behind the scenes. Like Jimmy Sangster, Michael Carreras had become weary of the horror market and so left Hammer in 1961 in search of pastures new, leaving the running of Hammer entirely in his father's hands. Michael did in fact return to Hammer on occasion throughout the sixties as a producer, director and (using the pseudonyms Henry Younger and Michael Nash) a scriptwriter. However, much of his time was taken up with the formation of a new company, Capricorn Films, for which he produced and directed a western, *The Savage Guns*, and a teenage musical, *What a Crazy World*. The less said about both movies the better.

Through one of their many subsidiary companies, ABPH, Hammer meanwhile released *Shadow of the Cat* in 1961 (though debate still rages as to whether this is an actual Hammer film). Scripted by George Baxt and directed in black and white with a certain flair by John Gilling (who had scripted *Room to Let* and *The Man in Black* for Exclusive back in 1950, and had almost directed *The Rape of Sabena* in 1960), this is a fairly familiar old dark house story, here involving a vengeful cat which kills the relatives responsible for the murder of its wealthy old mistress (Catherine Lacey).

A silly premise with an insufficiently frightening 'monster' (when did a vengeful cat movie last scare you?), the film nevertheless benefits from having been made by Hammer's top talent. Bernard Robinson produced some interesting sets (particularly the exterior of the creepy old mansion) through which Arthur Grant could rove his camera, whilst Greek composer Mikis Theodorakis (still three years away from *Zorba the Greek*) added an effectively offbeat score.

The cast, which includes such reliables as Barbara Shelley, Andre Morell, William Lucas, Conrad Philips and Freda Jackson, all give convincing performances given the material, and director Gilling makes the most of the film's creepy house setting, particularly during the cat attacks (filmed from the cat's point of view through a fish-eye lens) and the pre-requisite lightning storms.

Back at the ranch proper, Hammer's success at the box office continued to vary. Their big production for 1962 - one of only three films made by the studio that year - was a remake of *The Phantom of the Opera*. Yet despite the best efforts of director Terence Fisher, designer Bernard Robinson and producer-writer Anthony Hinds (writing as John Elder again), the film was shunned by fans and disdained by the critics ('The only shock is that the British, who could have had a field day with this antique, have wafted it back with a lick and a promise,' said *The New York Times*).

The reason for this seems to be that, despite criticism that their films were deemed too violent and gory, Hammer's *Phantom* was now considered too mild. Certainly, the film is by no means as shocking as some of their previ-

ous efforts, but this by no means makes it a lesser film. Indeed, its heavily romantic atmosphere is one of its greatest attributes. However, disappointed fans complaining at the lack of expected thrills should have laid the blame for this not on Hammer's doorstep, but on Cary Grant's!

For a while, Grant had seriously considered playing the Phantom in the film and, following his wishes, the script was accordingly given a more romantic feel to suit his screen image. When Grant finally pulled out of the project, which by then was ready to go, another Phantom had to be quickly found. This proved to be Herbert Lom (who had appeared in Exclusive's *Whispering Smith Hits London* back in 1951), who now found himself saddled with a script written for a totally different type of star personality. That he acquits himself so well under the circumstances is a credit to both himself and to Fisher.

Hammer's version of the Gaston Leroux novel was of course not the first to reach the screen. Back in 1925, Lon Chaney had starred in an elaborate silent production for Universal, which the studio remade in Technicolor in 1943 with Claude Rains in the title role. Universal even used the same sets from this remake in another thinly disguised variation on the story titled *The Climax*, in which Boris Karloff plays the Phantom-like role.

For *The Phantom of the Opera* (which, incidentally, was also backed and released by Universal), Hammer relocated the story from Paris to London and made the Phantom a more sympathetic character by making him wronged against rather than a wrong-doer. Thus, having had some music he's been working on stolen by the ruthless impresario Lord Ambrose D'Arcy (Michael Gough), Professor Petrie (Lom) attempts to get it back, only to be thrown into the street for his pains. Later, after accidentally dowsing himself with acid thinking it was water (go figure!), Petrie becomes The Phantom, haunting D'Arcy's theatre from an underground lair, where he works on an opera, *Joan of Arc*. To sing it, he abducts the theatre's leading lady, Christine Charles (Heather Sears) and rehearses her in his lair. But opera producer Harry Hunter (Edward de Souza) isn't far behind in his bid to rescue the diva.

Despite a spectacular fire in his lair which destroys most of his work, this isn't the end of the Phantom, though. He is finally killed while attempting to save Christine from a crashing chandelier, accidentally released from its moorings by his hunchbacked assistant (Ian Wilson) who is trying to escape from the police. For it is the dwarf and not the Phantom who has been carrying out the murderous acts around the opera house. This, combined with the evil deeds of the scenery-chewing Lord D'Arcy, help make the Phantom a more tragic figure than in previous versions, when it was the Phantom who released the chandelier onto the heads of the unsuspecting opera house audience.

Despite what the critics said, the film actually isn't without its shocking moments. The fire in the lair, the stabbing in the eye of a rat catcher (by the dwarf), scenes in a sewer and the bursting of a body through a piece of stage scenery on the end of a rope stay in the mind, though the unmasking of the Phantom (who rips his mask off to see better while saving Christine from the chandelier) could have had more impact, especially given Roy Ashton's mild make-up. Still, Fisher's direction is assured, the performances are fine and the theatre setting (actually the Wimbledon Theatre in London) is made the most of.

Nevertheless, the film, even though Hammer's most expensive to date and intended as a

major attraction, was often co-billed with their second release of 1962, *Captain Clegg* (aka *Night Creatures*). *The Phantom of the Opera*'s demise at the box office also resulted in a two-year departure by Terence Fisher from the company. Not idle during this period, he first went to Germany to direct Christopher Lee as Sherlock Holmes in *Sherlock Holmes and the Deadly Necklace*, which he followed back in England by the 'horror comedy' *The Horror of it All* and the science fiction thriller *The Earth Dies Screaming*, none of which rank with the best of his work. He eventually returned to Hammer (and to form) in 1964 with *The Gorgon*.

Captain Clegg, meanwhile, was Hammer's version of Russell Thorndike's novel *Dr Syn*, which had previously been filmed back in 1937 with George Arliss in the title role. Ironically, it was also the subject of a Disney film released in the same year as Hammer's version. Called *Dr Syn - Alias The Scarecrow*, this stars Patrick McGoohan and was originally intended as a three part television series to be shown in America. Instead it was edited together to form a feature, much to the consternation of James Carreras and his associates. However, the Disney film was a somewhat milder take on the story, leaving it to Hammer to give it the full-blooded treatment - which they certainly did.

Peter Cushing stars as the bespectacled Dr Blyss, the mild-seeming vicar of Dymchurch who is in fact a pirate called Captain Clegg. Using his disguise to avert suspicion from his smuggling activities, the good doctor also has his henchmen dress themselves and their horses up as skeletons (or 'Marsh Phantoms' as they call themselves) so as to frighten off any curious villagers, all of which recalls memories of the Will Hay comedy *Ask a Policeman*, in which a 'headless' coachman is used to frighten away locals from similar smuggling activities.

Co-starring Patrick Allen as the English army officer who eventually exposes Clegg, Oliver Reed and the seemingly ever-present Michael Ripper, the film was scripted by Anthony Hinds (using his John Elder pseudonym), performed with conviction by Cushing and helmed with with a certain degree of flair by Peter Graham Scott, an ex-television director whose only Hammer film this proved to be.

By no means Hammer's only piracy yarn, *Captain Clegg* was followed closely by *The Pirates of Blood River*, which stars Christopher Lee as La Roche, a pirate who forces one of his men (Kerwin Mathews, star of *The Seventh Voyage of Sinbad*) to lead his crew to his home town, a Puritan community presided over by his father (Andrew Keir), which apparently has hidden treasure. Though set in the West Indies, the film was actually shot on the back lot at Bray and in Black Park, Buckinghamshire. Yet it is lively enough to detract from these sometimes rather obvious English settings, thanks to the brisk direction of John Gilling (who had already tried his hand at this kind of stuff with the Peter Cushing vehicle *Fury at Smugglers Bay* for Regal Films in 1960) and highlights that included a piranha attack. Like *Captain Clegg*, the supporting cast again includes Oliver Reed and Michael Ripper, while the producing chores went for the first time solely to Anthony Nelson Keys, who had been Hammer's associate producer for a number of years. Double-billed with Columbia Picture's *Mysterious Island*, the two films proved to be a solid summer attraction.

Nevertheless, Hammer's fortunes continued to fluctuate in 1963, and though the films they made were quite varied in content, including thrillers and swashbucklers, they didn't make a single gothic horror - which was, after all, what they were now famous for.

Things started off badly with *Maniac*, a variation on his *Taste of Fear* script by Jimmy

Sangster, who wrote and produced again. This time the plot revolves around a series of murders by oxyacetylene torch, but director Michael Carreras and the cast (which includes Kerwin Mathews, Donald Houston and Nadia Gray) do little to bring the plot's convoluted twists and turns to life. In fact, so routine is the film that it was co-featured in Britain with *The Damned* (aka *These Are The Damned*), a not entirely successful adaptation of H. L. Lawrence's novel *The Children of Light*, which had actually been made back in 1961, but had been held up by Columbia (who didn't release it in America until 1965, minus ten minutes of footage). A sci-fi story about irradiated children, bred in an attempt to deal with the effects of radiation after a nuclear war, the film, directed by Joseph Losey (who'd been so unceremoniously dumped from *X - The Unknown*), has a certain sense of the visual. Yet despite the fact that it later won the Golden Asteroid Award at the 1964 Trieste Festival of Science Fiction Films, and features a solid enough cast (Macdonald Carey, Oliver Reed, Shirley Ann Field, Viveca Lindfors), it remains infrequently revived on television even today.

After this, writer-director John Gilling, who'd turned *The Pirates of Blood River* into a box office success, returned to Hammer to make their next swashbuckler, *The Scarlet Blade* (aka *The Crimson Blade*). A Technicolor romp in the best Saturday morning tradition, the film is set in 1648 and follows the cross-country pursuit of Charles I by Cromwell's troops, who take it upon themselves to hang royalist rebels along the way. However, they reckon without the interference of the Scarlet Blade, who insists on riding to the rescue just in the nick of time, much to their annoyance. Nicely photographed by Jack Asher and with another solid cast (the ever busy Oliver Reed, Lionel Jeffries, June Thorbun), the film fulfils its promise of providing entertainment for schoolboys of all ages.

Donald Houston wields the oxyacetyline torch in *Maniac.* Note the gauze on his stick-on moustache.

One of Hammer's best non-horror subjects followed this historical escapade. Called *Cash on Demand*, it stars Peter Cushing in one of his rare non-horror roles as a sniffy suburban bank manager who gets taken in by a high class robber (Andre Morell) posing as an insurance investigator. Scripted by Lewis Greifer and David T. Chantler from the play by Jacques Gillies, the film is tautly directed by Quentin Lawrence, who makes the most of the restricted settings and the inevitably low budget. Driven by excellent performances from

Cushing, Morell and supporting player Richard Vernon, the film has many tense confrontation scenes and a suitably claustrophobic atmosphere. A model of its kind, it still manages to engross today.

As does Hammer's second *Taste of Fear* variation, *Paranoic*. Scripted by Jimmy Sangster again (though this time produced by Anthony Hinds), it concerns another heiress (Janette Scott) who is rescued from a suicide bid by a young man (Oliver Reed) who claims to be her dead brother. Naturally, it isn't long before the heiress begins to doubt her sanity and the plot twists start to pile up. Yet thanks to the inventiveness of Sangster's script the results, though now formulaic, are still pretty diverting. Good performances by Reed and Scott also count, as does Freddie Francis's tight direction.

His first film as a director for Hammer (though he had photographed *Never Take Sweets From a Stranger* for them in 1960), Francis had helmed only two other films at this stage in his career: *Two and Two Make Six*, a romantic comedy that also features Janette Scott, and a horror film titled *Vengeance* (aka *The Brain*). However, he was also one of Britain's top cinematographers, having won an Oscar for *Sons and Lovers* in 1960. Francis's efforts as a director, almost wholly in the horror/thriller genre, were less distinguished, though the best of them being for Hammer, for whom he made another four films. Francis eventually returned to cinematography, where he won another Oscar for *Glory* in 1989.

The year finally came to a close with *The Old Dark House*, which proved to be one of Hammer's least successful films. Based on the J. B. Priestly novel *Benighted*, it had been filmed previously as *The Old Dark House* back in 1932 for Universal by director James Whale, who had also given the world *Frankenstein*, *The Invisible Man* and *The Bride of Frankenstein*. Sadly, Hammer's version, played mostly for cheap laughs, failed to live up to the classic status of its predecessor.

Shot in Technicolor but actually released in America in black and white on a double bill with *Maniac*, the film stars Tom Poston as Tom Penderel, an American who comes to England to visit his distant relatives, the Femm family, at their spooky manor. And a weird bunch they turn out to be, out to murder eachother for control of the family fortune.

Directed by American schlockmeister William Castle - whose previous productions include such gimmick-ridden shockers as *Macabre* (for which audiences were insured against death by fright), *The Tingler* (for which cinema seats were wired up to receive a mild electric shock) and *Thirteen Ghosts* (for which audiences were provided with anaglyph spectacles so as to see the ghosts) - the film was his only association with Hammer. Unfortunately, he wasn't quite in his element for it, and though the film has a good cast (Janette Scott, Robert Morley, Joyce Grenfell, Mervyn Johns, Fenella Fielding and Peter Bull - as twins), the results are pretty thin. 'This comedy-shocker is abysmal - repeat abysmal - from beginning to end,' said the *Monthly Film Bulletin* when the film was finally released in Britain in 1966, in colour but shorn of nine minutes of footage.

Hard to sit through today, the film's only memorable points prove to be the credit sequence, designed by Addams Family creator Charles Addams, and a shock moment involving a pair of knitting needles.

Thankfully, this brought to an end Hammer's most fallow period. What was called for was a return to gothic horror. And if that's what the public wanted, that's what they got with the studio's very next offering.

back to basics

Late 1963 finally saw the end of the Hammer's anaemic stretch and a welcome return to full-blooded gothic form with *Kiss of the Vampire* (aka *Kiss of Evil*), a *tour de force* in the studio's best manner.

Like *The Brides of Dracula*, it doesn't feature the Count himself (Christopher Lee was still refusing all entreaties to repeat the role) but another disciple, this time one Dr Ravna (Noel Willman), the leader of a vampire sect who plays host to the expected lost travellers - this time a honeymooning couple - only to have his ghoulish plans for them nipped in the bud by the Van Helsing-like Professor Zimmer (Clifford Evans).

To helm the film, Hammer relied on a number of its old guard, including producer Anthony Hinds, who also supplied the screenplay under his by now familiar pen name John Elder, production designer Bernard Robinson and composer James Bernard. However, with Terence Fisher absent from the studio after the disappointment over *The Phantom of the Opera*, it was decided to bring some new blood into the project. Consequently, the Tasmanian-born Don Sharp was signed to direct.

At this stage in his career, Sharp had only directed a few low budget films, such as the teen musicals *The Golden Disc* (aka *The In-Between Years*) with Terry Dene and *It's All Happening* (aka *The Dream Maker*) with Tommy Steele. Yet the popularity of these, combined with his impressive second unit work on such action films as *Carve Her Name With Pride*, made him the

Dr Ravna (Noel Willman) and his captive Marianne Harcourt (Jennifer Daniel) in *Kiss of the Vampire*.

ideal choice for the budget conscious Hammer. As it transpired, Sharp proved to be a chance worth taking, and not only went on to helm two more high profile projects for Hammer, but also enjoyed a successful career elsewhere both in and out of the horror genre, directing such classics as *The Face of Fu Manchu*, *Puppet on a Chain* and the 1978 remake of *The 39 Steps*, as well as the second unit sequences for *Those Magnificent Men in their Flying Machines*.

As the film was not to be directed by Fisher, cinematographer Jack Asher (whose painstaking working methods were now deemed too slow for Hammer) was replaced for this film by Alan Hume, a fast worker whose credits at this stage in his career included numerous *Carry Ons* and countless TV episodes (most notably for *The Avengers*). The cast also offered a mixture of old guard (Clifford Evans, Edward de Souza) and new (Noel Willman, Jennifer Daniel) in a bid to come up with an alternative to the by now firmly established partnership of Cushing and Lee.

Set in 1910 Bavaria, the film revolves round a British honeymooning couple, Gerald and Marianne Harcourt (Edward de Souza and Jennifer Daniel), who find themselves out of petrol while travelling through the Alps in their motorcar. Warned to get out of the area by the mysterious Professor Zimmer (Evans), seen previously in a brief pre-credit sequence in which he drives a shovel through the heart of his vampire daughter at her funeral, the couple find their way to the local inn where they meet Carl and Sabena Ravna, who have

journeyed from their father's nearby castle to invite them for dinner, the Doctor (Willman) having already spied their arrival through his telescope.

The evening goes well, and the couple are invited back the following night for a masked ball. What they don't realise is that the ball is actually a convening of Ravna's vampire sect, their intention being to initiate Marianne. Thus, during the course of the evening, Marianne is abducted and Gerald drugged and thrown out of the castle the next day, with all and sundry denying ever having seen his wife. Gerald consequently teams up with Professor Zimmer to rescue Marianne, after which Zimmer seals up the castle with garlic. Trapped inside, the vampires are finally destroyed by a horde of bats, summoned from hell by the Professor!

Far-fetched, certainly, but so briskly and efficiently handled is the material that this proves to be of no consequence. Indeed, the scenes in which everyone denies the existence of the kidnapped Marianne have a subtle echo of Hitchcock about them. Director Sharp's other memorable sequences include the eerie masked ball (parodied by Roman Polanski in his Hammer homage *Dance of the Vampires* [aka *The Fearless Vampire Killers*]), the scenes at the empty inn and the various woodland encounters, superbly photographed (in Black Park again) by Hume.

The finale, in which the bats descend and destroy the sect (compared by some to scenes from Hitchcock's *The Birds*, but actually shot a good year before), also leaves its mark, though as a climax it had originally been intended for *The Brides of Dracula*, but was discarded at the time as being too expensive to film. Yet despite

Frankenstein's latest creation (Kiwi Kingston) receives a helping hand from Katy Wild's mute beggar girl in *The Evil of Frankenstein*, the first Hammer Frankenstein able to use make-up approximating that of Boris Karloff's in the Universal movies, though here the results don't look too convincing.

Janet (Jenny Linden) gets a nasty surprise in *Nightmare,* one of Hammer's better psychological thrillers.

some obvious fakery and a few visible wires, it still manages to pack a punch.

Scriptwriter Elder/Hinds also plays around with vampire myth to the film's general benefit, for Ravna and his family are not only shown eating and drinking at dinner, his children also make daytime visits to the inn to see Gerald and Marianne, though under the cover of heavy cloud (just as Stoker's Dracula did during his stay in London). Vampirism, as it had been in *The Brides of Dracula,* is also equated with social and even venereal disease. As Zimmer reveals to Gerald at one point, the daughter he buried had similarly fallen prey to Ravna's powers. 'She came home eventually,' Zimmer tells him, to which he adds, 'She was riddled with disease - and she was a vampire.'

The performances are uniformly strong. Like Lee and Peel before him, Willman brings a touch a genuine nobility to his role as Ravna (played, according to the actor, with a single expression), while Evans's Professor Zimmer has a Van Helsing-like determination to destroy the vampires. Isobel Black's mysterious vampire (who turns out to be the inn keeper's daughter) adds a touch of mystery and sensuality to the proceedings, while Barry Warren and Jacquie Wallis are suitably double-edged as Ravna's children, making a hasty exit from the inn when the sun begins to break through the clouds ('Drive like the Devil', Carl informs the coachdriver as they hurriedly depart). Even Edward de Souza and Jennifer Daniel, despite playing archetypal British sticks, manage to court our sympathy.

The critics found things to like in the movie, too, particularly *Films and Filming,* which commented, 'All credit to Don Sharp for turning what could have been a creaking, monotonously predictable story into an exceptionally well-made and entertaining film.' At last, Hammer seemed to be back doing what they did best.

And much to the delight of audiences, they kept the impetus up throughout 1964, first reviving Frankenstein after a six year hiatus with *The Evil of Frankenstein*, the third episode in what was now an on-going series. By no means the best entry in the saga, the film nevertheless benefits from the presence of Peter Cushing as the Baron, and an atmospheric score by Don Banks. On the downside, the script by John Elder/Anthony Hinds is pretty mundane and the direction by Freddie Francis doesn't always make the most of the situation. (Terence Fisher was in Germany directing Christopher Lee in *Sherlock Holmes and the Deadly Necklace* at the time.)

Not a true sequel to *The Revenge of Frankenstein*, the film sees the Baron return to his home town after a long absence where he discovers one of his previous 'experiments' preserved in a glacier. Aided by his assistant Hans (Sandor Eles), he naturally attempts to revive the creature, but again has problems with its brain, which he eventually kick-starts with the help of a carnival hypnotist (Peter Woodthorpe). But the hypnotist has a few old scores to settle, and uses the creature to carry out his murderous revenge. Needless to say, everything is wrapped up neatly in a fiery finale in which the Baron and the monster are seen to perish in flames.

Thanks to their relationship with Universal, Hammer were this time able to use monster make-up which resembled that worn by Boris Karloff in the thirties films. Unfortunately, as designed by Roy Ashton, the results were ludicrously over the top, and the portrayal of the monster by wrestling star Kiwi Kingston (!) lacks the required pathos. Still, the lab scenes themselves worked well and the film had enough minor frissons to satisfy thrillseekers.

The film also remains of passing note for being the first Hammer production on which musical director Philip Martell worked, following the death of John Hollingsworth, the studio's previous department head, who had filled this important post from 1954 to 1963, in which capacity he assigned composers, oversaw composition and often conducted. Similarly, Martell would also remain associated with Hammer until his own death in 1994, supervising and/or conducting the music for all of their subsequent film and television productions.

The next of these proved to be *Nightmare*, yet another of writer-producer Jimmy Sangster's *Taste of Fear* variations which, like *Paranoiac*, was directed by Freddie Francis, with Jennie Linden as the girl being driven out of her mind this time. Yet despite the familiarity of its ingredients, the film manages to work up a certain degree of tension and remains one of the better examples of its kind.

1964 also saw Hammer's preoccupation with swashbucklers continue with another Saturday morning style adventure, this one titled *The Devil-Ship Pirates*. A straightforward romp, it stars Christopher Lee as Captain Roebels, a Spanish pirate whose ship puts in at a small Cornish fishing village to carry out repairs and terrorise the unfortunate locals. Generally quite lively if a little over-stretched, the film is kept moving by director Don Sharp, working from a script by Jimmy Sangster (did this guy ever sleep?), while the supporting cast includes the likes of Hammer regulars Andrew Keir, Duncan Lamont and Michael Ripper. By no means a classic of its kind, the film nevertheless remains of passing note for one specific reason: it was the first (English language) film actually to top-bill Christopher Lee, despite the fact that he'd played the title roles in both *Dracula* and *The Mummy* and was by now an international star of some repute (thanks to his success with Hammer).

Terence Fisher finally returned to the Hammer fold to direct the John Gilling scripted gothic horror *The Gorgon*, which was also released in 1964, and re-united him not only with composer James Bernard and production designer Bernard Robinson, but with Christopher Lee and Peter Cushing, too. This time, however, it is Lee who is the good guy. As Professor Meister, he travels to an isolated European village (aren't they always?) to discover what has become of his son.

As it transpires, the village is being terrorised by Magera, a Gorgon who can turn those who dare look into her eyes to stone, one of her victims being the good Professor's son. As she can also assume the identity of unsuspecting villagers, this makes her harder to track down

and destroy. Her 'cover' proves to be Carla Hoffman (Barbara Shelley), an assistant to the local doctor (Peter Cushing) who not only knows and shields her true identity, but is also lusting after her!

A rather talkative affair, the film is heavy on atmosphere if not thrills. Its best moments come when the action shifts to the crumbling castle where Magera lurks, waiting for her victims. Unfortunately, given the resources available, the writhing snakes in the title character's hair proved to be too much of a challenge for make-up man Roy Ashton. Consequently, the Gorgon is only briefly glimpsed. The fact that she is played by a different actress to Shelley (Prudence Hyman) also detracts from the overall effect.

Shelley had in fact suggested to the film's producers that they use live grass snakes for the sequences involving Magera, which she desperately wanted to play so as to maintain the character's continuity. Unfortunately, her idea was rejected, ultimately at a cost to the film's believability. Ironically, that same year, in the George Pal fantasy *The Seven Faces of Dr Lao*, Tony Randall also appeared briefly as a Gorgon, the snakes in his hair being of the rather more convincing stop-motion animated variety - as were those of the Medusa later seen in the 1981 Ray Harryhausen spectacular *Clash of the Titans*.

Still, despite its inadequate effects, *The Gorgon* has its admirers, and at the time *Variety* found things to praise in the film, particularly Fisher's direction, which it referred to as being, 'Restrained enough to avoid any unintentional yocks.'

The Gorgon could be considered a classic, however, when compared with the studio's next offering, *The Curse of the Mummy's Tomb*, the second and least effective of the four mummy films Hammer would eventually produce. Not

Christopher Lee's Pirate comes to a fiery end in *The Devil-Ship Pirates*.

a sequel to their 1959 film but a totally new story (or rather a new rehash of familiar ingredients), this one again involves an archaeological expedition whose various members, as to be expected, are killed off one by one by a revified mummy (Dickie Owen), this time at the urging of the mummy's twin brother (Terence Morgan), doomed to eternal life. Add to this a turn by Fred Clark as a vulgar American entrepreneur intent on making money out of the mummy by displaying it in a Barnum and Bailey-style roadshow and you have a momentary diversion from the familiar proceedings.

Otherwise the production (despite a solid £103,000 budget) is a slow moving and slackly handled affair which never overcomes its triple threat - all in the form of Michael Carreras, who was not only the film's producer, but also its director and, using the pen name of Henry Younger (a deliberate stab at Anthony Hinds' pseudonym) its scriptwriter, too.

As a producer, Carreras could best be described as being adequate if somewhat uninspired. However, as a director (particularly a self-appointed and self-accountable one) he was poor, with little grasp of technique, seeming merely to want to film each scene as quickly as possible. As a writer, meanwhile, he was able to turn even the most promising of subjects into slow-moving yawn-fests (particu-

larly when one compares his efforts here, say, to Anthony Hinds' script for *Kiss of the Vampire*, which took familiar ingredients and made something new out of them). Here, the Mummy's first appearance is painfully long in coming, the dialogue and situations in the meantime being dull and the characters barely two dimensional. Hampered by undistinguished widescreen photography (care of Otto Heller) with little to fill the canvas, the results are sadly amateur.

Still, occasional moments survive the morass. A scene on a foggy street stairway, in which the mummy sees off the showman, is eerily effective (thanks mostly to Bernard Robinson's otherwise undistinguished production design and the sound of the Mummy's 'breathing'), while the finale in the sewers of London (left over from *The Phantom of the Opera*) is well enough staged - though after nearly eighty minutes of dull chat it's a long time coming. Carlo Martelli's music meanwhile makes use of large chunks of Frank Reizenstein's score from Hammer's far superior 1959 film.

When paired with *The Gorgon* on a double bill, punters didn't complain, though. At least they were getting value for their money in quantity if not quality, spurred by the gimmick of free face masks at selected cinemas, should anyone 'Fear to look on the face of The Gorgon!'.

Michael Carreras (left) during the filming of the watery climax to *The Curse of the Mummy's Tomb*.

something old, something new

As they had done in 1964, throughout 1965 Hammer continued to offer the public a mixture of the tried and tested as well as the new and slightly more ambitious. The old proved to be another swashbuckler, *The Brigand of Kandahar* - a dully scripted and directed adventure from John Gilling, this time involving a Bengal Lancer who swaps his allegiance to a band of murderous bandits. Yet despite the presence of Oliver Reed in the lead, the film is a lacklustre affair and suffers from an overplus of unconvincing studio work standing in for 1850s India.

Equally lacking is *Hysteria*, another plot twister which again teamed producer-writer Jimmy Sangster with director Freddie Francis, the story this time involving an amnesiac (Robert Webber) who finds himself in the middle of a murder plot.

There was also another prisoner of war saga, *The Secret of Blood Island* which, rather improbably, has secret agent Barbara Shelley parachuting into a Jap camp to make a note of the atrocities before being smuggled out again. As scripted by John Gilling and directed by Quentin Lawrence, the results are so absurd as to be quite enjoyable.

Meanwhile, even more psychological pyrotechnics were to be found in *Fanatic* (aka *Die! Die! My Darling*), which stars Tallulah Bankhead as a religious maniac who decides to keep her dead son's fiancee prisoner when she comes to visit. Most notable for being Bankhead's last big screen appearance, the

Bette Davis in *The Nanny*, one of the triumphs of her later years.

actress looks suitably grim and threatening without any make-up on. Otherwise, the film stretches its premise too far, despite being scripted by noted fantasy writer Richard Matheson (from the novel *Nightmare* by Anne Blaisdell) and directed with occasional flair by Silvio Narrizano, who at least makes good use of colour and angles. Nevertheless, *Fanatic* was far outclassed by another psychological thriller, *The Nanny*, starring another Hollywood warhorse, the great Bette Davis.

Without doubt the best psychological thriller Hammer ever made, and certainly comparable with the work of Hitchcock in this field, *The Nanny* begins innocuously enough with the return home from school of ten-year-old Joey (William Dix), an obnoxious-seeming brat who, we are given to believe, was responsible for the drowning of his baby sister some years earlier. Much to the annoyance of his parents (Wendy Craig and James Villiers), Joey still accuses his nanny (Bette Davis) of the crime, and does everything in his power to annoy the kindly old woman, despite her best efforts to welcome him home.

As Joey is so relentlessly obnoxious to her, our sympathies naturally lie with poor put-upon Nanny, despite our better judgement (for why else would bad Bette be in the role?). And as the story progresses, it does indeed become apparent that Nanny is in fact one toy short of a nursery, and that she did kill Joey's sister, though a further twist reveals this to have been accidental... Having just received news that her own daughter has died during an abortion,

Nanny goes to draw the tot's bath, not realising that she has fallen in whilst playing with her doll and lies unconscious in the rising water, hidden by the drawn shower curtain.

Things gradually come to a head when Joey's sophisticated Aunt Pen (Jill Bennett) comes to stay and, getting up in the night, discovers Nanny hovering outside Joey's bedroom door, a pillow in her arms. Recalling that Nanny doesn't advocate extra pillows for fear that children might suffocate themselves, Pen confronts Nanny, only to suffer a fatal attack when she realises that Joey has been telling the truth about Nanny all along (this being a thriller, Pen naturally suffers from a weak heart!). Thus, with Aunt Pen conveniently out of the way, the path is clear for Nanny to do away with Joey, his parents being away for the evening.

What follows is one of the creepiest scenes in Hammer history, as Nanny slowly opens the door to Joey's room to carry out her deadly task. But unbeknownst to her, Joey has barricaded the door with a chest of drawers, the movement of which wakes the sleeping boy, who receives the shock of his life when he sees Nanny's face - shot in extreme close-up - grimacing round the door. With no music, dialogue or sound effects to punctuate the action, this remains one of the most chilling moments in the psycho genre, for straight away Joey knows Nanny's intent. And she knows he knows...

To reveal much more of the plot would spoil a superb film. Suffice to say that this remains one of Hammer's key films, thanks to the inspired direction by Seth Holt, who manages not only to make the very most of the opportunities available, but to also make believable what is basically a pretty convoluted piece of writing by producer Jimmy Sangster (based on the novel by Evelyn Piper).

As the title character Davis is simply superb. One of Hollywood's top actresses, her career began back in the early thirties in a number of movie potboilers, her performances gradually leading to above-the-title billing in countless thirties and forties classics, including *Dangerous* and *Jezebel*, both of which won her Oscars. However, by the early sixties, after over a quarter of a century at the top, her career had begun to slide. Luckily for her, *Whatever Happened to Baby Jane*, a horror drama in which she co-starred with Joan Crawford - whose own career was also on the slide - was just round the corner.

Ursula Andress takes time out for a cuppa during the location filming of *She*.

Ursula Andress, resplendent as Ayesha, She Who Must Be Obeyed.

Horror films of this nature were generally looked down upon by actresses of the stature of Davis and Crawford, yet they really weren't in a position to be grand about doing horror pictures at this stage in their careers. Their gamble paid off, and the huge international success of *Baby Jane* not only put them both back on the map, it also won Davis an Academy Award nomination (much to the chagrin of Crawford, with whom she continually battled on the set). *Baby Jane* had its price, though; for a long while after Davis was only offered 'crazy old lady' parts. Glad of the work, she was more than happy to accept them, however, and went on to appear in the likes of *Hush... Hush, Sweet Charlotte* (the semi-sequel to *Baby Jane*), *Dead Ringer* and, of course, *The Nanny*.

A highly volatile actress to work with, Davis didn't suffer fools gladly. That *The Nanny* came at a difficult point in her life didn't help matters for director Seth Holt, either. 'She was always telling me how to direct', he later said. That she had flu for most of the shoot and often held up filming while she took days off to recover also added to the production problems. Davis was worth the trouble, though, and Holt's conviction that his star was playing the part over-the-top proved to be his only misjudgement, for despite her usual penchant for going for the jugular, Davis was in fact a model of restraint in *The Nanny*, prompting *Herald Tribune* critic Judith Crist to comment: 'In this, her fourth venture into the Hitchcock-cum-horror milieu, Miss Davis is out for character rather than hoax and comes up with a beautifully controlled performance.'

Davis's performance wasn't the only good one in the film, however. As the seemingly spiteful Joey, nine-year-old William Dix is quite superb in what could have been a thankless role. Similarly, Jill Bennett as his sophisticated Aunt Pen gives a good account of herself, as does the icily suave James Villiers as his father, and

Wendy Craig as his long-suffering mother, herself still babied by Nanny.

Crisply photographed in black and white by Harry Waxman (colour would have been a mistake) and with an effective score by Richard Rodney Bennett, *The Nanny* is Hammer at its most professional and sophisticated. That it did very well at the box office, particularly in America where it became Hammer's second biggest success to date, must have pleased all concerned. Yet despite this, Davis herself didn't work for nearly three more years, finally returning again in triumph to Hammer in 1968 in *The Anniversary*.

But *The Nanny* wasn't the only fish Hammer had to fry in 1965. There was also their big budget adaptation of H. Rider Haggard's *She*, previously filmed back in 1935 by *King Kong* producer Merian C. Cooper, a remake of which was now suggested to Anthony Hinds by Kenneth Hyman, one of Hammer's American backers.

In the original book, ancient papers lead a Cambridge professor and his friends to a lost city in Africa where they discover Ayesha, a queen who cannot die until she falls in love, retaining her beauty in the meantime by bathing in the flame of eternal youth. For his version, Cooper had shifted the story from Africa to the Arctic with spectacular results. Hammer preferred to stick to the book, yet curiously lost the sense of mystery its predecessor had conjured up in the process. Still, the film isn't without its moments of spectacle, even if the overall feeling is one of claustrophobia.

For the role of Ayesha, Hammer cast ex-Bond girl Ursula Andress, who certainly had the required beauty, if not acting talent, to play the centuries old queen. For the leader of the expedition, Major Holly, the studio brought back the ever-reliable Peter Cushing, whose presence

Dracula (Christopher Lee) slips to a watery grave during the climax of *Dracula - Prince of Darkness*. Note the truck, top left.

at least helps to give the film's fantastic events a solid anchor. Hammer regulars Christopher Lee and Andre Morell also pop up in smaller roles, whilst Ayesha's love interest is provided by the comparatively unknown John Richardson, whose success in the role led to a number of other Hammer films.

Adequately directed by Robert Day (whose previous credits included such non-Hammer horrors as *Grip of the Strangler* and *Corridors of Blood*), the film did exceptionally well at the box office, despite its shortcomings, which were at least partially smoothed over by James Bernard's haunting score. The fact that Ursula Andress had helped to promote the film by appearing nude in the June 1965 issue of *Playboy* certainly didn't do anything to hurt box office receipts either, which were trumpeted

by Hammer in a *Variety* ad which read 'SHE-ing is believing!.

At this stage in the proceedings, Hammer, who in the past had received funding from a variety of sources, had an exclusive deal with Seven Arts, a future subsidiary of Warner Bros, for whom they would make eleven films, the first of which had been *The Nanny*. To this they quickly added four more horror films which, to further save on costs, they shot in pairs, back to back, on the same sets. An ingenious idea, it perhaps worked better in principle than in practice.

The first pair of films to go before the cameras was *Dracula, Prince of Darkness* and *Rasputin - The Mad Monk*, both of which top line Christopher Lee.

With *Dracula - Prince of Darkness*, Hammer finally persuaded Lee to return to the role of Dracula. Seven years and several films on, Lee felt the time was now finally right for a reprise, and so agreed to don the fangs, cape and red contact lenses once again. Similarly, Terence Fisher was brought back to direct the picture, while composer James Bernard revived his famous *Dracula* theme to give the film a sense of continuity, which is further established by the use of the climactic scenes from *Dracula* in a prologue to the new film, along with an explanatory narration.

The film's plot is simplicity itself. Two English couples, Alan and Helen (Charles Tingwell and Barbara Shelley) and Charles and Diana (Francis Matthews and Suzan Farmer) are travelling in the Carpathians and stop for the night at a village inn where they meet the earthy Father Sandor (Andrew Keir), a vampire hunter who predictably advises them all to leave the area for their own good. As to be expected, the travellers lose their way the next day and, spying Castle Dracula, decide to call in, hoping to find a room for the night. Here they are greeted by Klove (Philip Latham), a mysterious manservant who tells them that though his master is dead, he left provision in his will that all travellers be made welcome. Naturally, the two couples accept this offer and stay the night, during which one of them meets with a grisly end...

Woken by a curious noise, Alan naturally goes to investigate (this being a horror film) and discovers Klove dragging a large trunk down to the basement. His curiosity aroused, Alan follows Klove at a discreet distance to see what the retainer is up to. However, the moving of the trunk turns out to be a ruse simply to get Alan into the cellar, where Klove stabs him, then hoists his body up above a large sarcophagus into which he scatters his master's ashes. He then slits Alan's throat, the blood from

which flows onto the ashes and revivifies Dracula!

A superbly devised and realised sequence - and undoubtedly one of the film's highpoints - it nevertheless produced a major problem for the film's makers: after such a grand entrance, how could Dracula possibly live up to expectations? He couldn't now pop into the drawing room and greet his guests in the clipped manner he'd used in the original film - this would surely have provoked laughter. Consequently, it was decided that Dracula would remain mute throughout the film, influencing events by the sheer power of his presence, leaving any verbal instructions he might have to his fathful manservant Klove (even though Klove is not actually seen in the first film!).

As the plot picks up speed, Helen - something of a middle-aged frump - is given the bite by Dracula and transformed into a sensual vampire (later to be staked in a memorable scene), after which the Count focusses his attentions firmly on Diana, whom he wishes to make his new bride. To save her from this fate, her husband Charles enlists the help of Father Sandor who - after several incidents at his monastery where the Count is helped in his deeds by a Renfield-like character (Thorley Walters) -finally corners Dracula on the frozen moat of his castle, where a few well-aimed bullets crack the ice and send the Count to the icy depths (fresh running water being as fatal to a vampire as either a stake or a cross).

Production on *Dracula - Prince of Darkness* began on 26 April 1965, and progessed smoothly over the next five weeks. In fact, the only problems encountered in this phase came from the censors, the British Board of Film Classification, to whom Hammer, like all other British production companies, had to submit their scripts. What the BBFC objected to was the revivification scene, which originally had

Klove hoisting up Alan's body, severing his head and tossing it to one side. This was consequently altered to a mere throat-slitting, but even in this toned down version the scene still packs a wallop to this day.

Also nice to note is that, having been revived, Dracula lies naked in his sarcophagus rather than dressed in full evening garb - as was often the case in the old Universal films, such as *House of Dracula*, in which John Carradine transforms from a bare-boned skeleton to a fully dressed dandy in a few quick lap dissolves when the stake is removed from his heart. Thanks to Les Bowie's excellent effects, Dracula instead is seen gradually to build from ashes to skeleton to fleshy mess before emerging in human form in a clever reversal of the usual disintegration finale (though why Klove waited so many years to revive his master when he could so easily have abducted a local to do so is never explained).

Bowie was also responsible for the effects during the film's finale on the ice-covered moat, which were achieved by a variety of means, including shots of real ice in a swimming pool, wax on water and large slabs of plaster of Paris, one of which was mounted on a pivot to help give the illusion that the Count was slipping into the icy water beneath (a scene performed by Lee and his stuntman Eddie Powell).

The surrounding exterior castle sets - which differed from those seen in the 1958, which had long since been demolished - were designed as usual by Bernard Robinson, who got the most from his limited budget by relying on such age-old movie stand-bys as hardboard, plaster, canvas and scaffolding. The results are certainly convincing, even if they did stand just twenty feet high, any long shots being completed by models and matte paintings. The interior of Castle Dracula was also revamped to include a number of lengthy corridors, down which Terence Fisher was able to prowl his camera, a device he uses most effectively in the scenes just prior to Alan's murder, the movement of the camera down the empty corridors eerily suggesting an unseen but pervading presence of evil.

Scriptwise, the film offers few surprises, the stranded traveller situation being all too familiar, though the belated introduction of the fly-eating Renfield-like character Ludwig shows that Stoker's original novel was at least somewhere at the back of scriptwriter John Sansom's mind (Sansom was in fact a pen name for Jimmy Sangster, still trying to escape his image as a writer solely of horror films). But any defects the narrative might have are at least shored up by some strong performances. Andrew Keir's Father Sandor is a worthy substitute for Professor Van Helsing (Cushing being unable to return to the role because of prior commitments), while Barbara Shelley's seductive vampire brings an overt sexuality to the proceedings. Her character even introduces a certain element of sexual ambiguity when, fangs bared, she attempts to seduce Diana into the ways of the vampire, beckoning and murmuring 'You don't need Charles.'

As the young hero Charles, Francis Matthews is quite adequate if a little vapid, while Suzan Farmer's Diana has a suitably innocent air about her. Philip Latham, however, is excellent as the sinister Klove, as is Thorley Walters as the insect-eating Ludwig. Which only leaves Christopher Lee, who though he brings presence to the role of Dracula, is reduced to being little more than a walk-on in his own film. With no dialogue to speak, he is little more than a hissing bogey man. That he manages to pull this off with dignity is a tribute to is often under-rated skills as an actor. However, as if by compensation, his skills were more than called upon in *Rasputin - The Mad Monk*, the film made immediately following *Dracula - Prince of Darkness*.

violent end when murdered by Prince Youssoupoff. Unfortunately, Hammer soon found out that a representation of the actual facts would have resulted in their own undoing, as had been the case with MGM, who had made a version of the Rasputin story back in 1932.

At this time, the real Prince Youssoupoff was still alive, and though his name was changed to Prince Chegodieff for the film (in which he is played by John Barrymore), he sued MGM: not because the film accused him of murdering Rasputin, but because it implied that his wife had been raped by the monk. MGM settled out of court, paying Youssoupoff one million dollars. By the time Hammer came to make their version of events, Youssoupoff was dead, but his relatives were not. Not wishing a repeat of the MGM incident, John Elder/Anthony Hinds quickly revised the film's script, the result being that most of the characters, save for the royal family and Rasputin himself, were now fictionalised.

This wasn't the only problem the film encountered. Because of added expenses incurred by *Dracula - Prince of Darkness* (chiefly the re-acquisition of the opening flashback sequence from *Dracula*, which was now owned by Universal), *Rasputin's* budget was slashed by some £25,000 - the result being that further scenes had to be either cut or reshaped.

Despite these setbacks, Don Sharp delivered a workmanlike film. Yet its very subject matter means that it falls between two stools, for it is neither frightening enough to be classed as a true horror film - despite its determination to shock - nor faithful enough to the facts to be viewed as serious historical drama.

As the mad monk, Lee gives a good account of himself, yet so wide-eyed and energetic is his performance that at times it seems to overwhelm the film, leaving it to Tom Baker's

The dead that walk. A shocking moment from *The Plague of the Zombies.*

Similarly, *Rasputin* co-stars Barbara Shelley, Francis Matthews and Suzan Farmer. Other hold-overs included producer Anthony Nelson Keys, photographer Michael Reed and production designer Bernard Robinson, who now had the Castle Dracula exteriors suitably re-dressed so as to resemble the Russian winter palace. Meanwhile, newcomers included composer Don Banks, director Don Sharp (fresh from his sterling second unit work on *Those Magnificent Men in their Flying Machines*) and scriptwriter John Elder/Anthony Hinds (who had also supplied the story outline for *Dracula - Prince of Darkness*).

This time out, Lee plays the infamous Russian monk who successfully insinuates his way into the court of Tsar Nicholas II with the help of a compliant courtier, Sonia (Barbara Shelley). However, as history recalls, Rasputin came to a interpretation of the role in *Nicholas and Alexandra* (1971) to set the record straight. Something of a disappointment overall, *Rasputin - The Mad Monk* doesn't quite manage to overcome its various limitations, despite obvious effort all round.

Dracula and *Rasputin* weren't the only irons Hammer had in the fire at this stage, though. They were followed by the second of the back-to-back pairings, *Plague of the Zombies* (announced at various stages as *The Horror of the Zombie* and *Zombie*) and *The Reptile* (itself announced as *The Reptiles* and *Curse of the Reptile*), both of which were produced by Anthony Nelson Keys and directed by John Gilling. Energetic little pictures with tuppenny blood atmospheres, they were livelier affairs than both *Dracula* and *Rasputin*, despite being classed as second features, which meant even smaller budgets!

For these two films, Castle Dracula was again revamped by Bernard Robinson, though quite considerably this time, the end result being a small Cornish village! To achieve this, the 'ice'-covered moat was dug out and became a graveyard, while the walls of the castle were stripped of their hardboard and canvas and redressed as cottages, shops and an inn, though the drawbridge itself remained, becoming a rather more solid affair.

The first of the film's to be shot was *Plague of the Zombies*, which went before the cameras in late July 1965 and was completed in just twenty-eight days. For it, Hammer regular Andre Morell returned to star, this time as Sir James Forbes, a medical professor who, along with his daughter Sylvia (Diane Clare), travels to Cornwall to visit his friend and former pupil Dr Peter Thompson (Brook Williams) and his daughter Alice (Jacquline Pearce). Strange goings-on soon attract the attention of Sir James and Sylvia, who discover that the vil-

lage has recently suffered a number of mysterious deaths. Investigating, they discover that the local squire (John Carson), who has banned Dr Thompson from carrying out autopsies, is in fact using voodoo to resurrect the dead, in order to use them to work his tin mine!

As to be expected, the squire comes to a sticky end for his nefarious deeds, but not before the film has delivered its fair share of shocks and surprises, which in this case prove to be quite considerable. Even as the opening credits roll, we are treated to a torch lit voodoo ceremony in one of the tin mines, accompanied by thundrous drums care of James Bernard's score. Straight away we know that this is no ordinary Cornish village! The callous arrogance of the squire and his fellow aristocrats is also depicted early on: just as Sir James and his daughter are arriving in the village, a hunt careers through a funeral procession, knocking over the coffin, out of which tumbles the body. That the body has been mutilated immediately sets Sir James's mind working - as does the near-catatonic state of Alice, Dr Thompson's wife, who herself seems to be turning into a zombie.

The film's raison d'etre is undoubtedly the sequence in which Dr Thompson dreams of a mass rising of the dead in the local graveyard, brilliantly realised by director Gilling, who uses mist, green filters and tilted angles to achieve the required effect. Add to this a fire at the squire's manor, the decapitation of Alice and a blazing finale in which the zombies literally go up in smoke, and you have one of the most incident-packed ninety minutes Hammer ever produced.

Like Gilling's direction, all of the film's other technicalities are well up to scratch, including the script by Peter Bryan, Arthur Grant's photography and Roy Ashton's superb zombie make-up, seen at its best in a chilling scene when a zombie throws Alice's body down a mine shaft. Classy performances from Morell, Carson and Pearce are also a valuable asset to the film's overall effect (though gaffe spotters will notice a car speed by in the distance early on in the film, as well as the shadow of a rain machine during a storm).

However, out of the cast, it was only Jacqueline Pearce who crossed over to the second film, *The Reptile*, in which she was promoted to title character status. Again set in Cornwall, for which the village set was this time only slightly revamped, a few rowing boats being added to give the impression of a seaside town, its story (care of John Elder/Anthony Hinds) is a pretty straightforward affair. It transpires that the daughter of the local doctor (Noel Willman) periodically turns into a murderous reptile, a result of being cursed by a Malayan sect. This time it's the brother of one of the Reptile's victims who turns up to solve the mystery of the strange deaths in the village.

Unlike Hammer's previous female monster, the Gorgon - which had been played by both Barbara Shelley and Prudence Hyman - Jacqueline Pearce plays both the human and subhuman aspects of the Reptile, for which she underwent two-hour sessions in Roy Ashton's make-up chair to transform her into the title creature. The results are more than worth the discomfort the actress suffered, her various appearances in the film achieving the required impact, thanks to John Gilling's careful build up.

Filmed in just 32 days, *The Reptile* had gone into production just one week after the wrap of *Plague of the Zombies*, which made for a hectic schedule for Gilling, photographer Arthur Grant and producer Anthony Nelson Keys. Yet

it is to their credit that *Plague* and *The Reptile* still stand up as well as they do, both films being textbook manuals on how to make effective low budget horror films.

With all four films now complete, Hammer's initial idea seems to have been to release *Plague* and *The Reptile* on the same bill as co-features, which certainly would have revealed the fact that they were shot on the same sets. Luckily, common sense prevailed and *The Reptile* went out on a double bill with *Rasputin - The Mad Monk* early in 1966, for which the posters invited audiences to 'Scream through every second of them!'. As an extra come-on, ticket buyers were also given free Rasputin beards (blue for the boys, pink for the girls!), about which the pressbook rather condescendingly told cinema managers: 'Use the beard to get the younger crowd into the theatre. Youth nowadays are particularly susceptible to weird hair-dos and the beatnik look.'

Dracula - Prince of Darkness was teamed up with *Plague of the Zombies*, for which equally ludicrous freebies were given away to the public. This time the boys received paper fangs and the girls zombie eyes. William Castle would have been proud.

Despite these cheap gimmicks, the box office response to the films was strong. Even the critics found nice things to say about the quartet. 'Hokum? Yes. But acted with great competence and produced with great skill' said *The People* of *Dracula - Prince of Darkness*, while *Kine Weekly* described *The Reptile* as an 'excellent shocker'. Even *The Monthly Film Bulletin* called *Plague of the Zombies*: 'The best Hammer film for quite some time'.

It seemed the studio was on something of a roll.

jurassic larks

After the compactly budgeted Cornwall films, Hammer's next venture was something of an epic by comparison. Called *One Million Years BC* it was, like a good deal of their product, a remake, this time of the 1940 Hal Roach classic *One Million Years BC*. (aka *Man and His Mate*), which had the added box office fillip of being heavily promoted as Hammer's one-hundredth production (though in truth the figure was higher than this).

A prehistoric adventure which (anachronistically) pits humans against dinosaurs, the original stars Victor Mature, Lon Chaney Jr. and a number of magnified lizards posing as dinosaurs! For their version, Hammer for once decided to pull all the stops out and hired effects wiz Ray Harryhausen to provide the film with some rather more realistic-looking creatures.

An industry legend, Harryhausen's interest in stop motion effects was ignited in 1933 when, at the age of thirteen, he saw *King Kong*, with its superb animation by stop motion pioneer Willis H. O'Brien. Encouraged by it to make his own amateur films on 16mm, Harryhausen finally found professional work with producer George Pal in 1940, working on his famous Puppetoons. After serving in the army during the war, Harryhausen actually managed to get work with his boyhood hero O'Brien, whom he assisted on the *Kong*-like adventure *Mighty Joe Young*, after which he was sufficiently skilled to strike out on his own with such films as *The Beast From 20,000 Fathoms* and *20 Million Miles to Earth*.

In 1957, he teamed up with producer Charles

H. Schneer, with whom he would go on to make a number of classic fantasy adventures, including *The Seventh Voyage of Sinbad*, *Mysterious Island* and *Jason and the Argonauts*. It was after they had completed *The First Men in the Moon* that Hammer approached Harryhausen about doing the effects work for their *One Million Years BC* project.

The story is straightforward enough. In prehistoric times, a young girl from the Shell People falls in love with a young man from the Rock People, despite the fact that, like the houses of Montague and Capulet, their tribes are at war with eachother. Being ostracized is the least of the couple's worries, however - surviving attacks by pterodactyls and other dinosaurs being of greater importance. And it was Harryhausen's job to provide the film with these various creations, which he did with models in his usual, painstaking, frame by frame way (save one scene which utilised a real iguana, supposedly to make the later monsters appear even more realistic).

Such animation took months, sometimes even years, to complete, and had to be planned in advance of the live action shooting so that the actors could react to the 'imaginary' monsters they were supposedly fighting. Luckily for Harryhausen, the director assigned the task of bringing all this to the screen was none other than Don Chaffey, who a few years earlier had directed Harryhausen's biggest hit, *Jason and the Argonauts*. Thus, any worries that the film might go over budget (always a concern with Hammer) were generally allayed, though a

Meanwhile, the rest of the cast and crew headed off for the Canary Islands to film the live action footage into which Harryhausen would later painstakingly add his effects. Along with producer Michael Carreras, director Chaffey and cinematographer Wilkie Cooper (himself a *Jason and the Argonauts* veteran), this included leading lady Raquel Welch and her prehistoric beau John Richardson.

Welch had just come off her first major feature, Richard Flesicher's *Fantastic Voyage*, another big effects picture which she'd made for Fox. As it transpired, the last thing she now wanted to do was another effects picture - particularly a dinosaur film which required her to do little more than run around in a doeskin bikini (one of the film's many anachronisms, which also include false eye-lashes and modern-looking hairstyles).

That neither Welch nor the rest of the cast were required to speak any lines as such, save some made-up lingo which mostly consists of the words 'akeeta' and 'neetcha' repeated ad infinitum, didn't really endear the project to the star, either (though this at least saved the expense of dubbing or subtitling the film for its foreign release!). However, Richard Zanuck, then head of Twentieth Century Fox, the studio which owned Welch's contract, insisted that she do the picture on a loan out. Welch finally relented, and the film went on to become one of Hammer's and Welch's biggest hits - no doubt encouraged by the famous publicity shot (taken by Pierre Luigi) in which she is shown posing in her scanty doeskin bikini!

Helped along by Chaffey's assured direction, an atmospheric score by Italian composer Mario Nascimbene (which made excellent use of weird percussive sound effects, including rocks, bell sticks and the jawbone of an ass) and Harryhausen's superb stop motion work, the film could hardly have missed. Indeed, its

Creator and created - Peter Cushing and Susan Denberg in *Frankenstein Created Woman*.

sequence involving a brontosaurus was eventually dropped from Harryhausen's schedule for this reason. Some of the film's non stop-motion effects sequences were farmed out to Hammer's regular effects man Les Bowie so as to further save time. These included the opening scenes which saw the creation of the world in typical Hammer fashion, with porridge, red food colouring and gushing tap water standing in for molten lava!

eventual wordwide take topped $9 million. Encouraged by this success, Hammer immediately set up talks with Harryhausen about a remake of *King Kong*. Unfortunately, this never got past the discussion stage as RKO, who owned the rights, determined that no remakes of the story could be made - only sequels, which Hammer weren't interested in, especially given the disappointment of the Japanese follow ups (such as *King Kong vs Godzilla*), whose effects simply involved men romping about in rubber monster suits. Yet this setback didn't deter Hammer from making further prehistoric pictures of their own devising, the proliferation of which soon matched their previous obsession with swashbucklers.

In the meantime, it was business as usual back at the horror factory with *The Witches* (aka *The Devil's Own*), a rather disappointing effort given the talent involved in its making. Scripted by Nigel Kneale from the novel *The Devil's Own* by Peter Curtis (Nora Loftis), the film is a rather too genteel affair concerning a schoolteacher (Joan Fontaine) who moves to a quiet English village after a frightening experience in Africa involving witchcraft, only to discover more of the same on her doorstep!

The cast is certainly good, with Hollywood veteran Fontaine giving a good account of herself as the put-upon schoolmarm, ably supported by the likes of Kay Walsh (as the coven leader), Alec McCowen and Gwen Ffrangcon Davies. Sadly, the script is one of Kneale's lesser efforts and director Cyril Frankel fails to make the most of what few thrills there are available.

Which left it to Terence Fisher to redress the balance with *Frankenstein Created Woman* (announced as *The Fear of Frankenstein*), which saw Peter Cushing return to the role of Victor Frankenstien for the fourth time. Hammer had originally toyed with a similar title back in the late fifties, when they had intended *And Then*

Frankenstein Created Woman as a follow up to *The Curse of Frankenstein*, spoofing the title of the then popular Brigitte Bardot sizzler *And God Created Woman*. Luckily, they made *The Revenge of Frankenstein* instead.

Not a remake of *The Bride of Frankenstein*, as its title might suggest, but a new story entirely, *Frankenstein Created Woman* deals with the Baron's more esoteric experiments with soul transference. That he decides to transfer the soul of a wrongly executed man into the body of his dead fiancee (Susan Denberg, *Playboy's* Miss August, 1966) seems to be asking for trouble, though!

Lacking a monster in the true sense, the film is consequently a milder affair than Hammer's other Frankensteins. Having set up a promising situation, scriptwriter John Elder/Anthony Hinds curiously veers away from any overt references to the creation's presumably ambiguous sexuality, save for a scene in which 'she' uses her sexual allure to avenge her dead lover. That the film's central laboratory scene was excised just prior to release makes something of a mess of the narrative as well.

Nevertheless, there are compensations: Fisher's direction is as good as ever, as is the work of cinematographer Arthur Grant and composer James Bernard. There is also the added bonus of Thorley Walter's delightful turn as the Baron's fussy assistant Dr Hertz. This at least compensates for Denberg's lacklustre performance as the creature, which relies more on her bodily curves than her acting abilities.

Any gains Hammer made with *Frankenstein Created Woman* were quickly dispelled by their next film, though. Called *The Viking Queen*, it was filmed on location in Ireland and is one of their most hilariously inept productions - all the more remarkable because it was directed by Don Chaffey, who had recently done such a

(Opposite) Eddie Powell takes a well-deserved break during the filming of *The Mummy's Shroud*.

The Mummy (Eddie Powell) does its worst to Sir Basil (Andre Morell) as Haiti the Fortune Teller (Catherine Lacey) looks on.

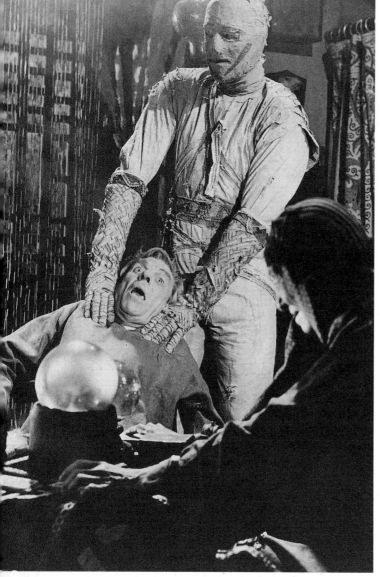

good job for them on *One Million Years BC*. That film at least had no dialogue. Unfortunately, *The Viking Queen* does, care of someone called Clarke Reynolds, most of which is unspeakable ('Bloody weather!' curses a rain-soaked Roman soldier as he trudges through Britain at one point).

The plot, such as it is, revolves round the Viking queen of the title (played by Carita), a Boudicea-like warrior who has an affair with an invading Roman soldier (Don Murray). A Romeo and Juliet story which might have passed muster with a better script, the results, unfortunately, are so bad as to be quite entertaining, especially given the film's frequent anachronisms which, as well as modern sounding dialogue, include the unintended appearance of a wrist watch!

Slightly better, but by no means a classic, is *The Mummy's Shroud* (originally announced as *The Mummy*), which proved to be writer-director John Gilling's last film for Hammer. Released on a double bill with *Frankenstein Created Woman*, Gilling based his script on a story by John Elder/ Anthony Hinds, which follows the old, old formula of a mummy being revived to avenge itself against the desecrators of its master's final resting place.

A less than routine affair, the film's few highpoints are the scenes in which the Mummy (Eddie Powell) makes his attacks, first appearing to his victims via a variety of distorted images (reflected in a tray of developing solution and a crystal ball, etc.), recalling Gilling's use of the fish-eye lens for the cat attacks in *Shadow of the Cat*. Yet despite a good cast (Andre Morell, John Phillips, Catherine Lacey, Michael Ripper) the film mostly seems to be going through its paces. The painfully low budget is obvious throughout, especially during the interminable opening sequence, supposedly set in Egypt, but looking suspiciously like a disused quarry. Gaffe spotters will also notice the casting of shadows across the cyclorama, supposedly representing the distant mountains, during this sequence.

Sadly, as well as being Gilling's last film for the studio, it was also the last Hammer film to be produced at their beloved Bray...

all change

The move from Bray was brought about primarily through Hammer's connection with the American company Seven Arts, with whom they had by now co-produced a number of successful features. Run by Eliot Hyman, Seven Arts was one of the cinema's largest independent film organizations, yet Hyman had aspirations to become a 'major', an ambition he achieved when he bought Warner Bros in April 1967 for the then staggering sum of $95 million. Consequently, the two companies merged to become Warner Bros-Seven Arts.

Hammer's ties continued with this new amalgamate, as they did with the British company Associated British Pictures, who themselves had ties with Seven Arts. The upshot of all this involved wheeler-dealing was that Hammer was requested to make use of the studios owned by ABPC at Elstree. They thus said goodbye to the homely Bray and hello to the Elstree film factory in mid 1967.

This move was by no means the end of Hammer. For the next few years they continued to make commercially viable films, some of which are good enough to be described as classics of their kind. What was gone, however, was the comfy, family atmosphere of Bray which, in essence, was Hammer Films.

Worries that their first post-Bray film might not live up to expectations proved ill-founded however, for *Quatermass and the Pit* (aka *Five Million Years to Earth*), the third episode in their on-going *Quatermass* series, turned out to be Hammer at its very best. Like its two predeces-

sors, it is based on a television serial by Nigel Kneale, which had been broadcast back in 1958 (again directed by Rudolph Cartier), with the role of Quatermass here played by Hammer regular Andre Morell, supported by Cec Linder, Christine Finn and Anthony Bushell. And just as the first two series had, it too cleared the streets on transmission evenings.

Hammer originally announced their film version of the series for production in 1963, with Anthony Hinds as producer, though it was 1967 before it finally went in front of the cameras with Anthony Nelson Keys now in charge of the production. As he had directed the first two Quatermass films for them, Val Guest was naturally Hammer's first choice to direct the third installment. Unfortunately, he was tied up with the James Bond spoof *Casino Royale*, so the megaphone instead went to Roy Ward Baker.

A highly respected director, Baker had helmed a number of classic British films in the forties and fifties, including *The October Man* with John Mills, *The One That Got Away* with Hardy Kruger and, most impressively, the *Titanic* reconstruction *A Night to Remember*. By the mid sixties his film career had gone into something of a decline, though, the result being that Baker had moved into television, where he successfully worked on episodes of *The Saint* and *The Avengers*, etc. Nevertheless, when the call came to work for Hammer he readily accepted, not having directed a feature since the Michael Crawford sex comedy *Two Left Feet* in 1963.

Quatermass and the Pit would mark a triumphant (if somewhat brief) return to form for Baker, who as a consequence would go on to direct a further six Hammer productions, though none of them would prove to be as well crafted as his brush with Quatermass.

Now that Hammer films were a world-renowned product, there was no longer any pressure to use an American star to play Quatermass, though Brian Donlevy (then 68) was briefly considered to reprise the role. Baker's own preferred choice was Kenneth More, with whom he'd successfully worked on *A Night to Remember* in 1958. This request was vetoed, however, and the part instead went to Hammer regular Andrew Keir (last seen in *The Viking Queen*) who proved to be more than up to

the challenge, even if he and Baker never actually saw eye to eye.

The rest of the cast were also well suited to their roles and include James Donald, Barbara Shelley and Julian Glover. Nigel Kneale, meanwhile, was commissioned to adapt his television series into movie form, while the film's technical aspects were in the practised hands of Arthur Grant (photography), James Needs (editing), Bernard Robinson (production design) and Les Bowie (effects).

The most involved of Kneale's Quatermass stories, the film revolves round the unearthing by workmen of mis-shapen skulls during excavations to extend London's underground. A large projectile, thought at first by the military to be

The Martian spaceship unearthed. Julian Glover (left, as the blinkered Colonel Breen) in *Quatermass and the Pit*.

Bette Davis as the venomous Mrs Taggart in *The Anniversary*. 'Snaps out her bitchy insults with all 57 varieties of relish' said the *Monthly Film Bulletin* of her performance.

had attempted to colonize earth. Unable to survive in the earth's atmosphere they had, like the monolith in *2001: A Space Odyssey*, thus played an integral part in the advancement of man, genetically re-engineering the apes then roaming the earth in an attempt to accelerate their development, imbueing them with telekinetic powers similar to their own. Consequently, the ship's force, now reactivated, reawakens these long dormant powers in those near enough to be susceptible to its transmissions. Under the ship's control, these people then attempt to destroy those about them not similarly gifted.

The fertility of Kneale's concept is perhaps a little too involved for a film just ninety-seven minutes long (the most persuasive of them being that man's image of the Devil derived from the horned Martians), yet so packed with incident and mayhem are the proceedings that the impenetrability of some of these ideas doesn't really matter. Scenes of genuine alarm in which inanimate objects fly about, minds are controlled and buildings destroyed at least put into more easily comprehendable visual terms what Kneale is attempting to get across in words, while the climax in which the 'Devil' is earthed with a giant crane as it rears over London brings things to a suitably exciting (if open-ended) conclusion.

Directed by Baker with an eye for the unnerving (the ground beneath an unfortunate workman is seen to ripple at one point when his long dormant powers are reactivated by the spaceship), the film produces many thrilling sequences once the main thrust of its story has been established, with Arthur Grant's sometimes stark photography giving the proceedings a suitably urgent feeling, particularly during the scenes of mob violence, when cinemaverite-style hand-held cameras are put to good use. Similarly, all the actors perform with conviction, particularly James Donald, top-billed

an unexploded German bomb left from World War Two, is also discovered soon after. But closer examination reveals it to be a spacecraft, millions of years old and made of an impenetrable substance unknown to man. When access is later gained into the spaceship's hull, it proves to be occupied by horned, locust-like creatures. Though the creatures themselves are long dead, the locusts' ship still exudes a mysterious force with the ability to control human minds.

Eventually it transpires that these insect creatures hailed from Mars five million years ago when, leaving their own dying planet, they above Keir as Dr Roney, the scientist first brought in to examine the unearthed skulls, Barbara Shelley as his assistant, and Julian Glover as the blinkered Colonel Breen, whose determination to pooh-pooh Quatermass's assertion that his 'unexploded bomb' is in fact an alien spacecreaft eventually proves to be his undoing.

Only Tristram Cary's music, which lacks the intensity that a James Bernard score might have produced, lets the proceedings down slightly, along with Les Bowie's variable effects work, in which tumbling masonry is too often seen to be bouncing styrofoam. But these are minor quibbles in a film whose fantastic developments, for the most part, keep one glued throughout, from the unearthing of the first skull to the final re-earthing of the Devil, making this one of Kneale's most symmetrical narratives.

It was Anne Pacey's comments about the film in *The Sun* (of all papers) that perhaps best summed up Kneale's script, though. 'The occasional references to witchcraft, devilry, gargoyles and the incarnation of true evil are thrown in probably to make the whole fantasy a lot weightier than it is. Those of us who know better can merely enjoy it for what it is; a colourful and imaginative enough load of .....!' And even if Kneale's story is little more than an elaborate con trick (he does in fact throw in certain ideas simply for effect, such as the unexplained discovery of claw marks in a derelict building), it certainly works a treat.

Which is more than can be said for Hammer's next film, *A Challenge for Robin Hood*, which stars Barrie Ingham in yet another variation on the old, old story.

At least late 1967 saw the return of battling Bette Davis to the Hammer fold for the second of her two films with them, an adaptation of

Bill McIlwraith's play *The Anniversary*. A black comedy drama, Davis stars as Mrs Taggart, a malevolent one-eyed matriarch who takes pleasure in goading her sons during an annual dinner to mark the death of her (much despised) husband. The film is a real showcase for the star, who spits out her bitcheries and put downs with relish ('Would you mind moving?' she asks her youngest son's girlfriend, who is sitting next to her on a sofa at one point. 'Body odour offends me!').

Just as she had been on *The Nanny*, Davis was not always easy to work with, though, and disagreements with the film's original director, the Canadian Alvin Rakoff, saw him replaced by her friend Roy Ward Baker, who Davis had met during his stint in Hollywood in the fifties when he'd directed her then-husband Gary Merrill in *Night Without Sleep*. The piece could have been a director's gift. However, Baker didn't quite rise to the challenge and made an adequate if unambitious film out of producer-screenwriter Jimmy Sangster's straightforward adaptation of the play.

Still, the performances shine, particularly James Cossins as Mrs Taggart's middle-aged son Henry, who it is revealed likes to dress up in women's clothes which he steals off neighbourhood washing lines, and Sheila Hancock as her daughter-in-law Karen, who has learned to fight back against the insults with as good as she receives. It's Davis's show, however, and she certainly seems to be enjoying herself in a role which could have been written especially for her.

The Vengeance of She, which followed *The Anniversary*, was an unfortunate regression to Hammer at its most inane. Originally announced as *Ayesha: Daughter of She*, the film was to have starred Ursula Andress, who eventually turned it down. The central role was then offered to Susan Denberg, whose shapely figure had

Filming *The Vengeance of She*. Note that two cameras are being used to capture the scene.

(Opposite) Jaqueline Pearce in full make-up as the Reptile. Note the forked tongue - or is that a fish she's eating?

graced *Frankenstein Created Woman*. Sadly, Denberg died from a drugs overdose before the film went before the cameras. Olinka Berova (formerly Olga Schoberova) was thus finally cast in the leading role in a story which revolves round a young woman (Berova) who turns out to be possessed by the dead queen Ayesha, much to the confusion of her lover (John Richardson again). Sadly, there is little in the way of true inspiration to the production, and the film's supporting cast (which includes Andre Morell, Noel Willman and Colin Blakely) is mostly wasted, while Miss Berova, though suitably endowed (as were most of Hammer's leading ladies), is no match for the charms of Ursula Andress.

Flabbily directed by Cliff Owen (more at home with comedies, such as *The Wrong Arm of the Law* and *Ooh, You Are Awful*) and unimaginatively scripted by Peter O'Donnell, the film nevertheless remains of passing note for being the first Hammer film to be produced by a woman, Aida Young - who had in fact joined Hammer back in 1963 as an associate producer and assistant to Michael Carreras, with whom she had worked on *One Million Years BC* and his non-Hammer films, *What a Crazy World* and *The Long Duel*. Now elevated to full producer status, she confirmed her abilities in this capacity later in 1968 when she was handed *Dracula Has Risen From The Grave*.

In the meantime, Hammer's old guard were re-united once more to adapt Dennis Wheatley's celebrated occult novel *The Devil Rides Out* for the screen, the result being yet another genre classic - and then some!

the devil made me do it!

When it came to writing stories about the
Occult, no one was more successful at it than
Dennis Wheatley who, beginning with *The
Forbidden Territory* in 1932, wrote over fifty
books during his career as an author, ten of
them dealing with the dark forces. However,
owing to their subject matter and the nature of
film censorship at the time of their writing, few
of these books made it to the screen, rare
exceptions being *Forbidden Territory* and *The
Eunuch of Stamboul*, which were filmed in
1938 and 1939 respectively.

By 1967 censorship had relaxed considerably
and a full-blooded version of Wheatley's *The
Devil Rides Out* (written back in 1934) now
seemed viable, especially given the author's
continued success in the world market.
Similarly, given their own success with the
horror genre, there seemed no one better
qualified to bring the novel to the screen than
Hammer.

Christopher Lee - who had met Wheatley at a
lecture in the mid-fifties and read all his books
- suggested to Hammer that they approach the
author about filming one of his works.
Hammer were quick to see the viability of
such a film and a contract was subsequently
negotiated, with *The Devil Rides Out* (described
by James Hilton as 'The best tale of its kind
since *Dracula*') agreed upon as the first subject,
to be closely followed by *The Lost Continent*,
based on *Uncharted Seas*.

It quickly became apparent that *The Devil Rides
Out* (aka *The Devil's Bride*) would be one of

Hammer's top flight productions when
Terence Fisher was signed to direct it and
Arthur Grant to photograph it, while to adapt
Wheatley's rambling narrative, Richard
Matheson (who had scripted *Fanatic* and an
unfilmed version of his book *I Am Legend* for
Hammer) was brought in, the result of his
efforts being ready to film at Elstree and on
location in Hertfordshire in August 1967.

Set in the mid-1920s, the film is a classic
struggle of good against evil and follows the
attempts by The Duc de Richeleau
(Christopher Lee) and his friend Rex Van Ryn
(Leon Greene) to rescue their protege Simon
Aaron (Patrick Mower), who has fallen in with
a group Satanists, led by a charismatic and
powerful figure simply known as Mocata
(Charles Gray). The Duc and Rex are fighting
for nothing less than Simon's soul, along with
that of a mysterious young girl called Tanith
(Nike Arrighi), all of which becomes apparent
when they encounter The Goat of Mendes, the
Devil himself (Eddie Powell), during a secret
initiation ceremony...

One of the rare occasions in which
Christopher Lee was allowed to play the hero
in a Hammer film, his performance as The Duc
de Richeleau is one of his very best and
remains a rare treat for those who can't see
beyond his Dracula persona. At once cool and
authorative, Lee brings the right aristocratic
bearing to the role and makes the character a
more than worthy adversary for Charles Gray's
Mocata, similarly one of the actor's finest
hours.

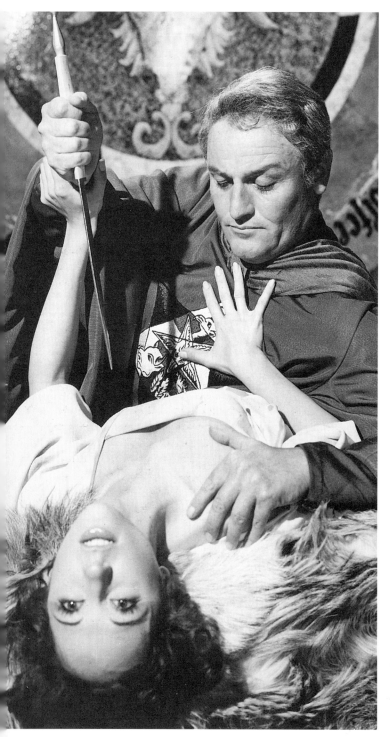

A stage actor of some presence, Gray's greatest asset is undoubtedly his mellifluent voice which, sounding not unlike that of Jack Hawkins, actually got him work dubbing Hawkins' voice in the sixties when the latter developed throat cancer. Gray's own film career has spanned a number of diverse projects, including two James Bond films (in one of which he plays Blofeld), *The Rocky Horror Picture Show* (in which he instructs us how to do the 'Time Warp') and *The Seven Per Cent Solution* (in which he plays Mycroft Holmes, a role he would reprise in the Jeremy Brett TV series). His work as Mocata in *The Devil Rides Out* is without question his most memorable screen role, however. In fact never did an actor exude such charm and menace at one and the same time. During one scene in which he unsuccessfully attempts to hypnotise a friend of Rex's into telling him the whereabouts of the girl Tanith, he exits with 'I shan't be back, but something will...,' a line he delivers with absolute relish.

Save for the role of Rex, which is played by Leon Greene but dubbed by Patrick Allen, owing to Greene's poor attempt at an American accent, the rest of the performances are also uniformally good, while Terence Fisher's direction is assured throughout - never more so, in fact.

A fast moving, episodic film, it contains many set pieces which stay in the mind, including the discovery by Rex and the Duc of the pentacle circle hidden in Simon's attic, the woodland initiation ceremony in which the Devil himself appears, and the climax in which a young girl is saved from sacrifice in a ceremony in which the Satanists are ultimately destroyed by the Duc. Most memorable of all, however, is the lengthy sequence in which the Duc, Simon and two of their friends (played by Paul Eddington and Sarah Lawson) fight off all manner of horrific apparitions (including a giant tarantula and the Angel of Death) from within the protection of a pentacle.

Charles Gray as the evil Mocata and Nike Arrighas as Tanith in a posed publicity still for *The Devil Rides Out*, one of Hammer's true classics.

Accompanied by the rat-a-tat-tat of James Bernard's powerful score and helped immeasurably by the lavish look of Bernard Robinson's production design, *The Devil Rides Out* is without question one of Hammer's classiest films, and certainly worthy of re-appraisal. There are, of course, occasional imperfections: the effects don't always convince (particularly the giant tarantula) and the continuity is a little shaky at times (day turns into night and back again within the space of the woodland initiation sequence), but these are nit-picking flaws in an otherwise fine film.

Even the critics had to admit that Hammer had got it right this time. 'Produced with the professional gloss and attention to period detail which we have come to expect from the best of Hammer films,' said *The Daily Cinema*. British audiences agreed, and turned the film into a local hit. Unfortunately, the same didn't happen for the film's American release, which immediately cast doubts over the filming of further Wheatley novels - which is a great shame, for one would have liked to have seen more of the Duc de Richeleau, particularly in the guise of Christopher Lee.

While working on *The Devil Rides Out*, scriptwriter Richard Matheson also found himself hired to work on Hammer's first foray into television, *Journey to the Unknown* (the second if one counts their aborted Frankenstein series, *Tales of Frankenstein*).

A collection of 17 hour-long 'twist in the tail' horror stories, the series was co-produced with Twentieth Century Fox (in a deal brokered by James Carreras) with an eye for American consumption. At Fox's insistence Joan Harrison, Alfred Hitchcock's long time assistant and sometime producer (especially on his long running TV series, *Alfred Hitchcock Presents*) was sent over as executive producer of the programmes, much to the chagrin of

Hammer's own producer Anthony Hinds who, as a consequence, left Hammer the following year (though he continued to write scripts for them under his familiar pen name, John Elder).

Not quite the success that had been envisaged, the series nevertheless produced some solid episodes and utilised a good deal of top talent. Among them were writers Robert Bloch and Alfred Shaughnessy, directors Peter Sasdy, Roy Ward Baker, Don Chaffey and Alan Gibson, and such stars as Vera Miles, Joseph Cotten, David Hedison, Roddy McDowall and Barbara Bel Geddes. Hammer's in-house musical director, Philip Martell, worked on every episode, and the catchy theme tune was supplied by composer Harry Robinson, soon to become a Hammer regular. Sadly, a second series, though mooted, was abandoned when the ratings of the first failed to live up to expectations.

Meanwhile, well before *The Devil Rides Out* had finished shooting, the second of Hammer's Wheatley films, *The Lost Continent*, had already gone into production. Described by *The Monthly Film Bulletin* as 'one of the most ludicrously enjoyable bad films ever made', the results are so silly as to be quite endearing. One of the studio's bigger-budgeted films of the late sixties, the thought of creating a camp classic can't have been their intended idea.

A tramp steamer, the *Carita*, making its way from Freetown in Africa to Caracas, finds itself waylaid in the Sargasso Sea where its passengers - a collection of British archetypes played by the likes of Eric Porter, Nigel Stock and Jimmy Hanley - encounter not only a curious community run by descendants of The Spanish Inquisition, but also some very phoney-looking monsters (created by Robert A. Mattey, who was later responsible for creating Bruce the shark for Spielberg's *Jaws*).

Scripted by Michael Nash (another Michael Carreras pseudonym, apparently his gardener's), the film emphasizes the book's more fantastical elements. Unfortunately, the production lacks the courage of its way-out convictions, and the direction - also by Carreras, who took over from Leslie Norman who was let go after just a couple of days - is, as usual for Carreras, pedestrian and unadventurous. Despite its shortcomings, the film nevertheless has its followers (though it fared badly at the box office), and at least Arthur Lawson's art direction is eye-catching (though again, Carreras could have made more of it). Very much a studio-bound film, even its storm sequences were filmed in a 175,000 gallon tank at Elstree, built especially for the film.

Unfortunately, *The Lost Continent* wasn't the only film Carreras inflicted on the public in 1968. He also wrote (as Henry Younger) and directed *Slave Girls* (aka *Prehistoric Women*), a romp involving a hunter's discovery of a hidden valley, a lost tribe of women (led by Martine Beswick) and a menacing white rhinocerous. Sadly, there are no Ray Harryhausen dinosaurs in this one to liven things up, and the film seems to be little more than an excuse to re-use Carl Toms' fur bikinis from *One Million Years BC*.

Luckily for them, 1968 also contained one of Hammer's biggest hits: their third Dracula film, *Dracula Has Risen from the Grave*. Neither the best nor the absolute worst entry in the series, the film is, with hindsight, something of a disappointment.

This time, the Count (Lee) is revived from his icy grave (into which he'd been plunged at the end of *Dracula - Prince of Darkness*) when a priest, who has been sealing the entrance to his castle with a giant gold cross, falls onto the ice and the blood from his injuries revives the Count. Following this, Dracula goes on the rampage,

avenging himself on a variety of locals.

Despite the fact that it doesn't rely on the familiar 'stranded travellers in peril' plot, the story for *Dracula Has Risen from the Grave* is a pretty routine effort from the pen of John Elder/ Anthony Hinds. In the hands of Terence Fisher (who would never again direct a Dracula film) it just might have passed muster. Unfortunately, Fisher broke his leg during the film's preparation period and the directorial reins for this episode were consequently handed to Freddie Francis who, despite his background as a cinematographer, makes heavy weather of the proceedings, his penchant for colour filters during several of the film's key scenes being an unwarranted and unsuccessful distraction.

The performances aren't quite up to scratch either. As the Count, Lee has too little to do, while the absence of Van Helsing means that his tasks again have to be carried out by a substitute, this time a another priest (Rupert Davies). The film's 'romantic' leads are a disappointment, too. As the young hero, Barry Andrews lacks charm and presence, while his girlfriend (Veronica Carlson), who falls under the spell of Dracula, seems to lack acting experience, though she certainly looks pretty.

The script even dares to play around with established vampire mythology when, staked through the heart, Dracula pulls the bloody stake out, the excuse being that it has been hammered in with insufficient religious conviction! The sequence has a certain impact, but just doesn't play fair with the legend, and caused Christopher Lee, who had become increasingly disillusioned with the series, to publicly criticize the film. 'The film was made with complete absence of style, taste or production quality', he said, while of the film's success he added 'I have got past understanding any of this by now.'

Indeed, the film broke box office records in its first two days in London, much to the mystification of the critics, who generally ripped the film to shreds ('A bloody bore', said Judith Crist). Still, the film has its good points: Bernard Robinson's design work is as usual top notch (particularly in those sequences set on the rooftops of the village), as is James Bernard's score, while the climax, in which the Count is impaled on the giant golden cross, is well-enough staged. The discovery of a young girl's body, stuffed into a giant bell, also remains in the mind.

The film's ad campaign, clearly aimed at the teenage market, was as unsubtle as the film itself, however. One poster featured a young girl with two band aids on her neck, accompanied by the tag line, 'Dracula has risen from the grave - obviously!' while the film's box office success was ballyhooed with the line, 'Dracula has risen to new heights!'. Hardly.

Hammer were little affected by the film's critical drubbing, though, particularly as, during its production, they had received the seal of royal approval...

Kari (Martine Beswick) comes to a sticky end in *Slave Girls*.

royal approval

Presented to Hammer on the set of *Dracula Has Risen from the Grave* during the filming of its bloody climax, The Queen's Award to Industry was given to the company in recognition of the fact that they had brought £1.5 million worth of US dollars into Britain during each of the previous three years - no mean feat given the size of Hammer's operation when compared to some of the bigger studios.

The award (which was shortly followed by the knighthood of James Carreras in the 1969 New Years Honours) came just in time, though, for it was during this period that the American studios began to pull out of the British film industry, a consequence of the huge losses they had suffered during the previous two years.

Prior to the sixties, it had long been the fashion that the British cinema followed the fads and dictates of Hollywood. However, thanks to the sudden international success of the Bond films, the music of the Beatles and the lure of 'Swinging London', Britain suddenly became the industry leader, and Hollywood, always quick to recognize a trend, jumped on the band wagon and began to invest heavily in the British film industry. At first, success followed success, with such films as *Tom Jones* and *Blow Up* racking up huge international grosses. By 1968, things had begun to sour, though, and a string of expensive miscalculations (such as *The Charge of the Light Brigade*), coupled with President Johnson's cutbacks on tax benefits for American investment overseas, saw a hasty pullout from the British market.

American subjects also came back into vogue, and during the following two years films such as *Butch Cassidy and the Sundance Kid*, *Midnight Cowboy* and *M*A*S*H* dominated the international box office. As a result, several of Hammer's announced films, such as *In the Sun* and *The Day the Earth Cracked Open*, were abandoned. However, Hammer seemed to take little notice of the cinematic winds of change and - some would say doggedly - continued to make the kind of gothic horrors they had originally become known for, even though the public's taste was beginning to change to the more visceral modern day horrors of *Rosemary's Baby* and *Night of the Living Dead* (both 1968).

Hammer's first release in 1969 seemed to be pretty much a safe bet though, for not only did *Frankenstein Must Be Destroyed* revive the Baron for the fifth time (and the fourth time under the aegis of Terence Fisher), it remains one of the best entries in the series.

Like Jimmy Sangster, who had started out life at Hammer as an assistant director, it was now the turn of the studio's current first assistant Bert Batt to have a bash at scriptwriting. And a respectable job he made of it too. Working from a story devised by himself and the film's producer, Anthony Nelson Keys, the film follows the Baron's attempts to transplant the brain of an ailing colleague (George Pravda) into a new body (played by Freddie Jones) so as to save the brain's scientific secrets.

As to be expected, Cushing again returned to

play the Baron, whose personality has become even colder by this stage. In a stunning pre-credits sequence, he makes his first appearance in a hideous mask, so as to disguise himself while beheading an innocent passer-by to provide further parts for his experiments. Later on he even rapes the fiancée of his assistant, simply to discipline her! Hardly the actions of a gentleman, and certainly gratuitous, even by Hammer's standards.

Nevertheless, the film is a lively and full-blooded production and was described by *Film Review* as having 'all the usual blood-gushing, scalpel-wielding, electrode-flashing and corpse-walking we expect of a Frankenstein film.' Yet there is more to the film than these fairground elements. It has a stronger sense of humour than its predecessors, thanks to

Thorley Walters' comic turn as Inspector Frisch, whose attempts to track down the Baron are almost as incompetent as Inspector Clouseau's, while as his sidekick, Geoffrey Bayldon as a police doctor is an excellent straight man.

The film also has moments of genuine pathos, thanks to Freddie Jones's sensitive performance as the creature. No mis-shapen monster he, but an intelligent and lucid being, who becomes dazed and confused when he discovers that his brain is now housed inside an alien body. The scenes where he attempts to speak to his wife - who of course does not now recognize him - are genuinely touching.

Meanwhile, as the Baron's assistant, the young Simon Ward gives a good account of himself,

Peter Cushing in his fright mask in the stunning pre-credit sequence to *Frankenstein Must Be Destroyed.*

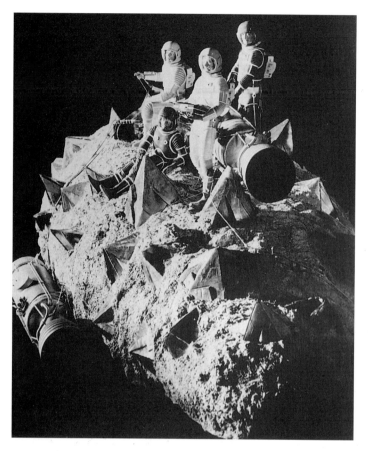

**A moment from
Moon Zero Two, one
of Hammer's wilder
miscalculations.**

Unfortunately, it was followed by *Moon Zero Two*, one of the studio's biggest blunders. Advertised as 'The First Space Western', it was made to cash in on the huge interest then surrounding the American moon landings. Compared to the previous year's 2001, it turned out to be something of an embarrassment for all concerned, though.

Set in 2021, the film stars James Olsen as Bill Kemp, a space pilot who is hired by a villainous millionaire (Warren Mitchell) to retrieve a solid sapphire asteroid and bring it back to his moon base. Also starring Hammer regulars Bernard Bresslaw, Michael Ripper and Adrienne Corri, the film was poorly directed on an insufficient budget by Roy Ward Baker, while the script by Michael Carreras (based on a story by Gavin Lyall, Frank Hardman and Martin Davidson) gives the impression of being written by a ten-year-old. Scott MacGregor's sets are also insufficiently eye-catching, and the inclusion of a number of songs (performed by the Go-Jos) only make matters worse. Deservedly, the film was a box office bomb.

as does Veronica Carlson as his fiancee, particularly in a scene where a water main bursts in her garden and 're-animates' the hand of a corpse the Baron has buried there. Superbly realised by Fisher, this sequence is perhaps the film's most memorable, though the finale, in which the creature carries Frankenstein into a burning building so that they will perish together, is also well staged.

As usual, all the other production elements are top notch, including James Bernard's music and Bernard Robinson's designs. Sadly, this proved to be Robinson's last film for the studio - he died in 1970. His work on *Frankenstein Must Be Destroyed*, which proved to be a popular box office attraction, was a more than worthy swan song, however.

As was the studio's next film, *Crescendo*, which also stars James Olsen. Yet another of Hammer's psychological thrillers, this one involves a young girl (Stephanie Powers) who goes to stay with the widow of a famous composer so as to research his life. But, as in all of Hammer's psychological thrillers, things aren't quite what they seem, and insanity is just a plot twist away. Scripted by Jimmy Sangster (who else?) and Alfred Shaughnessy, the film is almost rabid in its borrowings, yet director Alan Gibson manages to give the familiar proceedings a certain visual style.

The film's poor box office performance meant only one thing, though - it was time to revive Dracula and Frankenstein again!

a sense of deja vu

Something of a mixed year for Hammer, 1970 produced a few mild attempts to broaden the horizons of their horror output, as well as further variations on their established money-makers.

Taste The Blood of Dracula, their fourth Dracula movie, curiously fell between these two stools. While it offers yet another variation on the by now tried-and-tested revenge motif, this time the story is set in Victorian England (as was most of the Stoker novel) and involves the thrill-seeking escapades of three seemingly respectable Victorian gentlemen played by Peter Sallis, John Carson and Geoffrey Keen. (Vincent Price had originally been signed to play one of these characters, but was released from his contract when the film's budget was slashed). In their search for new pleasures, the gentlemen become involved with the mysterious Lord Courtley (Ralph Bates), a disciple of Dracula's who persuades them to procure for him a phial of the dead Count's dried blood so that he can resurrect his master. In the resulting ceremony, Courtley successfully revives the Count but dies in the process, leaving it for Dracula to exact his revenge on the three gentlemen and their families...

As much about the corruption of Victorian moral values (and the hypocrisy of those who would pretend to uphold them) as about the corruption of Dracula's victims, John Elder/ Anthony Hinds' script has more depth to it than the previous two sequels, though given his track record as a writer, one perhaps shouldn't approach his work here much more

seriously than usual. Nevertheless, debut director Peter Sasdy (a Hungarian with much television work to his credit) manages to imbue the proceedings with a certain European flavour, while James Bernard provides the film with one of his most romantic scores. Scott MacGregor's sets also successfully convey a sense of time and place, despite the film's shoestring budget.

Like the previous two Draculas, however, Christopher Lee is again given too little to do as the Count, except to lurk in the shadows and advance the action with an occasional bloody deed, leaving it to the children of the three corrupt gentlemen to carry the story. Unfortunately, some of these performers aren't quite up to the task. Neither is Ralph Bates as Lord Courtley. Nevertheless, Peter Sallis, John Carson and particularly Geoffrey Keen do well in their roles, and like *Dracula Has Risen From The Grave*, the film also has a stronger sexual content than its predecessors (as well as scenes in an East End brothel, Dracula's female victims submit to his will with even more relish). The climax, in which the Count is destroyed in a crumbling church, is also well staged.

But *Taste the Blood of Dracula* was not the only Dracula film to be released by Hammer in 1970. *Scars of Dracula* followed later in the year, performing badly at the box office, perhaps because audiences had by now had their fill of the Count (the film didn't get a US release for almost four years).

For this outing (again scripted by John Elder

Anthony Hinds), the story reverts back to the familiar setting of Dracula's castle, with a young man (Dennis Waterman) and his fiancée (a dubbed Jenny Hanley) turning up to discover what has happened to his missing brother (Christopher Matthews). After this, the plot quickly returns to form, though at least this time Lee has more dialogue, and previously unused fragments from the original Stoker novel (such as Dracula's descent down the castle wall) have been used. Still, the film's tight schedule (just three weeks) and low budget show, and director Roy Ward Baker gives the proceedings little visual flair. Van Helsing is also replaced by a vampire hunting priest again (this time played by Michael Gwynne).

The film also came in for comment for its stronger than usual violence, particularly Dracula's stabbing of a female vampire (Anoushka Hempel), from whose gashed stomach he then drinks blood, as well as a scene in which the Count is shown torturing his servant Klove (this time played by Patrick Troughton) with a whip and a red hot poker. The Count's death (he is struck by lightening during a fight on the castle turrets) is, by contrast, rather tame.

Though Scars of Dracula is by no means Hammer's best Dracula, it's certainly leagues ahead of the film it was double billed with, the pitiable Horror of Frankenstein, the first Hammer Frankenstein film not to star Peter Cushing as the Baron. Instead, the role went to Ralph Bates, whom Hammer seemed to be grooming for stardom.

Very much a jobbing actor when spotted by Hammer execs in Granada Television's acclaimed historical series The Caesars (in which he played Caligula), Bates was a competent actor who nevertheless lacked the presence horror films required. In Horror of Frankenstein he was also hampered by a particularly risible

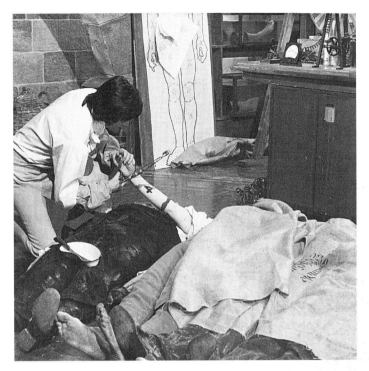

Christopher Lee and Isla Blair shelter from the rain during the filming of *Taste the Blood of Dracula* (opposite).

Victor Frankenstein (Ralph Bates) does it by numbers in *Horror of Frankenstein*. So did the film.

script (by Jeremy Burnham and Jimmy Sangster, who also produced and, for the first time, directed) and audience identification with Peter Cushing in the role.

A sorry mess indeed, the film was apparently intended by Sangster as a spoof on the original Curse of Frankenstein. Unfortunately, despite one or two mildly diverting moments (Frankenstein numbers the body parts he is amassing for his experiments akin to a painting by numbers kit), the film looks shoddy and suffers from uniformly poor production values. A good supporting cast (which includes Kate O'Mara, Veronica Carlson, Dennis Price, Jon Finch and James Cossins) is also defeated by the script, while the monster (played by Dave 'Darth Vader' Prowse, who had briefly appeared as the monster in the Bond spoof Casino Royale) lacks the required sympathy. That Frankenstein himself is now little more than a cold and calculating murderer doesn't help matters either, and the film

deservedly bombed at the box office.
'The film's basic weakness is a lack of feeling
for the genre', commented *Films and Filming*, a
prophetic turn of phrase which seemed to sum
up Hammer's attitude to the genre during the
early seventies.

Not all of Hammer's product at this time was
as bad as *Horror of Frankenstein*, though. *When
Dinosaurs Ruled The Earth*, a follow up to *One Million
Years BC*, was a box office success, thanks to the
inclusion of some more stop motion dinosaurs
- this time care of Jim Danforth and Roger
Dicken, who earned an Oscar nomination for
their pains.

This time, instead of Raquel Welch, the film
centres round the prehistoric adventures of
Victoria Vetri as Sanni, who escapes being sacri-
ficed by her tribe for having blonde hair, gets
swept out to sea during a storm and is later
befriended by a baby dinosaur (aah!). Written
and directed by Val Guest (returning to
Hammer for the first time since *The Full Treatment*
back in 1960), the film again lacks dialogue in
the true sense of the word (more 'akeeta' and
'neetcha'). The results are fairly childish but
quite enjoyable, let down chiefly by some poorly integrated studio work and a slimmed down
budget (hence the re-appearance of Carl Toms'
fur bikinis). On the plus side, though, there is
Mario Nascimbene's atmospheric score (more
percussive rock bashing) and the photography
by the unfortunately named Dick Bush.

The film went on to earn one-and-a-quarter
million dollars in its US release, though not
everyone was pleased with the results. J. G.
Ballard, who provided the film's story, said of
it, 'I'm very proud that my first screen credit
was for what is, without a doubt, the worst
film ever made,' to which *The Hollywood Reporter*
added, 'When a movie is this bad it's some-
how rather comforting.' The box office receipts
showed that Hammer hadn't quite lost their

golden touch, though - as did their next film,
The Vampire Lovers. Something of an experiment
for Hammer, the film was an attempt to try
something new within the framework of the
established gothic genre, and includes elements of lesbianism and nudity, added in an
attempt to spice up its commercial prospects.

An adaptation of J. Sheridan Le Fanu's novella
Carmilla, which had first been published in a
magazine titled *A Dark Blue* in 1871 (some six-
teen years before the appearance of Stoker's
Dracula), the idea for the film was brought to
Hammer by the independent producer Harry
Fine and his partner Michael Style (who had
produced an episode of Hammer's TV series,
Journey Into The Unknown). Given the go-ahead by
Sir James Carreras, who set up a deal for the
film with the American company AIP, Fine and
Style (whose own company, Fantale, was also
involved in the deal) thus brought in Tudor
Gates to write the screenplay, which proved to
be something of a rush job given that the film
was in front of the cameras just two months
after the deal was set up.

The first Hammer film to centre wholly round
a female vampire, *The Vampire Lovers* stars the
then relatively unknown Ingrid Pitt as Mircalla
Karnstein (alias Marcilla, alias Carmilla), a lady
vampire whose family has been destroyed by
vampire hunter Baron Hartog (Douglas
Wilmer). Naturally, Carmilla vows revenge and
years later insinuates herself into the household of one General Spielsdorf (Peter
Cushing), where she vampirizes his daughter
Laura (Pippa Steele), Laura's governess (Kate
O'Mara) and various other members of the
household. Moving on to the home of Roger
Morton (George Cole), Carmilla continues her
revenge afresh on his impressionable daughter
Emma (Madeleine Smith), but by this time
Baron Hartog and General Spielsdorf are in
pursuit and it isn't long before Carmilla is both
staked and beheaded.

Schoolteacher Giles (Ralph Bates) has a convenient crucifix to ward off Yutte Stensgaard's Mircalla in *Lust for a Vampire.*

Filmed in just six weeks on a budget of £170,000, *The Vampire Lovers* was directed by Roy Ward Baker with his by-now-customary lack of flair, save for the opening sequence in which the Karnstein family are destroyed by Baron Hartog. Nevertheless, despite its short-comings, the film went on to considerable box office success thanks to its nudity (pretty mild by today's standards) and occasional lesbian couplings (discreetly done). Performance-wise, Ingrid Pitt makes a strong impression as Carmilla, whilst Cushing is as reliable as ever as Spielsdorf, though some of the film's younger female players occasionally display their lack of experience.

An atmospheric score by Harry Robertson (who supplied the theme tune for Hammer's TV series *Journey Into The Unknown*) helps to glue things together and Scott MacGregor's sets convey the story's period well enough (though they lack the flair of Bernard Robinson's work). Though a box office success, critics weren't entirely satisfied with the film: 'Not up to the usual standard of Hammer offerings,' said the *Monthly Film Bulletin*, adding that it found Roy Ward Baker's direction 'surprisingly listless'.

The Vampire Lovers nevertheless has its admirers and its success not only took Hammer off into comparatively new directions (i.e. many of their films now contained nudity), it quickly provoked a sequel. However, while *The Vampire Lovers* was viewed by many as being merely adequate, *Lust for a Vampire* (originally titled *To Love a Vampire*) was judged as being completely dreadful.

Produced for Hammer and EMI by Harry Fine and Michael Style, the film was set up by James Carreras just two days after *The Vampire Lovers* had gone before the cameras and was

itself ready to go into production in July the same year. Again, Tudor Gates was brought in to write the script, which this time involves the reincarnation of Carmilla Karnstein (now played by Swedish starlet Yutte Stensgaard) who consequently wreaks havoc in a girls' finishing school (echoes of *Brides of Dracula*). Here she not only seduces the students but a weak-willed master (Ralph Bates) and a travelling writer (Michael Johnson) too, only to meet her fate in a fire, started by irate villagers, in which she is impaled on a falling beam!

Directorial chores on the film were originally intended for Terence Fisher. Unfortunately, he broke his leg in an accident again just three days prior to shooting, and the megaphone was thus handed to Jimmy Sangster who, as he had done with *Horror of Frankenstein*, accentuates the film's more puerile aspects. So much so that Ralph Bates (who stepped into the role of schoolteacher Giles Barton at short notice when Peter Cushing, for whom the part had been written, pulled out to look after his ill wife) described the final results as 'One of the worst films ever made.'

Poorly photographed by David Muir and with a score by Harry Robertson that includes an inapporpriate pop song titled 'Strange Love', the results are more often than not embarrassing, though Yutte Stensgaard's interpretation of Carmilla has its admirers, the publicity shot of her (not seen in the film) sitting topless in a blood-stained shroud having since passed into Hammer iconography.

Released so soon after *The Vampire Lovers*, *Lust for a Vampire* failed to repeat its predecessor's box office success, just as *Scars of Dracula* had failed to pull in the crowds so soon after *Taste the Blood of Dracula*. A re-think on production policy was obviously needed.

bosums, bums & buses

1971 began with the full-time return of Michael Carreras to the Hammer company as its managing director. Sir James Carreras had in fact been looking to retire since around 1968, but only now got around to doing so (though for several years he continued to advise Hammer and bring them the occasional project). Then, in 1972, when a company called Studio Film Labs attempted to buy Hammer and rid it of Michael Carreras in the process, Sir James sold all of his stock to his son, which gave Michael a controlling interest, thus keeping the company in the family as it had always been. But the almost complete withdrawal of American financing from the British film industry, followed by its virtual collapse, meant that Hammer had some hard times ahead. This, combined with some very poor film choices, seemed to doom the company. In the meantime, though, their release schedule was as busy as ever, and for the time being at least things still looked reasonably rosy.

Though by no means a hit, *Countess Dracula* continued Hammer's attempts to experiment and diversify within the text of the gothic genre, though the film's low budget and short shooting schedule ultimately work against it.

A re-telling of the Elizabeth Bathory legend, it stars Ingrid Pitt as Elizabeth Nadasdy, an ageing countess who discovers that by bathing in the blood of virgins she can restore her youth -albeit temporarily. She thus assumes the personality of her daughter (Lesley-Anne Down) who has been away at school and whom she now banishes to a woodcutter's cottage, leav-

ing herself free to fall in love with a handsome Hussar (Sandor Eles). But their wedding day ends in tragedy when the Countess reverts to her true age and attempts to murder her daughter (who has by now escaped) in another attempt to restore her youth. The film ends with the Countess being banished to her own dungeons, where she now is referred to by one and all as Countess Dracula.

A promising subject for Hammer, the film benefits chiefly from Ingrid Pitt's excellent performance as the Countess, sensuous as her younger self and totally believable in Tom Smith's make-up as an old hag. The supporting players are also in good form, particularly Patience Collier as Julia, the Countess's devoted servant, Nigel Green as her long-time advisor and admirer Captain Dobi, and Maurice Denham as her teacher, Master Fabio. On the production side, Peter Sasdy's direction and Ken Talbot's photography are generally well composed, given the time restrictions, while Harry Robertson's music (apparently written in just one week) has a distinct East European flavour to it thanks to his effective use of the Zimbalon. Unfortunately, Jeremy Paul's over-talkative script lacks action and the expected frissons never materialise. Moments do work, such as the discovery by Dobi of the Countess in her bloody bath, but otherwise the film lacks pace and excitement, while the title, which infers that the Countess is a vampire, is merely misleading (particularly when accompanied by ad lines which read, 'The more she drinks, the prettier she gets').

(Opposite above) Dracula does the unthinkable and removes his stake in *Dracula Has Risen from the Grave*.

(Opposite below) Reg Varney, Bob Grant and Michael Robbins in *On The Buses*.

(Next spread) One of the studio's most famous stills. Yutte Stensgaard as Mircalla in *Lust for a Vampire*.

(Next spread) Dr John Pritchard (Eric Porter) learns what it is to tangle with Jack the Ripper's daughter in *Hands of the Ripper*.

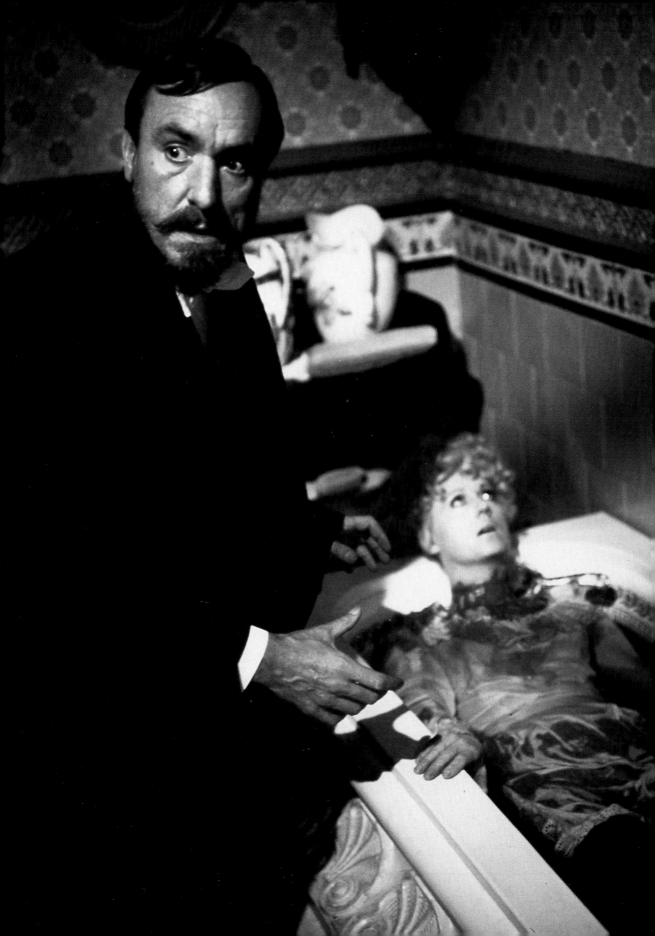

Still, the film was much better than Hammer's next release, another prehistoric romp entitled *Creatures the World Forgot*. Little more than a series of loosely-connected incidents involving a pre-historic tribe, the film was produced and scripted by Michael Carreras and directed with apparent indifference by Don Chaffey, who had previously made such a good job of *One Million Years BC*. With no dinosaurs to distract one's attention and little in the way of real excitement, the results prompted the critic from the *San Francisco Chronicle* to comment, 'Bang your club on the ground until they bring back *When Dinosaurs Ruled the Earth*, which at least had some humour, whimsy and a plot you could follow.' But did this daunt Michael Carreras? Not a jot, for he was about to release what, ironically, would turn into Hammer's biggest money spinner: *On The Buses*!

Produced for EMI, with whom Hammer now had a production deal following the evaporation of American investment, *On The Buses* had first aired on British television (LWT) in 1969, when it became an immediate hit. Like all sit-com successes, its concept was simple: each thirty minute episode follows the comic adventures of bus driver Stan Butler (Reg Varney), his conductor Jack (Bob Grant) and their mealy-mouthed inspector, Blakey (Stephen Lewis). Meanwhile, at home, the action revolves round Stan's mum (Cicely Courtneidge, later Doris Hare), his homely sister Olive (Anna Karen) and his idle brother-in-law Arthur (Michael Robbins).

As with most shows of this nature, each episode involves some sort of misunderstanding, opening the door for much insult and ribaldry in the British manner. Created and produced by Ronald Woolfe and Ronald Chesney, the show ran until 1975, and its 73 episodes were much repeated in the following years. But would audiences pay to see at the cinema what they could see for free at home? Having

had success with several radio and television spin-offs in the forties and fifties (most notably the Quatermass films), this wasn't an issue for Hammer - particularly as the budget allotted to the big screen version of *On The Buses* was parsimonious, given that no special effects or expensive gothic sets and costumes were required.

Thus, Ronald Woolfe and Ronald Chesney were invited by Michael Carreras to the horror factory to re-create for the big screen their biggest sit-com success. Directed by Harry Booth and starring all of the series' regulars, the film centres round the threat of women drivers at Stan and Jack's depot. Topical it is ('women's lib' was by then in full swing) but original it isn't - yet its cheap and cheerful vulgarity appealed mightily to British audiences

Ingrid Pitt as the aged Countess Elizabeth Bathory in *Countess Dracula*. The make-up was created by Tom Smith. Note the studio lights in the background.

(Opposite above) Dracula (Christopher Lee) gores poor Laura (Caroline Munro) in *Dracula A.D. 1972*.

(Opposite below) Michael Hordern stars in *Demons of the Mind,* a worthy but unpopular attempt to take Hammer horror out of the familiar gothic mould into more psychological territory.

reared on Benny Hill and a never-ending stream of *Carry On* films. Consequently, *On The Buses* went on to break box office records, pulling in a mighty one million pounds during the first six months of its British release. The fact that artistically the film isn't very good didn't seem to matter (except to the critics), and the results opened up new doors for Hammer. However, their output continued to be dominated by horror films for the time being, the next batch of releases displaying a partial return to classic form.

The first of these was *Hands of the Ripper*, a clever variation on the Jack the Ripper story in which his daughter Anna (Angharad Rees) displays signs of following in her father's footsteps. Having witnessed her father murder her mother as a child, she herself unconsciously resorts to violence later in life whenever kissed or shown affection. Taken into care by a psychologist, Dr Pritchard (Eric Porter), who tries to discover what drives Anna to commit these terrible murders, he soon discerns he has bitten off more than he can chew when Anna continues her murder spree in his own household.

An extremely polished production, the film was directed with flair by Peter Sasdy, who makes the very most of the film's often gory situations. Particularly memorable is the scene in which Anna impales a fake medium (Dora Bryan) on a bedroom door with a poker, along with a later scene in which she murders Dr Pritchard's housemaid (Marjie Lawrence), slashing her throat with a broken hand mirror. The killing of an East End prostitute with a bunch of hat pins and the running through of Dr Pritchard with a sword (which he extricates by hooking it onto a door handle!) are also effective. Best of all though is the film's climax, in which the dying doctor follows Anna to St Paul's Cathedral, where it seems she is going to kill his son's fiancée (Jane Merrow).

Things resolve themselves when Anna jumps from the Whispering Gallery, however, landing on top of the doctor, who has called her from below...

A psycho-sexual thriller with deeper meaning than most of Hammer's product, L. W. Davidson's script allows audiences to come to their own conclusions as to what has motivated Dr Pritchard to continually cover up Anna's crimes, while at the same time it successfully caters to thrill seekers simply out for a gory shock or two - which they certainly get.

As the misguided Dr Pritchard, Eric Porter is sufficiently cool and calculating, while as Anna, Angharad Rees exudes the required touch of deadly innocence. Backed up by Roy Stannard's excellent art direction, which truly captures the flavour of the late Victorian era, Kenneth Talbot's superb lighting and photography and a surprisingly romantic score by Christopher Gunning, *Hands of the Ripper* is a genuine Hammer classic. Sadly, it was one of their last.

The third of the studio's Carmilla/Karnstein films followed. Titled *Twins of Evil*, it brought the trilogy to a rousing conclusion. Again, production chores were handled by Harry Fine and Michael Styles, while for the third time the script was the responsibility of Tudor Gates. New onboard was director John Hough who, having directed many TV episodes at this stage in his career, brought a certain zip and style to the proceedings -which involve two beautiful twins, one of whom becomes a vampire after encountering the depraved Count Karnstein.

A sort of vampiric variation on *Witchfinder General* (aka *The Conqueror Worm*), the film has Frieda and Maria Geldhorn (Madeleine and Mary Collinson) arriving to stay with their puritanical uncle, Gustav Weil (Peter Cushing),

a witch hunter whose obsession with destroying evil takes on manic proportions. When he discovers that one of his nieces has become a vampire, his quandary proves to be to discover which one.

As with many Hammer films of this period, *Twins of Evil* features a certain degree of nudity to spice up the action (the Collinson twins were former *Playboy* centrefolds), while the gore content is again stronger than in previous years. Stake burnings, decapitations and a gruesome attack with a meat cleaver are all grist to this film's mill, though mercifully they don't take precedence over style and atmosphere. Like *Hands of the Ripper*, the film's script also has a little more depth than usual, with

A graphic moment from *Twins of Evil.*

Angharad Rees and Eric Porter on location during the filming of *Hands of the Ripper* (opposite).

Cushing's power-abusing witchfinder proving to be something of a religious hypocrite, (a suppressed, incestuous desire for his nieces is also hinted at.) Hampered only by the performances of the Collinson twins themselves (who were apparently dubbed because of their Maltese accents), *Twins of Evil* remains one of Hammer's better later vampire sagas, even if it is in no way comparable to the heydays of *Dracula* and *Kiss of the Vampire*.

Hammer's penchant for pouring old wine into new bottles continued further in 1971 with the release of *Dr Jekyll and Sister Hyde*, their third variation on the Robert Louis Stevenson classic following *The Ugly Duckling* and *The Two Faces of Dr Jekyll* (ironically, they never made a straight version of the story). This time Dr Jekyll (Ralph Bates) experiments with female hormones in his search for the elixir of life, only to discover himself turning into the evil Miss Hyde (Martine Beswick), in which guise she murders East End prostitutes so as to continue her experiments and, in a neat twist, unwittingly becomes the instigator of the so-called 'Jack the Ripper' murders.

Written by Brian Clemens (long associated with TV's *The Avengers*) and co-produced by Clemens and his partner Albert Fennell, the script also - anachronistically - throws grave robbers Burke and Hare into its brew of murder and mayhem, though it tends to veer away from the interesting sexual issues the story opens up, though these elements were played up in the original trade brochure. Mercifully, it avoids exploiting its elements of transsexuality, bisexuality, homosexuality and lesbianism for cheap sensationalism, yet by the same token the film could have made more of its central character's sexual ambiguity. Instead, it prefers to sweep such issues into the background and concentrate on the main task at hand - to shock in the tried and tested Hammer tradition.

Consequently, the film can be seen as something of a missed opportunity, lacking the courage of its convictions. Nevertheless, the results are good to look at, thanks to Norman Warwick's photography, if a little slowly paced by director Roy Ward Baker. Again, a good music score (by David Whitaker) helps to cover up the film's bigger cracks, while the performances of Bates and Beswick, who look surprisingly similar, are more than adequate (mercifully, Bates, who wanted to play both Jekyll and Sister Hyde, was prevented from doing so, as this really would have made a mockery of the film's sexual themes).

'The whole is irredeemably silly, even by recent Hammer standards,' summed up the *Guardian*, but there was more than enough going on to satisfy most paying horror fans.

Having experimented with the Jekyll and Hyde story, Hammer now turned their attention to the Mummy, whose last appearance had been in the disappointing *Mummy's Shroud* back in 1967. Unfortunately, those audiences who were lured in by the next film's misleading title, *Blood From The Mummy's Tomb*, left the cinema disappointed, for the story contains no sign of a marauding mummy!

Based on the Bram Stoker novel *Jewel of the Seven Stars* (which was later remade as *The Awakening*), the plot revolves round Tera, an Egyptian queen whose spirit manifests itself into the daughter of the archaeologist whose team has disturbed her tomb. In this guise she reverts to the standard mummy norm of extracting revenge on the desecrators, only to again end up swathed in bandages on a hospital bed when the archaeologist's house collapses about her when he tries to destroy the remains of the original mummy.

Produced on a budget of £200,000 by Hammer newcomer Howard Brandy (a former

Dr Jekyll (Ralph Bates) and Sister Hyde (Martine Beswick). But how can they be in the same room together?

publicity director whose first film this was), the film was a major disappointment to fans expecting 'the beat of cloth-wrapped feet' and it consequently flopped badly at the box office. To others, however, its attempt to play down the shocks in lieu of a more intellectual approach seemed to revitalize the genre, even if the final results aren't as satisfactory as they could have been.

In the capable hands of director Seth Holt, the film still manages to hold one's interest if one doesn't expect too much of it, thanks to the sincerity of its performers, who at least act out the plot's absurdities with suitably straight

faces - particularly Andrew Keir as the archaeologist and Valerie Leon as his possessed daughter.

Sadly, Holt died before filming had been completed, leaving it to Michael Carreras to finish the job. Also, Peter Cushing, who had been cast as the archaeologist, had to leave the project after just one day when his beloved wife Helen died, a loss which haunted him for the rest of his life.

As an experiment to instill new life into old formulas, the film also proved to be one of Hammer's last.

decline & fall

Though it is easy to chart Hammer's fall from box office grace with hindsight, in the early seventies it seemed that they were merely going through another slump of the kind they had outridden before. Unfortunately, the dearth of funding and the paucity of new ideas gradually took their toll on the company. Ironically, 1972 and 1973 proved to be their most prolific years with regard to output. Sadly, little of what they produced struck it big, and many of these films saw only limited release in America. Some didn't get released Stateside at all. Thus, with just the domestic market to rely on for their income, Hammer's days were truly numbered.

Though it didn't fare too well commercially, *Vampire Circus* -Hammer's first 1972 release - remains one of their better later films, even though it is little more than another attempt to instill something new into a tired genre. What helps to distinguish it is some classy direction by Robert Young, a livelier than usual script by the American writer Judson Kinberg (based on a story by George Baxt and the film's producer, Wilbur Stark) and a cracking good score by David Whitaker.

The film begins with a lengthy (twelve minute) pre-credit sequence which is almost a film in itself. In it, the evil Count Mitterhaus (Robert Tayman), who has been preying on the children of the nearby village of Schtettel, is staked in his castle by an angry mob headed by Mueller (Laurence Payne), who finishes the job by blowing up the castle. But not before a curse has been placed on the village and all its inhabitants.

Cut to fifteen years later and Schtettel is beset by the plague. Consequently, all roads in and out are blockaded to stop anyone from entering or leaving. But this doesn't prevent The Circus of Nights from getting through, their promise being to bring a little cheer to the unfortunate villagers. What the yokels don't realise, however, is that the circus is peopled by vampires with the ability to turn into animals. More importantly, it is led by a character called Emil (Anthony Corlan), a cousin of Count Mitterhaus, on whose behalf he has sworn revenge...

A film with many threads and twists, *Vampire Circus* is perhaps the most complexly plotted of all Hammer's vampire films, and consequently keeps moving at a fair old clip. The circus itself is naturally the main focus of the action, the sequences in which the villagers gape at the various acts being particularly well handled. Further sequences involving a mysterious hall of mirrors, a bloody attack on escaping villagers in the forest (usually cut for television) and a climax in which the resurrected Count Mitterhaus is beheaded by a crossbow also leave their mark. Most memorable, however, are the transformation sequences in which a pair of trapeze artists turn into bats in mid-air, and the scene in which a vampire turns into a leopard while running up a flight of stairs.

Filmed on a tight schedule and an even tighter budget, *Vampire Circus* made much use of sets already standing on the backlot at EMI (particularly the village square, previously seen in *Countess Dracula* and *Twins of Evil*), all of which

A bloody moment from
Vampire Circus, one of
Hammer's last true moments
of glory.

Dracula (Christopher Lee) lurks in the desanctified Chelsea church featured in *Dracula A.D. 1972*. Jessica Van Helsing (Stephanie Beecham) is his intended bride.

recalled the back-to-back filming of *Plague of the Zombies* and *The Reptile*. The church from *Taste the Blood of Dracula*, which had also been re-vamped for *The Scars of Dracula* and *Horror of Frankenstein*, also makes another disguised re-appearance. Such is Arthur Grant's photography, however, that few people noticed.

The film's cast, meanwhile, is top notch. Led by Adrienne Corri as a mysterious circus gypsy woman, it also boasts Thorley Walters as Schtettel's dithery village Burgermeister, John Moulder Brown as the young hero Anton, Lynne Frederick as the heroine, Dave Prowse as the circus strong man, Robin Sachs, Lalla Ward and Elizabeth Seal.

Despite its qualities, the critics were divided about the film when it finally appeared. 'Being facetious is the only defence against abysmal British films', said *The Sunday Telegraph* rather snootily, though *Cinefantastique* recognized the film's virtues, commenting that it was 'Divertingly entertaining, stylistically fresh and imaginatively produced.' Time has proved the latter comment to be the correct one, for the film is now something of a cult.

Less can be said of Hammer's next batch of releases, though. *Fear in the Night* was yet another stale variation on his *Taste of Fear* scenario by co-writer-producer-director Jimmy Sangster. This time Judy Geeson is the unfortunate woman being driven mad by her husband (Ralph Bates) and his mistress (Joan Collins). Also involved in this watchable but basically tired hokum are Peter Cushing (as Collins' one-armed husband) and James Cossins.

Much worse is *Straight On Till Morning* (aka *Till Dawn Us Do Die*) which stars Rita Tushingham as a naive Liverpudlian girl who moves to London and gradually comes to realise that her new boyfriend (Shane Briant) is a psychopath. Written by Michael Peacock and directed with

a bludgeon by Peter Collinson, the film was deemed something of a disappointment and was released on the bottom half of a double bill (titled 'Women in Fear') with *Fear in the Night*.

Rather better - though another commercial dud - is *Demons of the Mind* (aka *Blood Will Have Blood*), which also features Shane Briant who, along with Gillian Hills (in a part originally intended for Marianne Faithfull), play the children of a nineteenth-century Bavarian baron (Robert Hardy) who keeps them locked up, believing them to be the inheritors of the family's streak of insanity. A local doctor (Patrick Magee) reveals a series of local murders to be the baron's doing - the baron having 'projected' his bloody fantasies into the mind of his son, who thus carries them out!

Also starring Paul Jones (formerly the lead singer with Manfred Mann), Yvonne Mitchell and Michael Hordern, the film (scripted by Christopher Wicking, based on a story by its producer, Frank Godwin) is somewhat confusingly told, but first time director Peter Sykes at least makes sure the proceedings look good. EMI, who co-financed the film with Hammer, were unimpressed, though, and it received only a limited release.

A return to the on-going Dracula cycle followed. However, if Hammer were hoping to hit the jackpot again with this increasingly tired formula, they could not have been more wrong - especially given the finished product, the endearingly awful *Dracula A.D. 1972* (also known, at various times, as *Dracula Today*, *Dracula, Chelsea, 1972* and - most hilariously - *Dracula Chases the Mini Girls!*).

As the title suggests, the setting for this particular brew is 1970s London, though the plot is basically little more than a re-working of *Taste the Blood of Dracula*, involving the thrill-seeking

The delicacies of Brain surgery. Peter Cushing and Shane Briant and friend in *Frankenstein and the Monster From Hell*.

escapades of a group of teenagers who, with the assist of a Satanist called Johnny Alucard (spell it backwards) manage to revive the Count in a desanctified church in Chelsea. Unfortunately, from here on, the story resorts entirely to formula, with the teenagers now predictably in peril and the climax only a stake away.

Not entirely devoid of interest, the film at least re-unites Christopher Lee and Peter Cushing as adversaries, and gets off to a promising start with a flashback sequence involving a fight to the death between Dracula and Van Helsing atop a runaway coach in 1872, Dracula coming to a sticky end when the coach crashes and he is impaled on the wooden spokes of one of the wheels. A jet plane then flies overhead and we are transported to 1972, where all originality quickly disappears.

Here, Jessica Van Helsing (Stephanie Beecham), granddaughter of Professor Van Helsing (a descendant of the Van Helsing seen in the prologue), becomes involved in the resurrection of the Count. Naturally, it isn't long before her grandfather cottons on to what she's involved in and makes preparations to do away with Dracula - but not before the teens (who include Michael Coles, Caroline Munro and Michael Kitchen) get to drink lots of coffee at the 'trendy' Cavern Bar and speak some of the worst dialogue ever heard on the silver screen. Sounding like it had been written for a fifties dragstrip flick, the would-be hip dialogue was dated before the film was even released.

Described by the *Monthly Film Bulletin* as 'an abortive and totally unimaginative attempt to update the Bram Stoker legend to present-day Chelsea', the film suffers not only from Don Houghton's inane script, but from the lacklustre direction of Alan Gibson, an inappropriate score by Mike Vickers (another former Manfred Mann member) and the general

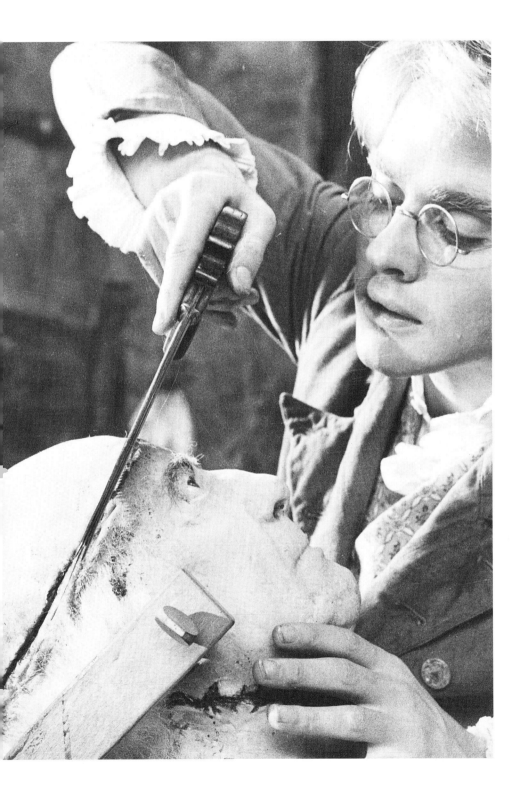

shoddiness of the enterprise. Under the circumstances, Peter Cushing acquits himself pretty well in his return to the role of Van Helsing for the first time since *The Brides of Dracula* back in 1960, though Lee, with even less to do than usual, does little but lurk about the desanctified church, failing to venture out into the modern world beyond (what on earth would he have done there anyway?).

Meanwhile, with Christopher Neame - who plays Johnny Alucard in the film - Hammer seemed to be grooming another up-and-coming youngster for stardom, as they were continuing to do with Ralph Bates and, less successfully, with Shane Briant. There were even rumours that Neame would inherit Lee's Dracula cape - but he all but disappeared from the horror scene after *Dracula A.D. 1972*, which is hardly surprising, as the film was a monumental flop.

The updating of the series was apparently foisted on Hammer by Warner Brothers who, in one of their last ventures in Britain, hoped to squeeze some more money out of the rapidly declining series, having seen the success which had greeted the low-budget modern day vampire saga *Count Yorga, Vampire* in America. Sadly, *Dracula A.D. 1972* lacked this film's fresh approach and all but finished off the series.

Undaunted, Hammer - never shy of exploiting past successes -returned to sit-com territory with a sequel to *On The Buses*. Titled *Mutiny On The Buses*, it re-unites the cast of the previous film in a story involving Stan's engagement, a trip to Windsor Safari Park and the arrival of a stern new supervisor who causes trouble at Stan and Jack's depot. A cheap-looking jaunt, it was again written and produced by Ronald Woolfe and Ronald Chesney and directed by Harry Booth, and - like many British comedies - it did well enough in its home market but failed to travel abroad.

1973 continued Hammer's downward spiral and saw the release of their last true Dracula film, *The Satanic Rites of Dracula* (aka *Count Dracula and his Vampire Bride/Dracula is Dead and Well and Living in London*). This had been commissioned by Warner before *Dracula A.D. 1972* had been released, so convinced were they that that film would be a success. Consequently, when *A.D.* bombed at the box office, *Satanic Rites* received only a limited release in Britain and none at all in the States (not until 1978, when an independent distributor acquired it).

Satanic Rites is actually a mark or two up on *A.D.*, despite being made by the same team. Here, Dracula poses as D.D. Denham, a reclusive Howard Hughes-like businessman (he even gets to speak a few lines in an American drawl). Dracula's mission is to destroy the world with a deadly bacteria developed for him by a misguided scientist (Freddie Jones). But Van Helsing (Cushing) is soon on the Count's trail when his granddaughter Jessica (now played by Joanna Lumley) is kidnapped by the Count's henchmen, a gang of sheepskin-clad motorcyclists!

Quite stylishly directed by Alan Gibson, with an eye for odd angles and set-ups, the film very much resembles an episode of *The Avengers*, with the Count's country hideaway guarded by all manner of Bond-style gadgetry and surveillance equipment. Again, nudity rears it head in an attempt to further spice up the action (one vampire woman is staked through her bare bosom), while the bike gang add a few violent moments of their own to the proceedings.

Yet despite these rather desperate attempts to modernize and prolong the series, it was really the end of the road. Lee's Dracula makes his final exit amid the thorns of a bramble patch, where he is staked for the last time with a handy fence post, bringing to an ignoble end Hammer's most profitable franchise. (Though in 1974 Lee did narrate *Dracula*, a Hammer/EMI record written by Don Houghton, with sound effects and music by James Bernard, which purported to tell the 'horrifying story of vampirism'. Though now a collectors' item and recently re-issued on CD, it wasn't deemed a success at the time).

Ironically, *That's Your Funeral*, another sit-com writ large, followed. Released on a double bill with Rank's *Carry On, Dick*, it was based on a seven part series (itself derived from *Last Tribute*, a *Comedy Playhouse* episode) and revolves round the goings on at a North of England undertakers. The film version involves the smuggling of drugs in a coffin, yet despite the efforts of stars Raymond Huntley, Bill Fraser and David Battley (all retained from the series) and an amusing car chase sequence involving two hearses, the end product is variably amusing at best.

It was then the turn of the *Frankenstein* series to come to the end of its [un]natural life with *Frankenstein and the Monster from Hell*. Unlike *Dracula*, however, this series went out with a bang rather than a whimper.

Peter Cushing was brought back to play the Baron for the sixth time, while the directorial chores were in the very capable hands of Terence Fisher (working on his fifth *Frankenstein*), whose last film this proved to be. Also re-united for the project were composer James Bernard, writer John Elder/Anthony Hinds and editor James Needs.

Not dissimilar to *The Revenge of Frankenstein*, this episode has the Baron, known here as Dr Victor, locked away in an insane asylum, where he uses the bodies of his fellow inmates to carry on with his experiments. Assisted by a mute girl called Angel (Madeline Smith) and Simon Hedler (Shane Briant, playing a young doctor who has been placed in the asylum for

carrying out his own grisly experiments), the Baron patches together a Neanderthal-like creature (Dave Prowse) which, like its predecessors, proves to have a taste for murder.

Working in a secret laboratory with the full knowledge of the asylum's director (John Stratton), the Baron all but runs the place in a clear case of the inmates having taken over the asylum. However, when his experiments become known to the other inmates, they rip the creature apart, leaving the Baron no choice but to begin again from scratch.

A sequel to *Frankenstein Must Be Destroyed* (the Baron's hands are little more than burned stumps, presumably a result of that film's fiery climax), the premise is a little on the silly side, as is the appearance of the Monster (care of make-up man Eddie Knight). Yet style in this case triumphs over content, and Fisher's direction (ably assisted by Brian Probyn's moody photography and Scott MacGregor's superior art direction) makes excellent use of the asylum's confined setting. Cushing gives his all in his final stab at the role that made him a worldwide star, and he is capably supported by Smith, Briant and Stratton, while such well known faces as Bernard Lee, Patrick Troughton (as a body snatcher) and Charles Lloyd Pack pad out the rest of the cast.

The laboratory scenes are directed with Fisher's accustomed skill (Frankenstein helps out with his teeth at one point, because his hands are so useless) and genuine sympathy is again generated for the unfortunate monster. Further helped by James Bernard's atmospheric score, the film actually received good notices from the press. 'Efficiently horrible', said *The Sunday Times*, while The Evening Standard added that, 'Terence Fisher's direction plays commendably straight-faced.' The film was hardly a box office gold mine, however.

Indeed, by this time, audiences were deserting the Hammer style of gothic horror in their droves for the far more sensational thrills of *The Exorcist*, which literally changed the horror genre overnight. The cosy, Victorian atmosphere of Hammer was no longer fashionable. It had been replaced by something far more visceral.

In the months and years to come, this area of filmmaking would come to be dominated by such big budget spectaculars as *The Omen* and *Alien* series and such low-budget splatter pictures as *The Texas Chainsaw Massacre*, *Halloween* and *Friday The* 13th. Curiously, Hammer seemed to ignore these very obvious winds of change and continued as they had done before, attempting to wring a last few bucks out of tried and tested formulas. The public weren't impressed, however, despite attempts to present old stories in new wrappings.

Sadly, this was the fate of *Captain Kronos: Vampire Hunter*, the first in what was planned as a series of adventures for the young hero of the title. Audience indifference saw it quickly die at the box office - which is a shame, for the film is actually rather good.

In it, Horst Janson plays the Aryan-like Captain Kronos, ex of the Prussian army who - with his hunchbacked assistant Professor Grost (John Cater) - roams the countryside in search of vampires (a result of having discovered that his mother and sister had been turned into vampires while he was away fighting in some war). Coming across a small township, Kronos and Grost find that a vampire has been sapping the very youth from the locals, turning beautiful young girls into dead hags. But the mystery is: who?

Aided in their task by a local, Dr Marcus (John Carson), the trio lay various traps for the vampire - who has the ability to move about during the hours of daylight - only to finally discover

Dave Prowse as the Neanderthal-like creature in *Frankenstein and the Monster from Hell.*

the perpetrator of the attacks to be the beauti-ful Lady Durward (Wanda Ventham) who, like many members of the aristocracy before and since, has literally been preying on the lower classes.

An entertaining blend of action, adventure, comedy, horror and swordplay, *Captain Kronos* was written and directed by Brian Clemens (making his debut with the megaphone) and was co-produced by Clemens and Albert Fennell. And like much of Clemens's work, the proceedings have a strong feeling of *The Avengers* about them, particularly during the action sequences. These include a number of well-staged sword fights, care of fight choreograph-er William Hobbs, who also plays Hagen, one of the film's villains.

Basically, the film is little more than a collec-tion of every horror cliche imaginable, yet so tempered with wit are they that they come up fresh and new. The film's most effective sequence revolves around the discovery that Dr Marcus has been infected by the vampire. He begs Kronos and the Professor to kill him. They thus tie Marcus to a chair and try first impaling him on a spear, but to no avail. Hanging and burning similarly fail, with the doctor waking from each attempt to kill him only to wait for the next. Only the accidental discovery that a crucifix has a deadly effect on vampires finally finishes him off.

Clever visual touches also abound. The wither-ing of woodland flowers when the cape-clad vampire passes by, and a scene in a church where the shadow of a giant cross gradually turns into something more sinister stay in the mind, as does the tear of blood which runs down the cheek of Lady Durward at the film's conclusion. Lively performances (patricularly by Cater as Professor Grost) and a pounding score by *Avengers* regular Laurie Johnson also add immeasurably to the proceedings.

Sadly, the film failed to find an audience and all future cases for Kronos were subsequently cancelled, though the film has since gone on to become a cult item.

So, it was back to sit-com territory next with a big-screen version of *Nearest and Dearest*, a North country comedy in which Hylda Baker plays Nellie Pledge, the owner of a run down pickle factory who, travelling to Blackpool for a holi-day with her scheming brother Eli (Jimmy Jewell), is pursued by one of his friends (Joe Gladwyn) for her money. A witless and vulgar romp, any charm the television series pos-sessed was lost on the big screen. Mercifully a sequel, *Nearer and Dearer*, never got made. Neither did *The Godmother*, a spoof on *The Godfather*, which was also set to star Baker.

Unfortunately, *Love Thy Neighbour* did get made. Another sit-com writ large, this one revolves round Eddie Booth (Jack Smethurst), a bigoted white socialist who has to come to terms with the fact that his neighbours (Rudolph Walker and Nina Baden-Semper) are not only black but staunch conservatives. A small-screen suc-cess, the series ran from 1972 to 1976 and derived a good deal of humour out of the touchy issue of race relations, usually at the expense of the bigoted Eddie. On the big screen, however, the situations come across as over-stretched and uncomfortable - not to mention artless - and like the series, its appeal quickly dated. Consequently, the film is little revived in these rather more politically correct times.

Television continued to supply Hammer with their main source of material through 1974, too. *Man at the Top* follows the further adven-tures of Joe Lampton (Kenneth Haig), the working class hero of the 1958 film *Room at the Top* and the acclaimed novel by John Braine. Here Lampton has risen to become an execu-tive for a pharmaceutical company, only to dis-

Opposite above: Peter Cushing as the Baron in *Frankenstein and the Monster from Hell*.

Opposite below: Frankenstein (Peter Cushing) and his assis-tants (Shane Briant and Madeline Smith) survey their handiwork in *Frankenstein and the Monster from Hell*, Terence Fisher's final movie for Hammer.

cover that they are marketing an unsafe drug. Like the TV series on which it was based, the film has plenty of sex, violence and boardroom intrigue, and proved to be one of Hammer's more popular efforts during this period.

Holiday On The Buses followed, the third and final entry in this increasingly desperate series (though a fourth installment, titled Still On The Buses, was planned then abandoned.) This itself was followed by Hammer's last true gothic exercise: The Legend of the Seven Golden Vampires (aka The Seven Brothers Meet Dracula).

A dispirited mess, the film was co-produced in Hong Kong with the Shaw Brothers (makers of chop-sockey actioners) and offers a curious blend of vampire hunting and martial arts, then all the rage in the West thanks to the success of the Bruce Lee films, a trend which Hammer seemed keen to hook up with.

Set in 1904 Chungking, it follows Professor Van Helsing's attempts to track down the six surviving members of a vampire cult, headed by Dracula himself (John Forbes-Robertson in a curiously green make-up!).

A slip-shod piece of filmmaking, the movie was perhaps scuppered by the fact that it was made in circumstances beyond director Roy Ward Baker's creative control. The majority of the actors spoke only Chinese and the film was shot 'silent' and later dubbed into various languages. Photographed in Panavision and in grainy-looking Eastmancolor, it is an amateur-looking affair, one of its few redeeming features being the presence of Peter Cushing in his last outing as Van Helsing. Christopher Lee, who refused to do any more Dracula films for Hammer, wisely refused to appear, even though he was approached to revive the part again. James Bernard's Dracula

theme also made a hasty final appearance when the film had to be quickly re-scored when the music provided for it by the Hong Kong producers (a collection library tracks) proved to be unusable.

Scripted by Don Houghton (who had made such a mess of the final two Draculas), the end product was mercifully seen by very few people outside the Far East, though a recording of the story, narrated by Peter Cushing and with music by James Bernard, appeared at the same time. Billed as 'The first Kung Fu horror sound track album' it is, like Hammer's Dracula album, now something of a collectors piece. A third album in which Peter Cushing narrated the Frankenstein story was also recorded around this time but never released, bringing Hammer's brief foray into the recording business to an unhappy close, too.

While in Hong Kong for the filming of The Seven Golden Vampires, Michael Carreras also set up a deal with the Shaw Brothers to make a modern day thriller, to be filmed back to back with the vampire saga. Called Shatter (aka Call Him Mr Shatter) it stars Stuart Whitman as a professional assassin who finds himself a marked man when tricked into an assignment in Hong Kong. Scripted by Don Houghton and co-starring Peter Cushing (in little more than a cameo) and Anton Diffring (in his first Hammer film since The Man Who Could Cheat Death back in 1959), it was originally to have been directed by Monte Hellman. Perhaps wisely, Hellman pulled out of the project at the last minute, leaving the directing chores to Michael Carreras, whose efforts were deemed so bad the film failed to get a theatrical release of any kind.

Hammer, it seemed, had come to the very end of its tether.

Opposite: Dave Prowse as the Creature in Frankenstein and the Monster from Hell.

last gasps

After the high productivity of the early seventies, Hammer's 1975 schedule contained just one release, yet another sit-com feature. This time it was the turn of *Man About The House* to get the big-screen treatment.

The series, a witty battle of the sexes, revolves around two girls (Paula Wilcox and Sally Thomsett) who share their flat with a young man (Richard O'Sullivan) simply because he's a trainee chef and good at cooking and housekeeping. Naturally, this arrangement is frowned upon by their landlords (Brian Murphy and Yootha Joyce) who continually misconstrue what is really going on.

A big hit on British television, 39 episodes were made between 1973 and 1976. The show also provoked two sequel series: *George and Mildred*, which centres round the two landlords (itself made into a film, produced by Hammer's Roy Skeggs) and *Robin's Nest*, in which O'Sullivan openes up his own restaurant. The Americans even borrowed the idea of *Man About the House* for their own highly successful sit-com *Three's Company*.

Sadly, all of these offshoots were much better than Hammer's sorry film version, in which the tennants find themselves fighting to prevent their building from being demolished. A lamentable exercise in poor scripting and artless direction, the jokes are tame and the performers (all recruited from the series) are left clutching at straws.

Similarly, 1976 saw only one release, the rather

Could this be the end of Hammer? Peter Cushing in *Silent Scream*, an episode from the *Hammer House of Horror* TV series.

better *To The Devil... A Daughter*, a somewhat belated attempt by Hammer to hitch themselves to the *Exorcist/Rosemary's Baby* bandwagon. Based on the novel by Dennis Wheatley, this nevertheless seemed a curious choice given the box office failure of Hammer's two previous Wheatley adaptations, *The Devil Rides Out* and *The Lost Continent*.

Co-produced with a German film company, Terra Filmkunst - when British backers failed to express any interest in the project - Hammer resorted to their old tactic of importing an American star to bolster the film's box office potential. They finally settled on Richard Widmark to play the film's leading character, John Verney, an occult writer who finds himself protecting a young girl (Nastassja Kinski) from a group of Satanists, led by an excommunicated priest (Christopher Lee).

Name directors steered clear of the project, which eventually fell into the lap of Peter Sykes, whose *Demons of the Mind* had been one of Hammer's recent flops. However, with a budget of one million dollars, this was going to be their most expensive picture to date. Written by Christopher Wicking (who had also scripted Sykes's *Demons of the Mind*), the final results are rather confused, despite the best efforts of Lee as the demonic Father Michael and a top notch supporting cast that includes Denholm Elliott, Honor Blackman, Derek Francis and Anthony Valentine.

Sykes's direction actually has a certain flair to it and makes good use of the film's London

locations (particularly St Katharine's Dock). Certain scenes remain in the mind, too, such as the birth of a devil child, which is forced to claw its way through its mother's stomach when her legs are tied together by Father Michael, and a sequence in which Elliott's character, fearing for his life, confines himself within a pentacle for protection. Yet despite its many qualities, the critics were generally harsh on the film and the public stayed away in their droves. Sadly, it would be another three years before Hammer produced another feature film.

But Michael Carreras wasn't idle in the meantime; there were many attempts to set up new productions, though none of them finally saw the light of day. Among these were *Nessie*, a $7 million Lock Ness Monster adventure to be co-produced with David Frost and Euan Lloyd, *Vampirella*, a comic strip romp to star Peter Cushing and Playboy Playmate Barbara Leigh, and *Vlad The Impaler*, which purported to tell the true story of the real Dracula. Several attempts to revive the defunct Dracula series itself were also bandied about, such as *Kali: Devil Bride of Dracula*, *The Dracula Odyssey*, *Dracula - The Beginning*, *Dracule* and *Dracula...Who?*

Stalled projects were nothing new to Hammer, though. In the past, attempts to make such films as *Zeppelin vs Pterodactyls*, *Victim of his Imagination* (based on the life of Bram Stoker), *Jack the Ripper Goes West*, *Mistress of the Seas* and the cumbersomely titled *Allan Quartermain Esq: His Quest for the Holy Flower* all floundered at various stages of production.

Yet interest in Hammer from its staunch army of fans continued to hold firm throughout these troubles times, and several magazines highlighting the studio's output and history appeared in the seventies, including *The House of Hammer* (aka *The Halls of Horror*) and *Little Shoppe of Horrors* (aka *The Hammer Journal*). The latter is still going strong today, and has since been joined

by *Dark Terrors*, and the excellent *Hammer Horror*, whose first issue appeared in January 1995.

It was 1979 when things finally came together for Hammer again, their choice of production this time being a remake of the Hitchcock classic *The Lady Vanishes*. Since Hammer's last feature film, the movie industry had changed considerably, and was now dominated by the blockbuster, the trend having been set by such films as *Jaws*, *Star Wars* and *Close Encounters*. Yet there was still room for the glossy, all star murder mystery, and such films as *Murder on the Orient Express* and *Death on the Nile* (both based on novels by Agatha Christie) had been very successful, as had been a remake of Hitchcock's *The 39 Steps*. A remake of *The Lady Vanishes* therefore didn't seem like a bad idea.

Co-produced with Rank, the film was similarly set up as an all-star extravaganza, with preferred choices for the two leading characters being Roger Moore and Faye Dunaway, followed by George Segal and Diane Keaton. Finally, Cybill Shepherd and Elliott Gould were chosen to play the madcap heiress and the American journalist caught up in a train-bound adventure involving the mysterious disappearance of a British nanny just before the outbreak of World War Two.

Also starring Angela Lansbury (as the missing nanny, Miss Froy), Ian Carmichael and Arthur Lowe (as Charters and Caldicott), Herbert Lom (returning to Hammer for the first time since *The Phantom of the Opera*) and Gerald Harper, the film was scripted by comedy specialist George Axelrod (who wisely stuck close to the original screenplay), directed by Anthony Page and photographed in Panavision by the great Douglas Slocombe.

A smart-looking film with solid production values, willing performances and a catchy score by Richard Hartley and Les Reed,

Hammer's *The Lady Vanishes* is an enjoyable enough romp if taken on its own count, rather than comparing it too heavily with Hitchcock's obviously superior original.

However, the critics took exception to it, seeing no reason why the film, like *Casablanca* or *Citizen Kane*, should have been remade in the first place. Audience reaction was also indifferent, and the movie quickly disappeared, though it now often pops up on television and is certainly worthy of re-appraisal.

As a consequence of the film's box office failure, Hammer almost disappeared completely. The receivers were brought in and Michael Carreras was forced to relinquish his post as the head of the company, which now owed in excess of £800,000. Finally, Roy Skeggs, who was asked to take over the running of the company by the creditors, bought Hammer for £100,000.

A former accountant, Skeggs had entered the film industry in 1956 as an assistant accountant, moving on to become Hammer's production accountant in 1963. This eventually led to Skeggs becoming the studio's production supervisor in 1970 and a credited producer for the first time with *Straight on Till Morning* in 1972. A variety of other Hammer productions followed, such as *Frankenstein and the Monster From Hell* and *Man About The House*.

In the late seventies Skeggs even formed his own company, Cinema Arts, with his then partner Brian Lawrence (himself a former Hammer board director during the sixties and seventies), and entered the TV spin-off market

with big screen versions of *Rising Damp* and *George and Mildred*. His acquisition of Hammer in late 1979 prevented the name of Hammer being lost forever.

Again, numerous theatrical features were announced, but it was on television that the name of Hammer survived, with *Hammer House of Horror*, a series of thirteen hour-long thrillers in the *Tales of the Unexpected* manner, which aired in late 1979/early 1980. Witchcraft, possession, reincarnation and lycanthropy were some of the themes used by the series, and old Hammer talent such as director John Hough, composer James Bernard and musical director Philip Martell were involved in various episodes. A reasonable success, this series was followed in 1983 by *Hammer House of Mystery and Suspense* (aka *Fox Mystery Theatre*), which used such Hammer talent as directors John Hough, Peter Sasdy and Val Guest, writers Brian Clemens and Don Houghton (who was also the series' story editor) and musical director Philip Martell.

Unfortunately, at the insistence of Twentieth Century Fox - who co-produced the series - the stories concentrated on mystery themes with a so-called twist in the tail. The results might have been entertaining in a thirty-minute slot, but each episode was padded out to fill a ninety-minute segment, which stretched many of the stories beyond snapping point. Shot in just two weeks each, the series was a disappointment to say the least (many segments are barely watchable) and a proposed second series never materialised.

Hammer, it seemed, was all but defunct.

the phoenix rises

Despite regular announcements that they were about to go back into production with some project or other (such as another TV series, *The Haunted House of Hammer*), all remained quiet on the Hammer front for over a decade after *The Lady Vanishes* debacle.

However, in 1993, it was announced that Hammer had joined forces with Warner Brothers and Donner/Schuler-Donner Productions, the idea being to produce remakes of a number of Hammer's classic back catalogue, including *Stolen Face*, *The Devil Rides Out* and a $30 million version of *The Quatermass Experiment* (a price tag which would have kept Hammer solvent throughout its entire history), as well as new material, such as *Hideous Whispers*, based on the novel *The Hiss* by Andrew Laurance. Further production deals with Rank, The Movie Group, Grundy International and Winchester Pictures to produce *The House on the Strand*, *Children of the Wolf*, *Vlad the Impaler* and a remake of Val Guest's *The Day the Earth Caught Fire* are also apparently in the works. Like Dracula, Hammer at last seems ready to rise from the grave - though what similarities there will be between the new company and the old one is open to debate.

Prior to this new spurt of activity, Hammer never quite disappeared from the public consciousness, despite its decade of production inactivity. Their library of films continued (and continues) to play on television around the world, while the video boom has seen numerous Hammer classics made available for collectors, particularly through Lumiere, who even

released a much-appreciated wide-screen version of *Dracula - Prince of Darkness* in 1995.

For the more serious Hammer fan there have not only been the journals (*Little Shoppe of Horrors*, *Dark Terrors*, *Hammer Horror* etc.), but regular Hammer conventions in both Britain and America, where star guests are invited to speak about their glorious pasts. The studio's impressive music catalogue has also been marketed in album form, the best example being Silva Screen's superb *Dracula - Classic Scores From Hammer Horror*, which contains suites from *Vampire Circus*, *Hands of the Ripper* and several of Bernard's Dracula scores. Silva Screen were also responsible for the rather more curious *Hammer Horror - A Rock Tribute to the Studio That Dripped Blood*, in which heavy metal group Warfare treat listeners to such high decibel numbers as 'Baron Frankenstein' and 'Plague of the Zombies', the noise from which is enough to raise the dead!

There have also been a variety of TV documentaries and tributes to the studio, including the BBC's half-hearted *The Studio That Dripped Blood* (1987), *The World of Hammer*, a 26-part Best of British-style compilation series (1990, though not aired in Britain until 1994), and the rather poorly produced *Flesh and Blood - The Hammer Heritage of Horror* (1994), a two-parter with narration provided by Lee and Cushing (who died shortly after completing his work on the project).

Meanwhile, in 1993, Hammer House of Horror Marketing (run by Gary Wilson and former Frankenstein monster Dave Prowse) launched a series of model kits based on the best known Hammer Horror characters, such as Lee's Dracula, Reed's werewolf and Prowse's own 'Monster from Hell'.

Since the glory days of Hammer, the fortunes of its stars and techicians have also varied considerably. After he lost control of the company in 1979, Michael Carreras was involved in a number of projects, including The Palladium Cellars, a Madame Tussaud-style horror exhibition which, though initially successful, quickly ran into financial trouble and closed. He died in 1994 at the age of just 66. His father, Sir James Carreras, died at the age of 81, just four years earlier in 1990.

Scriptwriter Jimmy Sangster finally left Britain in the mid-seventies and moved to the USA, where he continued successfully to ply his trade in television, before returning to Britain in the late eighties. Terence Fisher sadly died in 1980, while Peter Cushing, the star of Fisher's last film, followed in 1994. However, despite

his strong association with Hammer, Cushing's work for them wasn't the sum total of his career. His role as Grand Moff Tarkin in Star Wars introduced him to a whole new generation of movie-goers, and was followed up by roles in such diverse films as Top Secret! and Biggles.

Christopher Lee, meanwhile, remains as busy as ever, his more recent films including Gremlins 2: The New Batch, The Rainbow Thief, an all too brief cameo in the British-made Funnyman, and A Feast at Midnight, which saw him top-billed again. Sad though it may be that many of Hammer's greatest artists are no longer with us, we can still at least appreciate their work. For, as Denis Gifford wrote in the conclusion to his 1973 book A Pictorial History of Horror Films, 'They will be back, at the flicker of a projector, the touch of a TV switch, through their own medium - the only medium to revive the dead. The cinema.'

And long may it do so.

chronology, who's who & filmography

Hammer - a film chronology

1935
The Public Life of Henry the Ninth

1936
The Mystery of the Marie Celeste
  (aka The Phantom Ship)
The Song of Freedom

1937
Sporting Love
The Bank Messenger Mystery

1946
Old Father Thames
Cornish Holiday
Candy's Calendar

1947
Skiffy Goes To Sea
We Do Believe in Ghosts
Crime Reporter
Death in High Heels
Bred To Stay

1948
River Patrol
Who Killed Van Loon?
Dick Barton - Special Agent
  (aka Dick Barton - Detective)
The Dark Road

1949
It's A Dog's Life
Jack of Diamonds
Dr Morelle - The Case of the Missing
  Heiress
Dick Barton Strikes Back
Celia

1950
Yoga and You
The Adventures of P.C. 49
The Man in Black
Meet Simon Cherry
Room to Let
Someone at the Door
What the Butler Saw
Monkey Manners
Dick Barton at Bay

The Lady Craved Excitement

1951
Keep Fit With Yoga
Yoga and the Average Man
The Rossiter Case
To Have and to Hold
The Dark Light
Cloudburst
The Black Widow
Chase Me, Charlie
Village of Bray
A Case for P.C.49
Death of an Angel

1952
Queer Fish
Whispering Smith Hits London
  (aka Whispering Smith vs Scotland
  Yard)
The Last Page (aka Man Bait)
Never Look Back
Wings of Danger
Stolen Face
Lady in the Fog (aka Scotland Yard
  Inspector)
Mantrap (aka Man in Hiding)

1953
The Gambler and the Lady
River Ships
Four Sided Triangle
Spaceways
The Flanagan Boy (aka Bad Blonde)
The Saint Returns (aka The Saint's Girl
  Friday)
Sky Traders
Blood Orange (aka Three Stops to
  Murder)

1954
Face the Music (aka The Black Glove)
Life with the Lyons (aka A Family
  Affair)
The House across the Lake (aka Heat
  Wave)
The Stranger Came Home (aka The
  Unholy Four)
Five Days (aka Paid to Kill)
36 Hours (aka Terror Street)

Men of Sherwood Forest
Mask of Dust (aka A Race for Life)

1955
The Lyons in Paris
Third Party Risk (aka Deadly Game/Big
  Deadly Game)
Murder By Proxy (aka Blackout)
Cyril Stapleton and the Show Band
  (featurette)
The Glass Cage (aka The Glass Tomb)
The Eric Winstone Band Show
  (featurette)
The Quatermass Experiment (aka The
  Quatermass Xperiment/The
  Creeping Unknown)

1956
Break in the Circle
Just for You (featurette)
A Man on the Beach (featurette)
Parade of the Bands (featurette)
Eric Winstone's Stagecoach
  (featurette)
Women Without Men
Copenhagen (short)
X - The Unknown
Dick Turpin - Highwayman (featurette)

1957
The Edmundo Ross Half Hour
  (featurette)
The Curse of Frankenstein
The Seven Wonders of Ireland (short)
Italian Holiday (short)
Day of Grace (featurette)
The Steel Bayonet
Quatermass II (aka The Enemy from
  Space)
The Abominable Snowman (aka The
  Abominable Snowman of the
  Himalayas)
Danger List (featurette)

1958
Up the Creek
Clean Sweep (featurette)
The Camp on Blood Island
Dracula (aka Horror of Dracula)
The Snorkel
Further up the Creek

Man with a Dog (featurette)
The Revenge of Frankenstein

1959
I Only Arsked
The Hound of the Baskervilles
Ten Seconds to Hell
The Ugly Duckling
Ticket to Happiness (short)
Operation Universe (featurette)
Yesterday's Enemy
The Mummy (aka *Terror of the Mummy*)
The Man Who Could Cheat Death
Don't Panic, Chaps!

1960
The Stranglers of Bombay
Hell is a City
The Brides of Dracula
Never Take Sweets from a Stranger
The Two Faces of Dr Jekyll (aka *House of Fright/Jekyll's Inferno*)
Sword of Sherwood Forest

1961
Visa to Canton (aka *Passport to China*)
The Curse of the Werewolf (aka *The Wolfman*)
The Full Treatment (aka *Stop Me Before I Kill*)
A Weekend with Lulu
Taste of Fear (aka *Scream of Fear*)
Watch It, Sailor!
The Terror of the Tongs

1962
Highway Holiday (short)
The Phantom of the Opera
Captain Clegg (aka *Night Creatures*)
The Pirates of Blood River

1963
Maniac
The Old Dark House
The Damned (aka *These are the Damned*)
The Scarlet Blade (aka *The Crimson Blade*)
Cash on Demand
Paranoiac
The Devil-Ship Pirates

1964
Kiss of the Vampire (aka *Kiss of Evil*)
The Evil of Frankenstein
Nightmare
The Gorgon
The Curse of the Mummy's Tomb

1965
Fanatic (aka *Die! Die! My Darling!*)
She
The Secret of Blood Island
Hysteria
The Brigand of Kandahar
The Nanny

1966
Dracula - Prince of Darkness
Rasputin - The Mad Monk
Plague of the Zombies
The Reptile
The Witches (aka *The Devil's Own*)
One Million Years B.C.
Frankenstein Created Woman

1967
The Viking Queen
The Mummy's Shroud
Quatermass and the Pit (aka *Five Million Years to Earth*)
A Challenge for Robin Hood

1968
The Anniversary
The Vengeance of She
The Devil Rides Out (aka *The Devil's Bride*)
Slave Girls (aka *Prehistoric Women*)
Dracula Has Risen from the Grave
The Lost Continent

1969
Frankenstein Must Be Destroyed
Moon Zero Two
Crescendo

1970
Taste the Blood of Dracula
Horror of Frankenstein
Scars of Dracula
The Vampire Lovers
When Dinosaurs Ruled the Earth
Lust for a Vampire

1971
Countess Dracula
Creatures the World Forgot
On the Buses
Hands of the Ripper
Twins of Evil
Dr Jekyll and Sister Hyde
Blood from the Mummy's Tomb

1972
Vampire Circus
Fear in the Night
Straight on Till Morning
Demons of the Mind

Dracula A.D. 1972
Mutiny on the Buses

1973
The Satanic Rites of Dracula
That's Your Funeral
Frankenstein and the Monster From Hell
Captain Kronos: Vampire Hunter (aka *Kronos*)
Nearest and Dearest
Love Thy Neighbour

1974
Man at the Top
Holiday on the Buses
The Legend of the Seven Golden Vampires (aka *The Seven Brothers Meet Dracula*)
Shatter (aka *Call Him Mr Shatter*)

1975
Man About the House

1976
To The Devil... A Daughter

1979
The Lady Vanishes

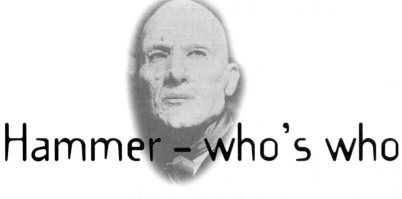

Hammer - who's who

An A-Z-style who's who featuring Hammer's most important contributors, be they writers, directors, producers, stars or make-up men, etc. Obviously, because of limited space, not everyone is included.

Arnold, Malcolm (1921 -)
Celebrated British composer/conductor whose many film scores include three for director David Lean, one of which, *The Bridge on the River Kwai*, won him an Oscar in 1957. Also a concert composer of some note; in 1953 he wrote 'Homage to the Queen' for the coronation. His three scores for Hammer in the early fifties were workmanlike but uninspired - as were the films they accompanied.

Hammer credits:
Stolen Face (1952), *Wings of Danger* (1952), *Four-Sided Triangle* (1953)

Asher, Jack (1916 - 1994)
Celebrated British cinematographer who entered the film industry in 1930 as an assistant cameraman for Gainsborough, becoming their resident camera operator in 1940. His first film as a director of photography was the Technicolor period piece *Jassy* in 1947, which was followed by *Lili Marlene*, *The Young Lovers*, *Reach for the Sky*, etc. His first film for Hammer was *The Curse of Frankenstein*, after which he went on to photograph some of their best films, which were noted for their subtle use of lighting and colour. The brother of director Robert Asher, he later photographed several of his brother's films, including *She'll Have To Go* (which he co-produced), *The Intelligence Men*, *The Early Bird* and *That Riviera Touch*.

Hammer credits:
The Curse of Frankenstein (1957), *The Camp on Blood Island* (1958), *Dracula* (1958), *The Revenge of Frankenstein* (1958), *The Hound of the Baskervilles*

(1959), *The Mummy* (1959), *The Man Who Could Cheat Death* (1959), *The Brides of Dracula* (1960), *The Two Faces of Dr Jekyll* (1960), *The Secret of Blood Island* (1965)

Ashton, Roy (1909 -1995)
Australian-born make-up artist who came to Britain in 1933 to study art and music, shortly after which he became an apprentice make-up artist at Gaumont. His first film was *Tudor Rose* in 1936, which he followed with *The Man Who Changed His Mind* (aka *The Man Who Lived Again*), etc. Following service in World War Two he became a singer with The English Opera Group. Returned to make-up in the late fifties when he became the head of Hammer's make-up department after the departure of Phil Leakey. Worked on all of the studio's key horror films. His other genre films include *Dr Terror's House of Horrors*, *Tales from the Crypt*, *Frankenstein - The True Story* and *The Monster Club*.

Hammer credits:
The Curse of Frankenstein (1957 - assistant), *The Hound of the Baskervilles* (1959), *The Ugly Duckling* (1959), *The Mummy* (1959), *The Man Who Could Cheat Death* (1959), *The Stranglers of Bombay* (1960), *The Curse of the Werewolf* (1960), *The Brides of Dracula* (1960), *The Two Faces of Dr Jekyll* (1960), *The Terror of the Tongs* (1961), *The Shadow of the Cat* (1961), *Captain Clegg* (1962), *The Phantom of the Opera* (1962), *The Damned* (1963), *Kiss of the Vampire* (1964), *Nightmare* (1964), *The Evil of Frankenstein* (1964), *The Curse of the Mummy's Tomb* (1964), *Fanatic*

(1965), *She* (1965), *Hysteria* (1965), *Dracula - Prince of Darkness* (1966), *The Plague of the Zombies* (1966), *Rasputin - The Mad Monk* (1966), *The Reptile* (1966), *The Old Dark House* (1966)

Astley, Edwin
British composer with many film and TV credits to his name, including catchy themes for *Danger Man* and *The Saint*, many episodes of which he also scored. Composed only two scores for Hammer, the full-blooded *Phantom of the Opera* being the better of the two.

Hammer credits:
Visa to Canton (1961), *The Phantom of the Opera* (1962)

Baker, Roy Ward (1916 -)
British film director who began his career at Gainsborough in 1934 as a third assistant, graduating to first assistant in 1938, in which capacity he worked with Alfred Hitchcock and Carol Reed. After war service, during which he was a part of the Army Kinematograph Unit, he returned to filmmaking, his first film as a fully-fledged director being the excellent character thriller *The October Man* in 1947. Experience in Hollywood (*I'll Never Forget You*, *Inferno*, etc.) was followed by a string of top class British productions, including *The One That Got Away* and *A Night to Remember*. During the sixties Baker's career seemed to go into decline and much television work followed. His first, and best, Hammer movie was *Quatermass and the Pit*, after which he became a proficient but unambitious genre director with such films as *Asylum*, *Vault of Horror* and *The Monster Club*.

Hammer credits:
Quatermass and the Pit (1967), *Moon Zero Two* (1969), *The Vampire Lovers* (1970), *Scars of Dracula* (1970), *Dr*

Jekyll and Sister Hyde (1971), *The Legend of the Seven Golden Vampires* (1974)

Banks, Don (1923 - 80)
Australian composer, long resident in Britain. One of Hammer's busiest musicians, he scored eight of their films in the 1960s, the income from which he used to support himself whilst working on his own classical pieces. Less brassy than the music of James Bernard, Banks' work for Hammer is surprisingly subtle, his key works for the company being *The Evil of Frankenstein* and *The Reptile*. His jazz score for *Hysteria* helped prove his diversity.

Hammer credits:
Captain Clegg (1962), *The Evil of Frankenstein* (1964), *Nightmare* (1964), *The Brigand of Kandahar* (1965), *Hysteria* (1965), *Rasputin - The Mad Monk* (1966), *The Reptile* (1966), *The Mummy's Shroud* (1967)

Barnes, Chris (1938 -)
British editor who began his career as an assistant editor on television in the fifties, progressing to films with *The Long Haul* and *The Trollenberg Terror*. Joined Hammer in 1958 as an assistant and worked on a number of films under the supervision of James Needs. Became a fully-fledged editor on *Dracula - Prince of Darkness* and remained with Hammer as either editor or co-editor until the mid seventies.

Hammer credits:
Dracula - Prince of Darkness (1966), *Plague of the Zombies* (1966), *The Witches* (1966), *The Mummy's Shroud* (1967), *A Challenge for Robin Hood* (1967), *The Lost Continent* (1968), *Taste the Blood of Dracula* (1970), *Crescendo* (1970), *Horror of Frankenstein* (1970), *Creatures the World Forgot* (1971), *Hands of the Ripper* (1971), *Demons of the Mind* (1972), *The Satanic Rites of Dracula* (1973), *Nearest and Dearest* (1973), *Man at the Top* (1973)

Bates, Ralph (1940 - 1991)
British actor, the great-great nephew of Louis Pasteur! Began his career in the theatre, having studied drama at Yale University. Early television

appearances include *Coronation Street*, *Imaginary Dialogues* and *The Caesars*, in which he played Caligula. It was this performance that led to his being cast in Hammer's *Taste the Blood of Dracula* in 1970, after which Hammer seemed to groom him for stardom. Other credits include *Persecution* and *I Don't Want to be Born*. Later television work includes *Poldark*, *Penmarric* and the sit-com *Dear John*.

Hammer credits:
Taste the Blood of Dracula (1970), *Horror of Frankenstein* (1970 - as Frankenstein), *Lust for a Vampire* (1971), *Dr Jekyll and Sister Hyde* (1971), *Fear in the Night* (1972)

Bennett, Richard Rodney (1936 -)
Respected British composer with many top class film scores to his credit, including *Murder on the Orient Express*, *Lady Caroline Lamb* and three for director John Schlesinger (*Billy Liar*, *Far from the Madding Crowd*, *Yanks*) not to mention *Four Weddings and a Funeral*. Trained at the Royal Academy of Music and entered films at the age of 20 with *Face the Night* (1956). Now working primarily in television (*Murder with Mirrors*, *Enchanted April*, *The Charmer* etc.), he provided three scores for Hammer, the best of which was for their excellent psychological thriller *The Nanny*.

Hammer credits:
The Man Who Could Cheat Death (1959), *The Nanny* (1965), *The Witches* (1966)

Bernard, James (1925 -)
British composer, one of Hammer's lynch pins, his scores for their horror classics being among the genre's very finest (his three-note *Dracula* motif practically became Hammer's signature tune). Began composing during his teenage years and, after wartime service in the RAF, went to study at the Royal College of Music at the suggestion of his friend, Benjamin Britten. Began his professional career scoring for the BBC, his music for a radio version of *The Duchess of Malfi* leading to *The Quatermass Experiment*, his first film for Hammer (the *Malfi* score had been conducted by his friend John Hollingsworth, then Hammer's

resident musical director). Won an Academy Award in 1950 for co-authoring the story (with Paul Dehn) for the thriller *Seven Days to Noon*. His work as a film composer has been almost exclusively for Hammer, exceptions being *Windom's Way* and *The Torture Garden* (with Don Banks)

Hammer credits:
The Quatermass Experiment (1955), *X - The Unknown* (1956), *Quatermass 2* (1955), *The Curse of Frankenstein* (1957), *Dracula* (1958), *The Hound of the Baskervilles* (1959), *The Stranglers of Bombay* (1959), *The Terror of the Tongs* (1961), *Kiss of the Vampire* (1962), *The Damned* (1963), *The Gorgon* (1964), *She* (1965), *Dracula - Prince of Darkness* (1966), *The Plague of the Zombies* (1966), *Frankenstein Created Woman* (1967), *The Devil Rides Out* (1967), *Dracula Has Risen from the Grave* (1968), *Frankenstein Must Be Destroyed* (1969), *Taste the Blood of Dracula* (1970), *Frankenstein and the Monster from Hell* (1973), *The Legend of the Seven Golden Vanpires* (1974), *Witching Time* (1980 - *Hammer House of Horror* episode)

Black, Stanley (1913 -)
Prolific British film composer/conductor/musical director (approaching 200 credits), former bandleader /arranger/record producer who conducted the BBC Dance Orchestra from 1944 - 54. His four Hammer credits comprise three thrillers and one comedy, all of which were fairly workmanlike. Perhaps best known for the three Cliff Richard musicals *The Young Ones*, *Summer Holiday* and *Wonderful Life* which proved so popular in the early sixties.

Hammer credits:
Further up the Creek (1958), *Hell is a City* (1960), *The Full Treatment* (1961), *Maniac* (1963)

Bloch, Robert (1917 -)
Celebrated genre writer (*Psycho, The Night Walker, The Skull, Asylum*) who contributed to two episodes of Hammer's television series *Journey to the Unknown*: *Indian Spirit Guide* (w), *Girl of my Dreams* (co-w)

Bowie, Les (1913 - 1979)
Prolific British special effects techni-

cian who worked on a good many of Hammer's classic films, his main task usually being to disintegrate Dracula. Other credits include work on *Great Expectations*, *The Red Shoes*, *The Trollenberg Terror*, *The Face of Fu Manchu*, *The Day The Earth Caught Fire*, *The Assassination Bureau*, *Star Wars* and *Superman*, for which he won an Oscar. Began his career as a scenic artist, which led to his first film, *The School for Secrets* (aka *Secret Fight*) in 1946. Much matte work followed. His first Hammer film was *The Quatermass Experiment*, for which he had a budget of just £30!

Hammer credits:
The Quatermass Experiment (1955), *X-The Unknown* (1956 - co-sp), *The Curse of Frankenstein* (1956), *The Curse of the Werewolf* (1961), *The Shadow of the Cat* (1961), *Captain Clegg* (1962), *The Old Dark House* (1962), *The Devil-Ship Pirates* (1963), *The Scarlet Blade* (1963), *Paranoiac* (1963), *Kiss of the Vampire* (1964), *The Evil of Frankenstein* (1964), *She* (1965 - co-sp), *Dracula - Prince of Darkness* (1966), *The Plague of the Zombies* (1966), *The Reptile* (1966), *Frankenstein Created Woman* (1966), *One Million Years B.C.* (1966 - co-sp), *The Mummy's Shroud* (1966), *Quatermass and the Pit* (1967), *Moon Zero Two* (1969 - co-sp), *Vampire Circus* (1971), *Dracula A.D. 1972* (1972), *The Satanic Rites of Dracula* (1973) *The Legend of the Seven Golden Vampires* (1974), *Shatter* (1974), *To The Devil...A Daughter* (1976)

Bresslaw, Bernard (1933 - 1993)
Tall, gormless-looking British comedy actor, a mainstay of the Carry On series (*Carry on Screaming*, *Carry on Camping*, etc.) and TV's *The Army Game* (filmed by Hammer as *I Only Arsked*). Was considered for the role of the Creature in *The Curse of Frankenstein*. Other films include *Vampira* (aka *Old Dracula*), *One of our Dinosaurs is Missing*, *Jabberwocky*, *Hawk the Slayer* and *Krull*.

Hammer credits:
Men of Sherwood Forest (1954), *The Glass Cage* (1955), *I Only Arsked* (1959), *The Ugly Duckling* (1959), *Moon Zero Two* (1969)

Briant, Shane (1946 -)
British actor whom Hammer seemed to be grooming for stardom for a while. Other credits include *Moving Targets*, *True Colors* and *Grievous Bodily Harm*.

Hammer credits:
Demons of the Mind (1972), *Straight on Till Morning* (1972), *Captain Kronos - Vampire Hunter* (1973), *Frankenstein and the Monster from Hell* (1973)

Bryan, Peter
British writer, producer and director, brother of Oscar-winning production designer John Bryan. Joined Hammer in 1949 as a camera operator on such films as *Dr Morelle*, *Meet Simon Cherry* and *Room to Let*. Directed a number of travelogue shorts and documentaries for them, including *Operation Universe*. Also wrote *The Hound of the Baskervilles* (1959), *Brides of Dracula* (1960 - with Jimmy Sangster and Edward Percy) and *Plague of the Zombies* (1966) for Hammer.

Budd, Roy (1949 - 1994)
Busy British composer and jazz pianist, most at home in the action genre (*The Wild Geese*, *The Sea Wolves*, *Get Carter*, etc.). His only Hammer credit was for *Man at the Top* (1973).

Bush, Dick (1931 -)
British cinematographer with several Ken Russell credits to his name (*Savage Messiah*, *Mahler*, *Tommy*, *Crimes of Passion*, *Lair of the White Worm*, etc). Other films include *The Legacy*, *Victor/Victoria*, *Little Monsters* and *Switch*.

Hammer credits:
When Dinosaurs Ruled the Earth (1970), *Twins of Evil* (1971), *Dracula A. D. 1972* (1972)

John Cacavas (1930 -)
Work-a-day American composer with many routine film and TV credits to his name, including *Airport 1975*, *Airport 1977* and many episodes of TV's *Kojak*. His one Avengers-style Hammer score, *The Satanic Rites of Dracula* (1973), was not deemed a success.

Carreras, Enrique (1880 - 1950)
Spanish-born entrepeneur who came to England in the early 1900s. After several business ventures, which met with variable success, formed Exclusive Films in the late twenties. Father of Sir James Carreras.

Carreras, Sir James (1909 - 1990)
Very much the driving force behind Hammer Films, his communications skills moved the company full steam ahead in the 1950s, his contacts in America with Robert Lippert assuring the studio's first big US distribution deal. A showman and bon viveur extraordinaire, he gave the public exactly what they wanted. Educated at Stonehurst, he served with the HAC during the war, was awarded an MBE in 1944 and was ultimately demobbed as a Lieutenant Colonel. Was knighted in 1970 and retired from Hammer in 1972, after which he concentrated on charity work. Though he was never actively involved in the making of films, his influence was present in all of Hammer's product.

Carreras, Michael (1927 - 1994)
British-born producer, executive producer, writer, director, studio head who, after national service in the Grenadier Guards (1946 - 8) worked his way up through the ranks at Exclusive, from the publicity department to assistant to the producer. Became a board director of Hammer Films after the death of his grandfather, Enrique Carreras, in 1950. First producer credit was for *The Dark Light* in 1951, after which he seemed to have a credit on the majority of Hammer/Exclusive's output, either as a producer or executive producer. Wrote his first script, *The Stranger Came Home*, in 1954, whilst in 1955 he produced and directed a number of musical featurettes for the company, all of which were shot in colour and scope. Left Hammer in 1961 to form Capricorn Films, for whom he made *The Savage Guns* and *What a Crazy World*, though he still regularly contributed to Hammer's output as either a writer, producer or director. His work as a writer (using the pen names Henry Younger and Michael Nash) and director was routine at best, however. Returned to Hammer full time in the early 1970s as Managing Director, purchasing the company following his

father's retirement and a hostile take-over bid. Unfortunately, this coincided with the collapse of the British film industry and the gradual decline and fall of Hammer in the mid-70s. His last credit was as an executive producer on the ill-fated remake of *The Lady Vanishes*. Following his departure from Hammer, he involved himself in several business ventures, including *The Palladium Cellars*, a Tussaud-like horror exhibition, and a travel company.

Hammer credits:
The Dark Light (1951 - p), *Never Look Back* (1952 - p), *The Last Page* (1952 - casting), *Mantrap* (1952 - co-p), *Stolen Face* (1952 - p), *Spaceways* (1952 - p), *Four-Sided Triangle* (1953 - p), *The Blood Orange* (1953 - p), *Face the Music* (1954 - p/d), *The Stranger Came Home* (1954 - w/p), *Mask of Dust* (1954 - exec p), *Men of Sherwood Forest* (1954 - p), *The Eric Winstone Band Show* (1955 - p/d), *Murder by Proxy* (1955 - p), *Copenhagen* (1956 -p/d), *Dick Turpin* (1956 - p), *Just for You* (1956 - p/d), *Parade of the Bands* (1956 - p/d), *The Curse of Frankenstein* (1956 - exec p), *The Edmundo Ros Half House* (1957 - p/d), *The Steel Bayonet* (1957 - p/d), *Quatermass 2* (1957 - exec p), *The Abominable Snowman* (1957 - exec p), *The Revenge of Frankenstein* (1958 - exec p), *The Snorkel* (1958 - p), *Dracula* (1958 - exec p), *The Camp on Blood Island* (1958 - p), *Clean Sweep* (1958 - exec p), *The Hound of the Baskervilles* (1959 - exec p), *Hell Is a City* (1959 - p), *The Mummy* (1959 - exec p), *Ticket to Happiness* (1959 - p), *The Ugly Duckling* (1959 - p), *The Man Who Could Cheat Death* (1959 - exec p), *Ten Seconds to Hell* (1959 - p), *Break in the Circle* (1959 - p), *The Stranglers of Bombay* (1960 - exec p), *Never Take Sweets from a Stranger* (1960 - exec p), *The Brides of Dracula* (1960 - exec p), *The Two Faces of Dr Jekyll* (1960 - p), *Visa to Canton* (1961 - p), *Watch It, Sailor!* (1961 - exec p), *Weekend with Lulu* (1961 - exec p), *Taste of Fear* (1961 - exec p), *The Terror of the Tongs* (1961 - exec p), *The Pirates of Blood River* (1962 - exec p), *Maniac* (1963 - d), *The Damned* (1963 - exec p), *Cash on Demand* (1963 - exec p), *The Curse of the Mummy's Tomb* (1964 - d/p/w [w as Henry Younger]), *Fanatic* (1965 - exec p), *She* (1965 - p), *One Million Years B.C.* (1966 - w/p), *Slave Girls* (1968

-d/w [w as Henry Younger), *The Lost Continent* (1968 - p/d/w [w as Michael Nash]), *Crescendo* (1969 - p), *Moon Zero Two* (1969 - w/p), *Creatures the World Forgot* (1970 - w/p), *Blood from the Mummy's Tomb* (1971 - co-d), *Straight on Till Morning* (1972 - exec p), *Fear in the Night* (1972 - exec p), *That's Your Funeral* (1973 - p), *Nearest and Dearest* (1973 - p), *Legend of the Seven Golden Vampires* (1974 - exec p), *Shatter* (1974 - co-p/d), *To the Devil... A Daughter* (1976 - exec p), *The Lady Vanishes* (1979 - exec p).

Cary, Tristam (1925 -)
British composer with a number of effective scores to his credit, including *The Ladykillers* (1955) and Hammer's *Quatermass and the Pit* (1967).

Chaffey, Don (1917 -)
British director on the international scene who began his career in the art department at Gainsborough. Many children's films to his credit (*Greyfriars Bobby, The Prince and the Pauper, Pete's Dragon, The Magic of Lassie*, etc.) as well as several genre entries, including *Jason and the Argonauts, Persecution* and *Chomps*.

Hammer credits:
One Million Years B.C. (1966), *The Viking Queen* (1967), *The Beckoning Fair One – Journey to the Unknown episode – 1969, Last Visitor, Creatures the World Forgot* (1971)

Clemens, Brian (1931 -)
Prolific British writer and producer with credits in television (*The Avengers, The Professionals, The New Avengers,* etc.) and films (*Station Six Sahara, And Soon the Darkness, Blind Terror, The Golden Voyage of Sinbad, Watcher in the Wood*, etc.), usually in association with his partner, producer Albert Fennell.

Hammer credits:
Dr Jekyll and Sister Hyde (1971 - w/co-p), *Captain Kronos - Vampire Hunter* (1973 - w/co-p/d), *Sweet Scent of Death* (1984 - w -*Hammer House of Mystery and Suspense TVM*), *Mark of the Devil* (1984 - w - *Hammer House of Mystery and Suspense - TVM*)

Corwithen, Doreen

British composer with a number of routine Hammer scores to her credit.

Hammer credits:
Mantrap (1950), *Men of Sherwood Forest* (1954), *Break in the Circle* (1955)

Court, Hazel (1926 -)
British actress, former model, who made her film debut in the Tommy Trinder musical *Champagne Charlie* in 1944. Has appeared in several genre pictures (*The Ghost Ship, Devil Girl from Mars, Dr Blood's Coffin*), including three for Roger Corman (*The Premature Burial, The Raven, The Masque of the Red Death*).

Hammer credits:
The Curse of Frankenstein (1957), *The Man Who Could Cheat Death* (1959)

Cushing, Peter (1913 - 1994)
British actor who, along with Christopher Lee, came to personify Hammer Films. Began his professional career as a surveyor, but a keen interest in amateur dramatics led to his joining the Worthing Repertory Company. After four years' experience, went to America in 1939 on a one-way ticket, where he worked on such films as *The Man in the Iron Mask* (as Louis Hayward's double) and the Laurel and Hardy comedy *A Chump at Oxford*. Returned to Britain in 1942 and joined Ensa, after which he was cast by Laurence Olivier as Osric in both his film and touring productions of *Hamlet*. In the fifties he tied his career to the burgeoning television industry and quickly became recognised for his sterling performances in such productions as *The Creature* and 1984, which won him the British Television Actor of the Year award and led to his being cast as Baron Frankenstein in *The Curse of Frankenstein*. Following this, Cushing became synonymous with the roles of both the Baron and Van Helsing, which he returned to numerous times, as well as the horror genre itself, despite his own mild manner. His association with Hammer was long and successful, though he didn't work exclusively for them. His other genre films (many of which weren't worthy of his presence) include *Dr Terror's House of Horrors, Dr Who and the Daleks, Scream and Scream Again, Horror*

Express, Legend of the Werewolf and *Star Stars*. The latter of which introduced him to a new generation of movie-goers.

Hammer credits:
The Curse of Frankenstein (1957), *The Abominable Snowman* (1957), *Dracula* (1958), *The Revenge of Frankenstein* (1958), *The Hound of the Baskervilles* (1959), *The Mummy* (1959), *The Brides of Dracula* (1960), *Cash on Demand* (1963), *The Evil of Frankenstein* (1964), *The Gorgon* (1964), *She* (1965), *Dracula - Prince of Darkness* (1966 - flashback only), *The Mummy's Shroud* (1966 - narrator only) *Frankenstein Created Woman* (1967), *Frankenstein must be Destroyed* (1969), *The Vampire Lovers* (1970), *Twins of Evil* (1971), *Fear in the Night* (1972), *Dracula A. D. 1972* (1972), *The Satanic Rites of Dracula* (1973), *Frankenstein and the Monster from Hell* (1973), *The Legend of the Seven Golden Vampires* (1974), *Shatter* (1974), *Silent Scream* (1980 - *Hammer House of Horror* episode)

Davis, Bette (1908 - 1989)
Celebrated American star actress who dominated the world's box office in the thirties and forties. When her career began to slide in the sixties she successfully turned to the horror genre with *Whatever Happened to Baby Jane?* and *Hush... Hush, Sweet Charlotte*. Other genre entries include *Scream, Pretty Peggy, Burnt Offerings, The Dark Secret of Harvest Home, Return to Witch Mountain, Watcher in the Woods* and *Wicked Stepmother*.

Hammer credits:
The Nanny (1965), *The Anniversary* (1968)

Diffring, Anton (1918 - 1989)
German-born actor usually stereotyped as a Nazi officer. Genre credits include *Circus of Horrors, The Beast Must Die* and Hammer's *The Man Who Could Cheat Death* (1959). Appeared as Baron Frankenstein in the pilot episode of Hammer's aborted TV series *The Tales of Frankenstein* (1958).

Donlevy, Brian (1899 - 1972)
Burly-looking Irish-American actor whose many films include such Hollywood classics as *Beau Geste, The Great Mcginty, Brigham Young* and *The Glass Key*. Was brought to England by Hammer to play Professor Quatermass in *The Quatermass Experiment* (1955), a role he reprised for the sequel, *Quatermass 2* (1956), much to the annoyance of the character's creator, writer Nigel Kneale, who referred to his performance as, 'A wet raincoat looking for somewhere to drip.'

Elder, John see **Hinds, Anthony**

Ellis, Don (1933 - 1978)
American jazz trumpeter and sometime composer of blaring, atonal action scores, perhaps best remembered for the two *French Connection* films and *The Seven-Ups*. His one jazz-style score for Hammer, *Moon Zero Two* (1969), is deemed one of their worst - as is the film it accompanies.

Evans, Clifford (1912 - 1985)
Welsh character actor, memorable as the vampire hunter in *Kiss of the Vampire*. Other films include *Love on the Dole, The Foreman went to France* and *Twist of Sand* as well as TV's *Stryker of the Yard*.

Hammer credits:
Man with a Dog (1958 - short), *Curse of the Werewolf* (1961), *Kiss of the Vampire* (1962)

Fine, Harry
Irish-born producer who, with his partner Michael Styles, produced Hammer's 'Carmilla' trilogy. A former actor, stage manager and television casting director (*Fabian of the Yard, the Invisible Man, Danger Man*, etc.) he became an associate producer on television's *Sir Francis Drake*, progressing to fully-fledged producer for TV's *Man of the World* and *Sentimental Agent*. First film as a producer was *The Pleasure Girls* in 1965, which he followed with *The Penthouse, Up the Junction, The Long Day's Dying, The Rise and Rise of Michael Rimmer*. Formed Fantale Films with Michael Styles and made

Fright, To Kill a Stranger, etc.
Hammer credits:
To Have and to Hold (1951 - actor), *The Madison Equation* (1969 - associate producer - *Journey to the Unknown* episode), *The Vampire Lovers* (1970 - co-p), *Lust for a Vampire* (1971 - co-p), *Twins of Evil* (1971 - co-p)

Fisher, Terence (1904 - 1980)
The director most associated with the look of Hammer Horror, Fisher began his film career as a clapper boy in 1928 after experience in the navy and as a department store window dresser. Worked his way up to become an apprentice editor, his first solo credit being *Brown on Resolution* in 1935. After editing several movies, became a trainee director with Rank, his first fully-fledged credit being for *Colonel Bogey* in 1947, which was followed by such films as *Portrait from Life, Marry Me, The Astonished Heart* and *So Long at the Fair*. His first film for Hammer/Exclusive was *The Last Page* (1952), which he followed with a number of undistinguished second feature thrillers and melodramas, none of which seemed to indicate the style he would invest in the gothic horrors he later became known for, the first of which was *The Curse of Frankenstein*. Television work includes many episodes of *Douglas Fairbanks Presents* (1954 - 6), whilst other genre films for studios other than Hammer include *Sherlock Holmes and the Deadly Necklace, The Horror of it all, The Earth Dies Screaming, Island of Terror* and *Night of the Big Heat*.

Hammer credits:
The Last Page (1952), *Wings of Danger* (1952), *Stolen Face* (1952), *Mantrap* (1952), *Four-Sided Triangle* (1953), *Spaceways* (1953), *Face the Music* (1954 - aka *The Black Glove*), *Blood Orange* (1954*), The Stranger Came Home* (1954), *Mask of Dust* (1954*), Murder by Proxy* (1955), *The Curse of Frankenstein* (1957), *Dracula* (1958), *The Revenge of Frankenstein* (1958), *The Hound of the Baskervilles* (1959), *The Mummy* (1959), *The Man Who Could Cheat Death* (1959), *The Stranglers of Bombay* (1960), *The Brides of Dracula* (1960), *The Two Faces of Dr Jekyll* (1961), *The Phantom of the Opera* (1962), *The Gorgon* (1964), *Dracula - Prince of Darkness* (1966), *Frankenstein*

Created Woman (1966), *The Devil Rides Out* (1968), *Frankenstein Must be Destroyed* (1969), *Frankenstein and the Monster from Hell* (1973)

Francis, Freddie (1917 -)
Celebrated British cinematographer who, after experience as a stills photographer, joined Gaumont as a clapperboy in 1936, where his first film was *Joy Ride*. Work as a camera assistant at Pinewood followed, whilst during the war he joined the Army Kinematograph Services. After this he became a camera operator on such films as *The Macomber Affair* and *Mine own Executioner*, and second unit photographer on John Huston's *Moby Dick* (1956). First film as a fully-fledged cinematographer was 1957's *A Hill in Korea*, which was followed by such films as *Room at the Top, Sons and Lovers* (which won him an Oscar) and *The Innocents*. Turned to direction in 1962 with *Two and Two Make Six*, which he followed with *Vengeance* later the same year, after which he seemed to slip into the horror genre. Despite his abilities as a cinematographer, his work as a director is frequently flat and uninventive, lacking the pictorial qualities that had distinguished his earlier work. His first film for Hammer was the psychological thriller *Paranoiac* in 1963 (though he'd photographed *Never Take Sweets From a Stranger* for them in 1960). This was followed by numerous low budget entries for both Hammer and other companies, including *Dr. Terror's House of Horrors, The Skull, Trog, The Vampire Happening, Craze, The Ghoul* (for Tyburn, a film company formed by his son Kevin), *Legend of the Werewolf* (Tyburn) and *The Doctor and the Devils*. He returned to cinematography in 1981 with *The French Lieutenant's Woman*, which was followed by sterling work on *The Elephant Man, Dune, Glory* (which won him a second Oscar), *Cape Fear* and *The Princess Caraboo*.

Hammer credits:
Never Take Sweets From a Stranger (1960) Paranoiac (1963), *Nightmare* (1964), *The Evil of Frankenstein* (1964), *Hysteria* (1964), *Dracula Has Risen from the Grave* (1968)

Frankel, Benjamin (1906 - 1973)
British composer and musical director

with many important credits to his name (*The Seventh Veil, Mine Own Executioner, Night of the Iguana*, etc.). Of his three Hammer credits, *The Curse of the Werewolf* is undoubtedly the best.

Hammer credits:
I Only Arsked (1959), *The Curse of the Werewolf* (1960), *The Old Dark House* (1962)

Frankel, Cyril (1921 - 1983)
British director with generally routine productions to his credit, the best examples being *On the Fiddle and the Tygon Factor*.

Hammer credits:
The Witches (1966), *Tennis Court* (1984 - *Hammer House of Mystery and Suspense* TVM)

Gamley, Douglas (1924 -)
Australian-born composer, long in Britain. Has many genre scores to his credit, a good deal of them for Amicus (*Tales from the Crypt, Asylum, From Beyond the Grave*, etc.), though his two films for Hammer were comedies.

Hammer credits:
The Ugly Duckling (1959), *Watch It, Sailor!* (1961)

Gates, Tudor
British screenwriter and novelist, former stage manager. Penned Hammer's 'Carmilla' trilogy. Other credits include TV's *The Avengers* and such films as *Barbarella, Cry Nightmare, Fright*, etc. Also wrote and co-directed *Sex Thief* and *Love Box*, two soft-core sex films.

Hammer credits:
The Vampire Lovers (1970), *Lust for a Vampire* (1971), *Twins of Evil* (1971)

Gibson, Alan (1938 - 1987)
Canadian-born director, came to Britain in 1967. An ex-actor, he trained at the Bristol Old Vic School of Drama before becoming a trainee director with the BBC. Started out in television before making the move to films, where his strong visual sense was best displayed in genre films. Credits include *Goodbye Gemini, Witness for the*

Prosecution (TV remake) and the much derided *Dracula A.D. 1972*.

Hammer credits:
Jane Brown's Body (1969 - *Journey to the Unknown* episode), *Somewhere in a Crowd* (1969 - *Journey to the Unknown* episode), *Poor Butterfly* (1969 - *Journey to the Unknown* episode), *Crescendo* 1969), *Dracula A. D. 1972* (1972), *The Satanic Rites of Dracula* (1973), *Silent Scream* (1980 - *Hammer House of Horror* episode)

Gilling, John (1912 - 1985)
British writer, producer and director, former clerk, extra and stuntman. Began working as an assistant director for BIP in 1933. Served in the Royal Naval Volunteer Reserve during the war, after which he turned his talents to writing, his first screenplay being *Black Memory* in 1947. His first film as a director was *Escape from Broadmoor* in 1948, after which he churned out all manner of low budget crime thrillers and horror films, including *Mother Riley Meets the Vampire, The Flesh and the Fiends, The Night Caller* and *The Gamma People*, etc. His first film for Hammer was as a co-writer (with Godfrey Grayson) on *Room to Let* in 1950.

Hammer credits:
Room to Let (1950 - co-w), *The Lady Craved Excitement* (1950 -co-w), *Whispering Smith Hits London* (1952 - w), *Wings of Danger* (1952 - w), *Shadow of the Cat* (1961 - d), *The Pirates of Blood River* (1962 - co-w/d), *The Scarlet Blade* (1963 - w/d), *The Gorgon* (1964 - w), *The Brigand of Kandahar* (1965 - w/d), *Plague of the Zombies* (1966 - d), *The Reptile* (1966 - d), *The Mummy's Shroud* (1967 - w/d)

Glass, Paul
British composer whose only score for Hammer was for their last horror film to date, *To the Devil... A Daughter* (1976).

Goodwin, Harold (1917 -)
Chirpy British character actor, usually in gormless, dim-witted roles, of which he played several for Hammer. Other film credits many.

Hammer credits:
The Last Page (1952), *The Mummy*

(1959), *The Ugly Duckling* (1959), *The Terror of the Tongs* (1961), *The Phantom of the Opera* (1962), *The Curse of the Mummy's Tomb* (1964), *Frankenstein must be Destroyed* (1969)

Gough, Michael (1917 -)
British actor, on stage since 1936 and in films since 1947 with *Blanche Fury*. Despite his reputation as a serious actor, he has appeared in all manner of low budget genre films (*Horrors of the Black Museum, Konga, The Black Zoo, Berserk, Satan's Slaves,* etc.) as well as *Batman, Batman Returns* and *Batman Forever*, in which he plays Alfred the butler. Made a rather half-hearted Arthur Holmwood in Hammer's *Dracula*, his first genre film.

Hammer credits:
Dracula (1958), *The Phantom of the Opera* (1962)

Grainer, Ron (1922 - 1981)
Australian composer, long in Britain. Perhaps best remembered for his various TV themes which include *Dr Who, Steptoe and Son* and *Man in a Suitcase*. His one Hammer credit was for the 'comedy' *Mutiny on the Buses* (1972).

Grant, Arthur (1915 - 1972)
Busy British cinematographer who, along with Jack Asher, was regarded as Hammer's top lighting cameraman. Equally at home with black and white or colour, he began his career in 1929 at the studios of Cecil Hepworth where he made himself useful in various capacities. Graduated to camera operator in 1947 with *When you come Home*, and cinematographer in 1950 with *The Dragon of Pendragon Castle*. His first film for Hammer was *The Abominable Snowman* in 1950, which was followed by many of their top genre productions. Work elsewhere includes *The Tomb of Ligeia* (for Roger Corman), *Jigsaw* and *80,000 Suspects*.

Hammer credits:
The Abominable Snowman (1957), *Up the Creek* (1958), *Clean Sweep* (1958 - short), *Man With a Dog* (1958 - short), *Yesterday's Enemy* (1959), *The Stranglers of Bombay* (1960), *Hell is a City* (1960), *Curse of the Werewolf*

(1960), *Terror of the Tongs* (1961), *The Shadow of the Cat* (1961), *Visa to Canton* (1961), *Watch It, Sailor!* (1961), *The Pirates of Blood River* (1962), *Captain Clegg* (1962), *The Phantom of the Opera* (1962), *The Damned* (1963), *Paranoiac* (1963), *The Plague of the Zombies* (1966), *The Reptile* (1966), *The Old Dark House* (1966), *The Witches* (1966), *Frankenstein Created Woman* (1967), *The Mummy's Shroud* (1967), *Quatermass and the Pit* (1967 aka *Five Million Years to Earth*), *The Devil Rides Out* (1968), *Dracula has Risen from the Grave* (1968), *Frankenstein Must be Destroyed* (1969), *Blood from the Mummy's Tomb* (1971), *Fear in the Night* (1972), *Demons of the Mind* (1972)

Grant, Moray (1917 - 1977)
British cinematographer (no relation to Arthur Grant) who began his career as a clapper boy at Denham in 1935, moving to British National in 1937 where he became an operator. Subsequent films many and various, though work mainly routine.

Hammer credits:
The Dark Light (1951 - ph), *Up the Creek* (1958 - camera operator), *Hell is a City* (1960 - cam op), *Kiss of the Vampire* (1962 - cam op), *The Mummy's Shroud* (1966 - cam op), *The Devil Rides Out* (1968 - cam op), *The Horror of Frankenstein* (1970 -ph), *Scars of Dracula* (1970 - ph), *The Vampire Lovers* (1970 -ph), *Vampire Circus* (1972 - ph), *Love Thy Neighbour* (1973 - ph)

Grayson, Godfrey
British writer and director, involved in many of Hammer/Exclusive's early second features. Work unambitious at best. Other credits include *The Fake, An Honourable Murder*.

Hammer credits:
Dr Morelle - The Case of the Missing Heiress (1949 - d), *Dick Barton Strikes Back* (1949 - d), *The Adventures of P. C. 49* (1949 - d), *Meet Simon Cherry* (1950 - co-w/d), *Room to Let* (1950 -co-w/d), *Someone at the Door* (1950 - co-w/d), *What The Butler Waw* (1950 - d), *Dick Barton at Bay* (1950 - d), *To have and to Hold* (1951 - d)

Green, Philip (1917 -)
British composer/musical director with

countless films to his credit, including a good many comedies, of which his only Hammer score, *Don't Panic, Chaps!* (1959), was one.

Guest, Val (1911 -)
Prolific British actor, writer, producer, director and lyricist who began his career writing about the entertainment industry in both Britain and America (for the *Hollywood Reporter* and the *Los Angeles Examiner* among others). Upon returning to Britain in 1932 he gained experience as an actor (in *Innocents in Chicago*) and, more successfully, as a scriptwriter on a number of classic British comedies (*The Maid of the Mountains, Good Morning, Boys, Okay for Sound, Oh, Mr Porter, Alf's Button Afloat, The Frozen Limits,* etc.) featuring such talent as Will Hay, Arthur Askey and The Crazy Gang. First film as a director was the Arthur Askey comedy *Miss London Ltd.* which was followed by all manner of comedies and lightweight musicals (*Mr Drake's Duck, The Runaway Bus, Penny Princess*, etc.). His first film for Hammer was the domestic comedy *Life with the Lyons* in 1954, which was followed by more lightweight material. However, it was his work on *The Quatermass Experiment* that changed not only the course of his own career, but that of Hammer's too. Further films for Hammer were many and various over the years, whilst elsewhere he was responsible for a wide variety of comedies, thrillers and science fiction pieces, among them *Expresso Bongo, The Day the Earth Caught Fire, Jigsaw, 80 000 Suspects, Casino Royale* and *Confessions of a Window Cleaner*, as well as TV's *Shillingbury Tales*.

Hammer credits:
Life with the Lyons (1954 - co-w/d), *Men of Sherwood Forest* (1954 - d), *The Lyons in Paris* (1955 - w/d), *The Quatermass Experiment* (1955 - co-w/d), *Break in the Circle* (1956 - w/d), *Quatermass 2* (1957 - co-w/d), *The Abominable Snowman* (1957 - d), *The Camp on Blood Island* (1958 - co-w/d), *Up the Creek* (1958 - w/d), *Further up the Creek* (1958 - co-w/d), *Hell is a City* (1960 - w/d), *Yesterday's Enemy* (1960 - d), *The Full Treatment* (1960 -p/co-w/d), *When Dinosaurs Ruled the Earth* (1970 - w/d), *In Possession* (1984 - d - *Hammer House of Mystery and Suspense* TVM), *Mark

of the Devil (1984 - d - Hammer House of Mystery and Suspense tvm), Child's Play - d - Hammer House of Mystery and Suspense tvm)

Gunning, Christopher

British composer whose lush and sur-prisingly romantic score for Hands of the Ripper is regarded by many as one of Hammer's best.

Hammer credits:
Hands of the Ripper (1971), Man About the House (1974)

Harris, Max

British composer whose one Hammer score was for On the Buses (1971).

Harryhausen, Ray (1920 -)

Celebrated American stop motion spe-cial effects wizard, began his career experimenting with home movies after seeing King Kong. One of these, Evolution of the World, led to his becoming an animator on George Pal's Puppetoon series (Mother Goose Presents Humpty Dumpty, Mother Goose Presents Old Mother Hubbard, etc.) in the early forties. Worked with his King Kong idol Willis H. O'Brien on Mighty Joe Young, after which he carved out a successful solo career (usually in association with producer Charles H. Schneer) on such films as The Beast from 20 000 Fathoms, The Seventh Voyage of Sinbad, Mysterious Island, Jason and the Argonauts, The Valley of Gawngi and Clash of the Titans. His only film for Hammer was One Million Years B.C., though a remake of King Kong for them was mooted at one stage.

Hartley, Richard

Busy British composer (Galileo, Dance with a Stranger, The Railway Station Man, etc.) whose one score for Hammer, co-written with Les Reed, was for the studio's under-rated remake of The Lady Vanishes (1979).

Harvey, James (Jimmy)

British cinematographer who worked on a good many of Hammer/Exclusive's early films.

Hammer credits:
The Rossiter Case (1951), To Have and to Hold (1951), Lady in the Fog (1952), Face the Music (1954), Blood Orange (1954), The House Across the Lake (1954), The Stranger Came Home (1954), Five Days (1954), 36 Hours (1954), Men of Sherwood Forest (1954), Mask of Dust (1954), The Lyons in Paris (1955), Third Party Risk (1955), Murder by Proxy (1955)

Harvey, Walter

British cinematographer who worked on many of Hammer/Exclusive's early second features.

Hammer credits:
Someone at the Door (1950), The Lady Craved Excitement (1950), Cloudburst (1951), The Black Widow (1951), A Case for P. C. 49 (1951), Death of an Angel (1952), Whispering Smith Hits London (1952), The Last Page (1952), Wings of Danger (1952), Stolen Face (1952), The Gambler and the Lady (1953), The Flanagan Boy (1953), The Saint's Return (1953), Life with the Lyons (1954), Break in the Circle (1955), The Glass Cage (1955), The Quatermass Experiment (1955), The Right Person (1955 - short), Women Without Men (1956)

Heneker, David

British composer, best known for writ-ing the songs for the stage musical Half a Sixpence, which was filmed in 1967. His only Hammer score (co-writ-ten with Monty Norman) was for The Two Faces of Dr Jekyll (1960).

Henried, Paul (1907 - 1992)

Austrian-born leading man who found fame in Hollywood in such films as Night Train to Munich, Now Voyager and Casablanca. Was brought over to appear in two Hammer/Exclusive films to bolster their US box office potential.

Hammer credits:
Stolen Face (1952), Mantrap (1952)

Hinds, Anthony (1922 -)

British producer and writer (under the pseudonym John Elder), son of William Hinds (aka Will Hammer, who founded Exclusive Films with Enrique Carreras). Joined Exclusive for a brief period in 1939 as a bookings clerk before war service in the RAF. Re-joined Exclusive in 1946 and gained experience over-seeing the quota quickies produced on their behalf, which led to himself becoming a fully-fledged producer when Hammer turned to production them-selves, producing 37 of the studio's first 50 films. Produced many of their classic horror films (The Quatermass Experiment, The Curse of Frankenstein, Dracula, The Revenge of Frankenstein, etc.) and scripted such films as The Curse of the Werewolf, The Phantom of the Opera and The Reptile. Left Hammer in 1969 after producing Hammer's TV series Journey to the Unknown, after which he provided scripts for two Tyburn hor-ror films, The Ghoul and Legend of the Werewolf. Only other Hammer credit after 1969 was in 1980 for Visitor from the Grave, an episode of The Hammer House of Horror TV series.

Hammer credits:
The Adventures of P. C. 49 (1949 - p), Dick Barton Strikes Back (1949 - co-p), Meet Simon Cherry (1949 - p), Dr Morelle - The Case of the Missing Heiress (1949 - p), Celia (1949 - p), What the Butler Saw (1950 - p), Someone at the Door (1950 - p), Room to Let (1950 - p), The Rossiter Case (1950 - p), A Case of P. C. 49 (1950 - p), The Lady Craved Excitement (1950 - p), The Man in Black (1950 - p), Whispering Smith Hits London (1951 - p), Cloudburst (1951 - p), Black Widow (1951 - p), The Dark Light (1951 - exec p), Death of An Angel (1951 - p), Wings of Danger (1952 - p), Stolen Face (1952 - p), Lady in the Fog (1952 - p), The Last Page (1952 - p), Thirty-Six Hours (1953 - p), The Saint Returns (1953 - co-p), The Flanagan Boy (1953 - p), The House Across the Lake (1953 - p), The Gambler and the Lady (1953 - p), Five Days (1954 - p), The Man on the Beach (1955 - p), The Glass Cage (1955 - p), The Quatermass Experiment (1955 - p), The Curse of Frankenstein (1956 - p), Women Without Men (1956 - p), X - The Unknown (1957 - p), Danger List (1957 - p), Quatermass 2 (1957 - p), Man with a Dog (1958 - p), Clean Sweep (1958 - p), Dracula (1958 - p), The Camp on Blood Island (1958 - p), The Revenge of Frankenstein (1958 - p), I Only Arsked (1959 - p), To Have and To Hold (1959 - p), The Hound of the Baskervilles (1959 - p), The Man Who Could Cheat Death (1959 - p), The

Stranglers of Bombay (1960 - p), *The Brides of Dracula* (1960 - p), *Never Take Sweets from a Stranger* (1960 - p), *Curse of the Werewolf* (1961 - w/p [w as John Elder]), *The Phantom of the Opera* (1962 - w/p [w as John Elder]), *Captain Clegg* (1962 - co-w [w as John Elder]), *The Old Dark House* (1962 - co-p), *The Damned* (1963), *Paranoiac* (1963 -p), *Kiss of the Vampire* (1964 - w/p [w as John Elder]), *The Evil of Frankenstein* (1964 - w/p [w as John Elder]), *Fanatic* (1965), *Dracula - Prince of Darkness* (1966 - story [as John Elder]), *The Reptile* (1966 - w [as John Elder]), *Frankenstein Created Woman* (1967 - w [as John Elder]), *The Mummy's Shroud* (1967 - story [as john Elder]), *Dracula Has Risen from the Grave* (1968 - w [as John Elder]), *Scars of Dracula* (1970 - w [as John Elder]), *Frankenstein and the Monster from Hell* (1973 - w [as John Elder]).

Hollingsworth, John (1916 - 1963)
British conductor who, in 1954, became Hammer's first in-house musical supervisor, a post he kept until his death in 1963, when he was succeeded by Philip Martell. Trained at London's Guildhall School of Music. Joined the RAF during the war, following which he conducted several orchestras, including those at the Royal Opera House and the BBC (where he spotted the talents of James Bernard).

Holt, Seth (1923 - 1971)
Palestinian-born director who began his career as an editor at Ealing where he worked on such classics as *Mandy*, *The Lavender Hill Mob* and *The Titfield Thunderbolt*, etc. His first film as a director was *Nowhere To Go* in 1958. His three Hammer films aside, he only directed two more films: *Danger Route* and *Station Six Sahara*. When in top form (as he was with Hammer), his work is comparable to that of Hitchcock. Died just days before completing his last film.

Hammer credits:
Taste of Fear (1961), *The Nanny* (1965), *Blood from the Mummy's Tomb* (1971)

Hotchkis, John
British composer whose two Hammer

scores were both for shorts: *Copenhagen* (1956), *A Man on the Beach* (1956).

Hough, John (1941 -).
British director from television. Has a strong visual sense, seen at its best in genre films. His credits include *Wolfshead*, *Eye Witness*, *The Legend of Hell House*, *Escape to Witch Mountain*, *Watcher in the Woods* and *The Howling IV*.

Hammer credits:
Twins of Evil (1971), *Czech Mate* (1984 - *Hammer House of Mystery and Suspense* TVM), *A Distant Scream (1984 - Hammer House of Mystery and Suspense TVM), Black Carrion (1984 - Hammer House of Mystery and Suspense TVM)*

Houghton, Don (c.1933 - 1991)
Paris-born British screenwriter and story editor (for *Hammer House of Mystery and Suspense*), the son of novelist George W. Houghton. Began writing for television on such series as *Emergency Ward Ten*, *Dr Who* and *The Flaxton Boys*. Came to Hammer in the early seventies to work on the dismissed *Dracula A.D. 1972*. Also scripted the dialogue for Hammer's two records: *Dracula* and the *Legend of the Seven Golden Vampires*.

Hammer credits:
Dracula A. D. 1972 (1972), *The Satanic Rites of Dracula* (1973), *Legend of the Seven Golden Vampires* (1974), *Shatter* (1974), *Black Carrion* (1984 - *Hammer House of Mystery and Suspense TVM*)

Hughes, Gary
British composer who provided reasonably lusty scores for four of Hammer's action-adventure pics.

Hammer credits:
Devil-Ship Pirates (1963), *The Scarlet Blade* (1963), *A Challenge for Robin Hood* (1967), *The Viking Queen* (1967)

Hume, Alan (1924 -)
Prolific British cinematographer who began his career as a camera operator on the *Carry Ons* and TV's *The Avengers*. Photographed many of the later *Carry Ons* before moving on to bigger films. Other credits include *The*

Legend of Hell House, The Land That Time Forgot, Trial by Combat, Bear Island, Eye of the Needle, For Your Eyes Only, Return of the Jedi, Octopussy, Supergirl, A View to a Kill, Lifeforce, A Fish Called Wanda and *Eve of Destruction.*

Hammer credits:
Kiss of the Vampire (1964)

Huntley, Raymond (1904 - 1990)
British character actor, usually in supercilious roles in countless films such as *Night Train to Munich* (aka *Night Train*), *Passport to Pimlico* and *Hobson's Choice*. Played Dracula on stage in the original London production.

Hammer credits:
Last Page (1952), *The Mummy* (1959), *That's your Funeral* (1973)

Jeffries, Lionel (1926 -)
British comedy actor who later turned to direction with equal success (*The Railway Children*, *The Amazing Mr Blunden*, *Baxter*, etc.).

Hammer credits:
The Quatermass Experiment (1955), *Up the Creek* (1958), *The Revenge of Frankenstein* (1958), *Further up the Creek* (1958), *The Scarlet Blade* (1963)

Johnson, Laurie (1927 -)
British composer/conductor, trained at the Royal College of Music. Best known for his various TV themes and scores for the likes of *The Avengers*, *The Professionals* and *The New Avengers*. Stage shows include *Lock Up Your Daughters* and *The Four Musketeers*. A longtime friend of composer Bernard Herrmann, after whose death he adapted his *It's Alive* (1974) score for *It's Alive 2* (1976 - aka *It Lives Again*). He also conducted a recording of Herrmann's *North by Northwest* in 1979, whilst his own *First Men in the Moon* (1963) score has more than a touch of Herrmann about it - as does his only Hammer score, *Captain Kronos: Vampire Hunter* (1974), whose driving title theme is one of the studio's best.

Jones, Kenneth V. (1924 -)
British composer with many scores to

his credit, including Roger Corman's *The Tomb of Ligeia* (1964). His only Hammer credit was for the drama *Ten Seconds to Hell* (1959).

Josephs, Wilfred
British composer with various film and TV credits to his name, including several genre entries (*The Deadly Bees, Dark Places, The Uncanny*, etc.).

Hammer credits:
Cash on Demand (1963), *Fanatic* (1965), *Carpathian Eagle* (1980 - *Hammer House of Horror* episode)

Keir, Andrew (1926 -)
Scottish character actor who made an excellent Professor Quatermass in *Quatermass and the Pit*. Other credits include *The Maggie, Zeppelin* and *Rob Roy*.

Hammer credits:
The Lady Craved Excitement (1950), *The Pirates of Blood River* (1962), *The Devil-Ship Pirates* (1964), *Dracula - Prince of Darkness* (1966), *The Viking Queen* (1967), *Quatermass and the Pit* (1967), *Blood from the Mummy's Tomb* (1971)

Keys, Anthony Nelson (1913 - 1985)
British producer, son of actor-comedian Nelson 'Bunch' Keys, brother of editor Roderick Keys, associate producer Basil Keys (who was associate producer on *Phantom of the Opera* and *Paranoiac*) and director John Paddy Carstairs (who directed *Weekend with Lulu*). Began his career as a recordist for HMV in 1928. After the war, during which he was a paratrooper, he went to work for Gainsborough as a production manager, then for Romulus. First film for Hammer was *Never Look Back* in 1952, on which he acted as production manager. Joined Hammer full time in 1956 as an associate producer, a role a fulfilled throughout the fifties. Graduated to producer in 1962 with *The Pirates of Blood River*. Was also General Manager of Bray studios in the 60s and co-wrote the screenplay for *Frankenstein must be Destroyed* in 1969. Formed Charlemagne productions in 1972 with Christopher Lee, but their only film was *Nothing but the Night*, which did badly at the box office.

Hammer credits:
The Curse of Frankenstein (1956 - associate p), *Dracula* (1958 - associate p), *The Revenge of Frankenstein* (1958 - associate p), *The Man Who Could Cheat Death* (1959 - associate p), *The Terror of the Tongs* (1961 - associate p), *The Pirates of Blood River* (1963 - p), *The Scarlet Blade* (1963 - p), *The Devil-Ship Pirates* (1964 - p), *The Secret of Blood Island* (1964 - p), *The Gorgon* (1964 - p), *The Brigand of Kandahar* (1965 - p), *Dracula - Prince of Darkness* (1966 - p), *Rasputin - The Mad Monk* (1966 - p), *Plague of the Zombies* (1966 - p), *The Reptile* (1966 - p), *Frankenstein Created Woman* (1966 - p), *The Mummy's Shroud* (1966 - p), *The Witches* (1966 - p), *Quatermass and the Pit* (1967 - p), *The Devil Rides Out* (1968 - p), *Frankenstein Must Be Destroyed* (1969 - p/co-w)

Kneale, Nigel (1922 -)
Manx-born writer who became a staff writer for the BBC just after the war where he became the creator of such television classics as *The Quatermass Experiment* (originally written to fill a gap in the schedules), *Quatermass 2, Quatermass and the Pit, The Creature* and, later, *The Sex Olympics, Beasts, Kinvig* and a fourth Quatermass series. The film rights to the original Quatermass series were of course bought by Hammer, whose success with which altered the course of the studio's history. Kneale's other film credits include *Look Back in Anger, The Entertainer, The First Men in the Moon* and *Halloween III: Season of the Witch* (from which he had his name removed).

Hammer credits:
Quatermass (1955 - series only), *Quatermass 2* (1956 - co-w), *The Abominable Snowman* (1957 - w), *The Witches* (1966 - w), *Quatermass and the Pit* (1967 - w)

Lawrence, Brian (1920 -)
British executive and executive producer who joined Exclusive in 1945 after experience in the Anglo American Film Corp during the war. Became Exclusive's Sales Manager in 1950, then General Manager and assistant to James Carreras in the late fifties. Became a Hammer board direc-

tor in the mid sixties. Formed Cinema Arts with Roy Skeggs in 1979, with whom he took control of Hammer when it collapsed in 1979. Executive produced *The Hammer House of Horror* (1980) and *Hammer House of Mystery and Suspense* (1984) before retiring in 1986.

Leakey, Phil (1908 - 1992)
British make-up artist who, having trained at Shepperton Studios in the mid forties, joined Hammer/Exclusive in 1947, where he worked on many of their second feature mysteries (*Meet Simon Cherry, Room to Let, Someone at the Door*, etc.). Worked on several of their key fifties horror films (*The Curse of Frankenstein, Dracula, The Abominable Snowman*, etc.). Left Hammer after the completion of *The Revenge of Frankenstein* in 1958, having become disillusioned with their continued horror output. Other credits include *Only Two Can Play, Sammy Going South, The Ipcress File, Far from the Madding Crowd* and *The Belstone Fox*.

Lee, Christopher (1922 -)
British actor whose prolific output has mostly been in the horror genre. Regarded by many as the definitive screen Dracula, he began his career after military service during World War Two, winning a seven year contract with Rank in 1947. However, his height proved to be a restriction, and he found himself playing bit parts in all manner of films, such as *Corridor of Mirrors, Hamlet* (he didn't share any scenes with Peter Cushing), *Prelude to Fame, A Tale of Two Cities* and *Valley of Eagles*. His height did win him the role of the Creature in Hammer's *The Curse of Frankenstein* though, which led to the title roles in *Dracula* and *The Mummy*. International fame in the horror genre followed, where he appeared in such variable films as *City of the Dead, Hercules in the Haunted World, The Face of Fu Manchu, Scream and Scream Again* and *The Wicker Man*. His gradual dissatisfaction with Hammer's treatment of him in the Dracula series led to a break from horror films in the mid-70s, when he appeared in such films as *The Three Musketeers, The Man with the Golden Gun* (as James Bond's nemesis Scaramanga), *The Four Musketeers* and *1941*, though he remains indelibly

linked with the genre.
Hammer credits:
The Curse of Frankenstein (1957),
Dracula (1958), *The Hound of the
Baskervilles* (1959), *The Man Who
Could Cheat Death* (1959), *The Two
Faces of Dr Jekyll* (1960), *Taste of
Fear* (1961), *The Terror of the Tongs*
(1961), *The Pirates of Blood River*
(1962), *The Devil-Ship Pirates* (1963),
The Gorgon (1964), *She* (1965),
Dracula - Prince of Darkness (1966),
Rasputin - The Mad Monk (1966), *The
Devil Rides Out* (1967), *Dracula Has
Risen From The Grave* (1968), *Taste
the Blood of Dracula* (1970), *Scars of
Dracula* (1970), *Dracula A.D. 1972*
(1972), *The Satanic Rites of Dracula*
(1973).

Lippert, Robert (1909 - 1976)
American producer, director and
exhibitor through whom
Hammer/Exclusive gained Stateside
releases for many of their early films,
in return for which Exclusive gained
the rights to release such Lippert-produced films as *Rocketship XM* and
The Lost Continent in Britain.

Lom, Herbert (1917 -)
Czech-born character actor (real name
Herbert Charles Angelo Kuchacevich
ze Schluderpacheru!), equally adept at
comic or sinister roles, though proba-
bly best remembered as Inspector
Dreyfus in the Pink Panther films. Was
a memorable Phantom for Hammer, a
role he inherited from Cary Grant.
Other genre films include *And Now
The Screaming Starts, Doppelganger,
Murders in The Rue Morgue, And
Then There Were None* and *The Sect.*

Hammer credits:
Whispering Smith Hits London (1951),
The Phantom of the Opera (1962), *The
Lady Vanishes* (1979)

Losey, Joseph (1909 - 1984)
American director (*The Boy with
Green Hair, M, The Prowler,* etc.) who
came to Britain after being blacklisted
in the McCarthy witchunts. Worked on
a couple of films for Hammer, but was
taken off *X - The Unknown* at the
request of its star, Dean Jagger, and
replaced by Leslie Norman. Other
films include *The Servant, Accident,
Boom* and *The Go-Between.*

Hammer credits:
Man on a Beach (1956 - short), *The
Damned* (1962).

Lugosi, Bela (1882 - 1956)
Celebrated Hungarian horror star, best
remembered as the stage and
screen's first Dracula. His only
Hammer film was *Mystery of the
Mary Celeste* made in 1935. He died
before Hammer's later horror revival.

Lutyens CBE, Elizabeth
British composer, trained at the Royal
College of Music. Numerous genre
credits to her name, including several
for director Freddie Francis (*Dr Terror's
House of Horrors, The Skull, The
Psychopath*). The daughter of architect
Sir Edwin Lutyens, she has done
much film, television and radio work
as well as concert work.

Hammer credits:
Never Take Sweets from a Stranger
(1960), *Paranoiac* (1963)

MacGregor, Scott (1914 - 1973)
Scottish art director/production design-
er who, after Bernard Robinson left
Hammer, became their most prolific
art director. An former stage designer,
he entered the film industry in 1941 as
an assistant to art director Edward
Carrick and workerd on such films as
Western Approaches and *Target for
Tonight.* Other films (usually as assis-
tant art director) include *The Day they
Robbed the Bank of England,
Cleopatra, Day of the Triffids, The
Vengeance of Fu Manchu, The
Vengeance of She,* etc.

Hammer cedits:
Don't Panic, Chaps (1959), *The
Vengeance of She* (1968 - co ed),
Moon Zero Two (1969), *Taste the
Blood of Dracula* (1970), *Crescendo*
(1970), *Horror of Frankenstein* (1970),
Scars of Dracula (1970), *The Vampire
Lovers* (1970), *On the Buses* (1971),
Blood from the Mummy's Tomb
(1971), *Vampire Circus* (1972), *Straight
on Till Morning* (1972), *Mutiny on the
Buses* (1972), *That's your Funeral*
(1973), *Frankenstein and the Monster
from Hell* (1973), *Nearest and Dearest*
(1973)

Mainwairing, Bernard

British director who helmed Hammer's
very first film, *The Public Life of Henry
the Ninth,* in 1935.

Martell, Philip (1915 - 1993)
British conductor who succeeded
John Hollingsworth as Hammer's resident musical supervisor, a role he
retained until his death. Worked on all
of Hammer's film and television pro-
jects from *The Evil of Frankenstein*
onwards, including their records of
*Dracula, The Legend of the Seven
Golden Vampires* and Silva Screen's
Music from the Hammer Films (aka
*Dracula - Classic Scores from Hammer
Horror*). Trained at London's Guildhall
School of Music. Entered the film
industry in the late twenties as an
arranger. Formed his own orchestra
and often performed on BBC radio.
Was also the musical director for
Tyburn Films.

Martelli, Carlo
British composer (despite the name)
with numerous genre credits (*It,
Witchcraft, Catacombs, The Murder
Game*), including two competent if
uninspired scores for two less than
competent and inspired Hammer
films.

Hammer credits:
The Curse of the Mummy's Tomb
(1964), *Slave Girls* (1968)

McCabe, John
British composer/conductor/pianist, a
principal at the London College of
Music. Hammer scores workmanlike
but fairly uninspired.

Hammer credits:
Fear in the Night (1970), *Guardian of
the Abyss* (1980, *Hammer House of
Horror* episode)

Matheson, Richard (1926 -)
American novelist and short story
writer with many genre films to his
credit, including several of Roger
Corman's Poe adaptations (*The Pit and
the Pendulum, Tales of Terror, The
Raven,* etc.) as well as such classics as
*The Incredible Shrinking Man, Duel,
The Legend of Hell House* and
Somewhere in Time. Attempted to get
a film version of his novel *I am
Legend* made with Hammer, for whom

he also adapted *The Devil Rides Out.*
Hammer credits:
Fanatic (1965), *The Devil Rides Out*
(1968), *Girl of my Dreams* (1969 -
story - *Journey to the Unknown*
episode)

Mathews, Kerwin (1926 -)
American leading man, best remem-
bered as Sinbad in *The Seventh
Voyage of Sinbad.* Other genre movie
include *The Three Worlds of Gulliver,
Jack the Giant Killer, Battle Beneath
the Earth, Octaman* and *The Boy who
Cried Werewolf.*

Hammer credits:
The Pirates of Blood River (1962),
Maniac (1963)

Matthews, Francis (1927 -)
Debonair British leading man with a
strong line in superior upper crust
types. Much stage and television
work. Film credits include *Corridors of
Blood* (aka *Doctor from Seven Dials),
That Riviera Touch, Crossplot.*

Hammer credits:
The Revenge of Frankenstein (1958), *I
only Arsked* (1959), *Dracula - Prince of
Darkness* (1966)

Mingaye, Don
British art director, trained at London's
St. Martin's School of Art. Began
working in films in 1945 as a junior
scenic artist at Gainsborough's
Islington studios. Began working for
Hammer in the late fifties as an assistant, gradually working his way up to
fully-fledged art director, often
co-working with production designer
Bernard Robinson.

Hammer credits:
Watch It, Sailor! (1961 - co-ad), *The
Phantom of the Opera* (1962 - co-ad),
Captain Clegg (1962 - co-ad), *The
Pirates of Blood River* (1962 - co-ad),
The Damned (1963 - ad), *The Scarlet
Blade* (1963 - ad), *Cash on Demand*
(1963 - ad), *Paranoiac* (1963 -co-ad),
Kiss of the Vampire (1963 - ad), *The
Evil of Frankenstein* (1964 - ad),
Nightmare (1964 - co-ad), *The
Devil-Ship Pirates* (1964 - co-ad), *The
Gorgon* (1964 - co-ad), *She* (1965 -
co-ad), *The Brigand of Kandahar* (1965
- ad), *Dracula - Prince of Darkness*
(1966 - ad), *Plague of the Zombies*

(1966 - ad), *Rasputin - The Mad Monk*
(1966 - ad), *The Reptile* (1966 - ad),
The Witches (1966 - ad), *Frankenstein
Created Woman* (1967 - ad), *The
Mummy's Shroud* (1967 - ad), *Lust for
a Vampire* (1971 - ad)

Morell, Andre (1909 - 1978)
Reliable British character actor who
played well-bred authority figures.
Made an ideal Watson to Peter
Cushing's Holmes in *The Hound of the
Baskervilles.* Other credits include
*Flesh and Blood, Seven Days to Noon,
Ben-Hur, The Slipper and the Rose* and
The First Great Train Robbery.

Hammer credits:
Stolen Face (1952), *The Camp on
Blood Island* (1958), *The Hound of the
Baskervilles* (1959), *The Shadow of
the Cat* (1961), *Cash on Demand*
(1961), *She* (1965), *Plague of the
Zombies* (1966), *The Mummy's
Shroud* (1967), *The Vengeance of She*
(1968)

Nascimbene, Mario (1916 -)
Italian composer, trained at Milan's
Giuseppe Verdi Conservatory. Has various sword and sandal epics to his
credit (*Alexander The Great, Solomon
and Sheeba, Barabbas,* etc.), of which
The Vikings (1958) is his best and
best-known. His atmospheric score for
Hammer's *One Million Years B.C.* was
followed by several other prehistoric
adventures, each of which made
effective use of odd-sounding percussion.

Hammer credits:
One Million Years B.C. (1966), *The
Vengeance of She* (1968), *When
Dinosaurs Ruled the Earth* (1970),
Creatures the World Forgot (1971)

Nash, Michael see **Carreras, James**

Needs, James
British editor/supervising editor, a
Hammer mainstay since 1950.
Worked on practically all of their films
up until the mid seventies.

Hammer credits:
A Case for P.C.49 (1950 - ed), *Room to
Let* (1950 - ed), *Black Widow* (1951 -
ed), *The Dark Light* (1951 - ed),
Whispering Smith Hits London (1951 -
ed), *Wings of Danger* (1952- ed),

Mantrap (1952 - ed), *Lady in the Fog*
(1952 - ed), *Thirty-Six Hours* (1953 -
ed), *The Flanagan Boy* (1953 - ed), *The
Saint Returns* (1953 -co-ed), *The
House Across the Lake* (1953 - ed),
Men of Sherwood Forest (1954 - ed),
Five Days (1954 - ed), *The Glass Cage*
(1955 - ed), *Cyril Stapleton and the
Showband* (1955 - ed), *Third Party Risk*
(1955 - ed), *The Quatermass
Experiment* (1955 - ed), *The Curse of
Frankenstein* (1956 - ed), *Dick Turpin*
(1956 - ed), *Women Without Men*
(1956 - ed), *X - The Unknown* (1956
-ed), *The Edmundo Ros Half House*
(1957 - ed), *Danger List* (1957 - ed),
Quatermass 2 (1957 - ed),*Clean
Sweep* (1958 - ed), *Dracula* (1958 -
co-ed), *The Camp on Blood Island*
(1958 - co-ed), *The Revenge of
Frankenstein* (1958 - co-ed), *The
Snorkel* (1958 - co-ed), *The Mummy*
(1959 - co-ed), *The Man Who Could
Cheat Death* (1959 -co-ed), *Hell Is a
City* (1959 - ed), *I Only Arsked* (1959 -
co-ed), *The Hound of the Baskervilles*
(1959 - co-ed), *Man with a Dog* (1959 -
ed), *Yesterday's Enemy* (1959 - co-ed),
The Ugly Duckling (1959 - co-ed), *Ten
Seconds to Hell* (1959 - co-ed), *To
Have and To Hold* (1959 - ed), *The
Stranglers of Bombay* (1960 - co-ed),
Sword of Sherwood Forest (1960 -
co-ed), *Never Take Sweets from a
Stranger* (1960 - co-ed), *The Two
Faces of Dr Jekyll* (1960 -co-ed), *The
Brides of Dracula* (1960 - co-ed), *The
Shadow of the Cat* (1961 - ed), *The
Curse of the Werewolf* (1961 - co-ed),
Taste of Fear (1961 - co-ed), *Terror of
the Tongs* (1961 - co-ed),*Visa to
Canton* (1961 - co-ed), *Watch It, Sailor!*
(1961 - co-ed), *Weekend with Lulu*
(1961 - co-ed), *The Old Dark House*
(1962 -ed), *Kiss of the Vampire* (1962 -
ed), *Captain Clegg* (1962 -co-ed), *Cash
on Demand* (1963 - co-ed), *Paranoiac*
(1963 - ed), *The Damned* (1963 -
co-ed), *The Scarlet Blade* (1963 -
co-ed), *The Pirates of Blood River*
(1963 - co-ed), *Maniac* (1963 - ed), *The
Gorgon* (1964 - co-ed), *The Devil-Ship
Pirates* (1964 - ed), *The Evil of
Frankenstein* (1964 - ed), *The Secret
of Blood Island* (1964 - ed), *The Curse
of the Mummy's Tomb* (1964 - co-ed),
Nightmare (1964 - ed), *The Nanny*
(1965 - co-ed), *The Brigand of
Kandahar* (1965 - ed), *Hysteria* (1965 -
ed), *She* (1965 - co-ed), *Fanatic* (1965 -
co-ed), *Dracula - Prince of Darkness*
(1966 -co-ed), *Rasputin - The Mad
Monk* (1966 - co-ed), *The Plague of
the Zombies* (1966 - co-ed), *The*

Reptile (1966 -ed), *The Witches* (1966 - co-ed), *One Million Years B.C.* (1966 - co-ed), *Frankenstein Created Woman* (1966 - co-ed), *The Mummy's Shroud* (1966 - co-ed), *Quatermass and the Pit* (1967 - co-ed), *The Viking Queen* (1967 -ed), *A Challenge for Robin Hood* (1967 - ed), *Dracula Has Risen from the Grave* (1968 - co-ed), *The Devil Rides Out* (1968 -co-ed), *Slave Girls* (1968 - co-ed), *The Anniversary* (1968 -co-ed), *The Lost Continent* (1968 - co-ed), *The Vampire Lovers* (1970 - ed), *Scars of Dracula* (1970 - ed), *Dr Jekyll and Sister Hyde* (1971 - co-ed), *Holiday on the Buses* (1973 - ed), *Dracula A.D. 1972* (1972 - ed), *Captain Kronos - Vampire Hunter* (1973 -ed), *Love Thy Neighbour* (1973 - ed), *Frankenstein and the Monster from Hell* (1973 - ed)

Parker, Clifton (1905 -)
British composer/musical director with many films to his credit (*Night of the Demon, Sink the Bismark, The Informers*), but only one Hammer Horror, the *Les Diaboliques* - like *Taste of Fear* (1961).

Pearce, Jacqueline
British actress who made a mark as the title character in Hammer's *The Reptile*. Other credits include *Sky West and Crooked, White Mischief* and TV's *Blake's Seven*.

Hammer credits:
Plague of the Zombies (1966), *The Reptile* (1966)

Pitt, Ingrid (1944 -)
Glamorous, under-used Polish actress in international films, with experience in East Germany and Spain (where she was a member of the Spanish National Theatre). Broke into films in Spain in 1964 with *El Sonido Prehistorico* (aka *Sound of Horror*) which led to work on *The Megans* and *Where Eagles Dare*, after which she became Hammer's leading lady vampire. Other genre films include *The House That Dripped Blood* and *The Wicker Man*. More recent films include *Who Dares Wins, Wild Geese II* and *Parker*. Also harbours aspirations to be a writer.

Hammer credits:
The Vampire Lovers (1970), *Countess Dracula* (1970)

Probyn, Brian
British cinematographer who worked on several of Hammer's later productions.

Hammer credits:
Straight on till Morning (1972), *The Satanic Rites of Dracula* (1973), *Frankenstein and the Monster from Hell* (1973), *Man at the Top* (1973), *Shatter* (1974 - co-ph)

Prowse, Dave
Tall (6'7") British actor and stunt man, best remembered for playing Darth Vader in the *Star Wars* films. Has played Frankenstein's monster three times to date (the first time as a gag cameo in *Casino Royale*). Other credits include *Up the Chastity Belt*.

Hammer credits:
Horror of Frankenstein (1970), *Vampire Circus* (1971), *Frankenstein and the Monster from Hell* (1973)

Reed, Michael (1929 -)
British cinematographer with several large-scale productions to his credit, including *On Her Majesty's Secret Service, The Mackenzie Break, Shout at the Devil* and *The Wild Geese*.

Hammer credits:
The Devil-Ship Pirates (1964), *The Gorgon* (1964), *Dracula -Prince of Darkness* (1966), *Rasputin - The Mad Monk* (1966), *Slave Girls* (1968)

Reed, Oliver (1938 -)
British actor, nephew of director Sir Carol Reed (for whom he appeared in the film version of *Oliver!* as Bill Sykes). Began his film career as an extra, graduating to bit parts in such films as *The League of Gentlemen, The Bulldog Breed* and *The Rebel*. A brief role as a nightclub rowdy in his first Hammer film, *The Two Faces of Dr. Jekyll*, led to his being cast as the wolfman in *The Curse of the Werewolf*, which he followed with a number of Hammer projects, including a handful of swashbucklers. Upon leaving Hammer in a bid to escape genre films, he found international fame in such productions as *The Jokers, Hannibal Brooks, Women in Love, The Three Musketeers* and *The Four Musketeers*, though he has since starred in such genre offerings as *Zero

Population Growth, And Then There Were None, Burnt Offerings, The Brood, Dr Heckyl and Mr. Hype, Venom, etc. Also narrated the Hammer compilation series *The World of Hammer* in 1990.

Hammer credits:
The Two Faces of Dr Jekyll (1960), *The Curse of the Werewolf* (1961), *Captain Clegg* (1962), *The Damned* (1962), *The Pirates of Blood River* (1962), *Paranoiac* (1963), *The Scarlet Blade* (1964), *The Brigand of Kandahar* (1965)

Reizenstein, Franz (1911 - 1968)
German-born composer/concert pianist whose only score for Hammer was for *The Mummy* (1959). One of the studio's very best scores, its imposing use of full orchestra, choir and percussion adds atmosphere a-plenty to an already fine film (parts of it were even re-used for *Curse of the Mummy's Tomb*).

Richardson, John (1934 -)
Handsome British leading man on the international scene in all manner of films, including *Ivanhoe, Black Sunday* and *Torso*, though perhaps best remembered as Raquel Welch's leading man in Hammer's *One Million Years B.C.*

Hammer credits:
She (1965), *One Million Years B. C.* (1966), *The Vengeance of She* (1968)

Ripper, Michael (1913 -)
British character actor who began his career in rep in 1924. Broke into films in 1935 with *Twice Branded* which he followed with countless minor roles in such films as *Prison Breaker, The Heirloom Mystery* and *If I Were Boss*, usually as a crook, cabby or the comic relief. His first Hammer film was *The Adventures of P.C. 49* in 1949, after which he became a regular feature of many of their films (six in 1958 alone), either as a coachman, yokel or bait for their many monsters. Other films include *The Belles of St. Trinian's, Blue Murder at St. Trinian's, Geordie, Richard III, Sink the Bismarck, No Sex Please - We're British* and *The Creeping Flesh*.

Hammer credits:

The Adventures of P.C. 49 (1949), A Case for P.C. 49 (1950), A Man on the Beach (1956 - short), X - The Unknown (1956), The Steel Bayonet (1957), Quatermass 2 (1958), Up the Creek (1958), The Camp on Blood Island (1958), I Only Arsked (1958), The Revenge of Frankenstein (1958), Further up the Creek (1958), The Man Who Could Cheat Death (1959), The Ugly Duckling (1959), The Mummy (1959), The Brides of Dracula (1960), The Curse of the Werewolf (1961), The Pirates of Blood River (1962), Captain Clegg (1962), The Phantom of the Opera (1962), The Scarlet Blade (1963), The Devil-Ship Pirates (1963), The Curse of the Mummy's Tomb (1964), The Secret of Blood Island (1964), Plague of the Zombies (1966), The Reptile (1966), The Mummy's Shroud (1967), The Lost Continent (1968), Dracula Has Risen from the Grave (1968), Moon Zero Two (1969), Taste the Blood of Dracula (1970), Scars of Dracula (1970), That's your Funeral (1972)

Robertson, Harry see **Robinson, Harry**

Robinson, Bernard (1912 - 1970)
Distinguished British art director and production designer with a talent for making the very most of limited budgets and cramped studio space (ie: Bray!). A Hammer mainstay, he was responsible for the look of many of their classic horror films, to which he added both visual flair and a sense of Victorian clutter. After being educated at the Liverpool School of Art he began in the industry as a draughtsman at Warner's Teddington studios, but quickly graduated to art director in 1939 for British Lion. During the war he lent his expertise as a camouflage and decoy expert, after which he returned to films (The Shop at Sly Corner, While I Live, Double Confession, Carve Her Name with Pride, Reach for the Sky, etc.), joining Hammer in 1956, where he stayed until his death in 1970, working on few non-Hammer projects in between.

Hammer credits:
Quatermass 2 (1956), X - The Unknown (1956), The Curse of Frankenstein (1957), The Abominable Snowman (1957), Day of Grace (1957 - short), Dracula (1958), The Revenge of

Frankenstein (1958), Yesterday's Enemy (1959), The Mummy (1959), The Ugly Duckling (1959), The Man Who Could Cheat Death (1959), The Stranglers of Bombay (1960), The Two Faces of Dr Jekyll (1960), Never Take Sweets from a Stranger (1960), Visa to Canton (1961), Watch It, Sailor! (1961), Taste of Fear (1961), Terror of the Tongs (1961), The Brides of Dracula (1960), Shadow of the Cat (1961), The Curse of the Werewolf (1961), The Phantom of the Opera (1962), The Pirates of Blood River (1962), Captain Clegg (1962), The Damned (1963), The Devil-Ship Pirates (1963), Paranoiac (1963), Kiss of the Vampire (1963), Nightmare (1964), The Secret of Blood Island (1964), The Gorgon (1964), The Curse of the Mummy's Tomb (1964), The Secret of Blood Island (1965), Dracula - Prince of Darkness (1966), Rasputin - The Mad Monk (1966), Plague of the Zombies (1966), The Reptile (1966), The Brigand of Kandahar (1965), The Old Dark House (1966), The Witches (1966), Frankenstein Created Woman (1967), The Mummy's Shroud (1967), Quatermass and the Pit (1967), The Devil Rides Out (1968), Dracula has Risen from the Grave (1968), Frankenstein Must be Destroyed (1969)

Robinson, Harry
Scottish musician, former pop arranger/composer/producer, also known as Harry Robertson, under which name he produced the 1980 sword and sorcery adventure Hawk the Slayer for ITC. Wrote a number of atmospheric scores for Hammer in the late sixties and early seventies, as well as the title theme to their 1969 TV series Journey to the Unknown. Also responsible for such genre entries as The Oblong Box, Fright, Legend of the Werewolf and The Ghoul. The less said about his pop song 'Strange Love', written for Lust for a Vampire, the better, however.

Hammer credits:
Journey to the Unknown (1969 - TV - title theme and episode scores for Eve, Somewhere in the Crowd, The Beckoning Fair One and Miss Belle), The Vampire Lovers (1970), Lust for a Vampire (1971), Countess Dracula (1971), Twins of Evil (1971), Demons of the Mind (1972)

Robinson, Margaret
British prop maker, wife of designer Bernard Robinson. Work for Hammer includes making the Egyptian artefacts for The Mummy (1959) and the dreadful papier mache mask for Colonel the dog for The Hound of the Baskervilles (1959).

Salzedo, Leonard (1921 -)
British composer. Studied at the Royal College of Music. Several concert works and ballets to his credit. Of his six Hammer scores, only the ambient Revenge of Frankenstein (1958) was a genuine horror film, the others being run-of-the-mill programmers.

Hammer credits:
Mask of Dust (1954), The Glass Cage (1955), Women Without Men (1956), The Steel Bayonet (1957), The Revenge of Frankenstein (1958) The Silent Scream (1980 - Hammer House of Horror episode)

Sangster, Jimmy (1927 -)
British writer, producer and director who scripted many of Hammer's classic genre films in the late fifties and early sixties. After service in the RAF during World War Two, he joined Hammer as a third assistant director and gradually worked his way up to first assistant at the age of just 19. In 1954 he began work as a production manager then became assistant to executive producer Michael Carreras. His first script was for the short A Man on the Beach, which was followed by his first full-length screenplay X - The Unknown. The Curse of Frankenstein put him on the map, after which he worked regularly for Hammer and other studios as a writer on such genre pictures as The Trollenberg Terror, Jack the Ripper and Blood of the Vampire. Turned to psychological thrillers in 1960 with A Taste of Fear (which he also produced) in a bid to escape genre pictures, only to now find himself equally tied to similar thrillers (Nightmare, Paranoiac, etc). Turned director with less success in 1970 on Horror of Frankenstein. Finally left Hammer in the mid-seventies and went to America, where he carved out a niche for himself as a writer of movies and TV movies (Scream, Pretty Peggy, Phobia, etc.). Sometimes uses the pen-name John

Sansom.
Hammer credits:
A Man on the Beach (1955 - w- short),
X - The Unknown (1956 - w), *The
Curse of Frankenstein* (1957 - w),
Dracula (1958 - w), *The Revenge of
Frankenstein* (1958 - w), *The Mummy*
(1959 - w), *The Man Who Could Cheat
Death* (1959 - w), *Taste of Fear* (1961 -
w/p), *Maniac* (1963 w/p), *Paranoiac*
(1963 - w/p), *Hysteria* (1965 - w/p),
The Nanny (1965 - w/p), *Dracula -
Prince of Darkness* (1966 - as John
Sansom), *The Anniversary* (1968 -
w/p), *Crescendo* (1969 -w/p), *The
Horror of Frankenstein* (1970 - w/p/d),
Lust for a Vampire (1970 - w/d), *Fear in
the Night* (1972 - co-w/p/d)

Peter Sasdy (1934 -)
Hungarian director with many TV credits to his name (including two
episodes of Hammer's *Journey to the
Unknown*) and experience as a theatre
producer and critic. Came to Britain
after the uprising and studied drama at
Bristol University, after which he
joined the BBC. His first feature film
was Hammer's *Taste the Blood of
Dracula* in 1970, to which he brought a
certain visual flair, though his best film
for them is undoubtedly *Hands of the
Ripper*. Other genre films include
*Nothing but the Night, Doomwatch, I
Don't Want to be Born* and *Welcome
to Blood City*.

Hammer credits:
The New People (1969 - *Journey to
the Unknown* episode), *Girl of my
Dreams* (1969 - *Journey to the
Unknown* episode), *Taste the Blood of
Dracula* (1970), *Countess Dracula*
(1970), *Hands of the Ripper* (1971),
Sweet Scent of Death (1984 -
*Hammer House of Mystery and
Suspense* TVM), *The Late Nancy
Irving* (1984 - *Hammer House of
Mystery and Suspense* TVM, *Last
Video and Testament* (1984 - *Hammer
House of Mystery and Suspense* TVM)

Schurmann, Gerard (1928 -)
British composer with several concert
works and operas to his credit. Best
known, however, for a handful of
throat-grabbing horror scores, the
most infamous of which is for *Horrors
of the Black Museum* (1959).

Hammer credits:
The Camp on Blood Island (1958),

The Lost Continent (1968)
Searle, Francis (1909 -)
British writer and director with many
second features to his credit (*A Girl in
a Million, Never Look Back, Dead
Man's Evidence, Night of the Prowler*,
etc.), many of them for either Hammer
or Danziger. Work mainly routine.

Hammer credits:
Celia (1949 - co-w/d), *The Man in
Black* (1950 - story/d), *Someone at the
Door* (1950 - d), *The Lady Craved
Excitement* (1950 -co-w/d), *The
Rossiter Case* (1951 - co-w/d),
Cloudburst (1951 -co-w/d), *A Case for
P. C. 49* (1951 - d), *Whispering Smith
Hits London* (1952 - d), *Never Look
Back* (1952 - co-w/d)

Sewell, Vernon (1903 -)
British writer, producer and director
with experience as an editor and art
director. Many low budget films to his
credit, including *The Ghosts of
Berkeley Square, The Ghost Ship,
House of Mystery, The Blood Beast
Terror, Curse of the Crimson Altar* (aka
The Crimson Cult) and *Burke and
Hare*.

Hammer credits:
The Jack of Diamonds (1949 - p/d),
The Dark Light (1951 - w/d), *The Black
Widow* (1951 - d).

Sharp, Don (1922 -)
Tasmanian-born director who began
his career as an actor. Came to Britain
after World War Two and went to
work with Group Three. Began directing low budget thrillers and musicals
in the mid 50s (*The Golden Disc, The
Adventures of Hal 5, It's all
Happening*, etc.) before graduating to
genre films, his first for Hammer being
Kiss of the Vampire. Was also responsible for the stunning second unit
work on *Those Magnificent Men in
their Flying Machines*, and *Puppet on
a Chain*, as well as such films as
*Witchcraft, The Face of Fu Manchu,
Vurse of the Fly, The Brides of Fu
Manchu, Taste of Excitement,
Psychomania, The Thirty-Nine Steps*
and *Bear Island*. TV work includes the
popular mini-series *A Woman of
Substance* and TV sequels.

Hammer credits:
Kiss of the Vampire (1963), *The
Devil-Ship Pirates* (1964), *Rasputin -
The Mad Monk* (1965)

Shelley, Barbara (1933 -)
Beautiful, sadly under-used British
actress who began her career as a
model before taking on small parts in a
number of Italian films. Made her
genre debut with *Cat Girl* in 1957 after
which she became something of a
Hammer mainstay, her first film for
them being *The Camp on Blood Island*
in 1957. Other genre entries include
*Blood of the Vampire, Village of the
Damned* and *Ghost Story*.

Hammer credits:
The Camp on Blood Island (1957),
Shadow of the Cat (1961), *The Gorgon*
(1964), *The Secret of Blood Island*
(1964), *Dracula -Prince of Darkness*
(1966), *Rasputin - The Mad Monk*
(1966), *Quatermass and the Pit* (1967)

Skeggs, Roy (1934 -)
British producer and executive who
began his career as an accountant,
first working for Douglas Fairbanks
Productions in 1956. In 1963 he
became Hammer's production accountant, then company accountant and
secretary. Became a production supervisor in 1970 on such films as *Blood
from the Mummy's Tomb* and *Dr
Jekyll and Sister Hyde*, etc. Produced
his first film, Hammer's *Straight on Till
Morning*, in 1972. Formed Cinema
Arts in 1979 with then partner Brian
Lawrence and produced *George and
Mildred* and *Rising Damp*. Took control
of Hammer with Brian Lawrence after
its collapse in 1979 and produced
Hammer House of Horror (1980) and
*Hammer House of Mystery and
Suspence* (1984) for television. Is now
working with Warner and
Donner-Schuler-Donner on a number
of Hammer remakes.

Hammer credits:
Straight on till Morning (1972), *The
Satanic Rites of Dracula* (1973),
*Frankenstein and the Monster from
Hell* (1973), *Love Thy Neighbour*
(1973), *Man at the Top* (1973 - exec p),
Man About the House (1975), *To the
Devil... A Daughter* (1976)

Slaney, Ivor
British composer with many forget-
table second feature scores to his
credit, a good many of them for
Hammer. Took over as Hammer's resident composer after the departure of

Frank Spencer at the end of 1952. Other scores include *Prey, Terror* and *Death Ship*.

Hammer credits:
The Flanagan Boy (1953), *The Gambler and the Lady* (1953), *The Saint's Return* (1953), *Spaceways* (1953), *Face the Music* (1954), *Blood Orange* (1954), *Five Days* (1954*), The Stranger Came Home* (1954), *Murder by Proxy* (1954)

Spencer, Frank
British composer whose credits include a good many of Hammer's early second feature mysteries, his work for which was adequate but unambitious - as were the films.

Hammer credits:
Dr Morelle - The Case of the Missing Heiress (1949), The Adventures of P.C. 49 (1949), *Dick Barton at Bay* (1950), *The Lady Craved Excitement* (1950), *The Man in Black* (1950), *Meet Simon Cherry* (1950), *Room to Let* (1950), *Someone at the Door* (1950), *A Case for P.C. 49* (1950), *Cloudburst* (1951), *The Dark Light* (1951), *To Have and to Hold* (1951), *Death of an Angel* (1952), *The Last Page* (1952)

Stannard, Don (1916 - 1949)
British actor who played special agent Dick Barton in three films for Hammer/Exclusive. Died in a car crash before a fourth Barton was filmed.

Hammer credits:
Death in High Heels (1947), *Dick Barton - Special Agent* (1948 - aka *Dick Barton - Detective*), *Dick Barton Strikes Back* (1949), *Dick Barton At Bay* (1950)

Stannard, Roy
British art director who worked on two of Hammer's later films, most notably *Hands of the Ripper*.

Hammer credits:
Hands of the Ripper (1971), *Twins of Evil* (1971)

Stapleton, Cyril
American bandleader who appeared in a couple of Hammer's musical shorts.

Hammer credits:
Cyril Stapleton and the Showband

(1955), *Just for You* (1956)
Styles, Michael (1933 -)
British producer who, after a time in Canada, returned to Britain in 1958 when he joined ATV as a sports producer, graduating to drama with *A Month in the Country* and *Luther*. First film as a producer was *Monique* for Tyburn, after which came Hammer's "Carmilla" trilogy with his partner Harry Fine, with whom he also formed Fantale Films (*Fright, To Kill a Stranger*, etc.).

Hammer credits:
The Vampire Lovers (1970 - co-p), *Lust for a Vampire* (1971 -co-p), *Twins of Evil* (1971 - co-p)

Sykes, Peter (1939 -)
Australian-born director, a former actor and dancer. Came to Britain in 1963, where he found work in television (*The Avengers*, etc.). Directed Hammer's last genre film, *To the Devil... A Daughter*. Other credits include *Steptoe and Son Ride Again, The House in Nightmare Park, Venom* and *Crazy House*.

Hammer credits:
Demons of the Mind (1972), *To the Devil... A Daughter* (1976)

Tucker, Forrest (1919 - 1986)
American leading man (*The Yearling, The Sands of Iwo Jima, The Wild Blue Yonder*, etc.), brought over to bolster the American box office potential of a couple of Hammer films.

Hammer credits:
Break in the Circle (1956), *The Abominable Snowman* (1957)

Troughton, Patrick (1920 - 1987)
British character actor. Was TV's first Robin Hood and second Doctor Who. Film credits include *Jason and the Argonauts, The Omen, Sinbad and The Eye of the Tiger*.

Hammer credits:
The Curse of Frankenstein (1957), *The Viking Queen* (1967), *Scars of Dracula* (1970)

Tully, Geoffrey M. see **Tully, Montgomery**

Tully, Montgomery (1904 -)
British director with many second features to his credit, including *Murder in Reverse, The Hypnotist, Clash by Night, Battle Beneath the Earth* and *The Terrornauts*.

Hammer credits:
Five Days (1954), *36 Hours* (1954*), The Glass Cage* (1955*), I Only Arsked* (1959)

Varney, Reg (1917 -)
British comedy actor on television (*The Rag Trade, On The Buses*) and film (*The Great St Trinian's Train Robbery, The Best Pair of Legs in the Business*, etc.).

Hammer credits:
On the Buses (1971), *Mutiny on the Buses* (1972), *Holiday on the Buses* (1973)

Vickers, Mike
British composer, former member of Manfred Mann, whose only score for Hammer was for the badly mis-judged *Dracula A.D. 1972*. Other credits include *At the Earth's Core, Warlords of the Atlantis,* etc.

Walters, Thorley (1913 - 1991)
British comedy character actor with a penchant for buffoons and fussy officials. One of Hammer's very best supporting players. Other credits include *Carleton Browne of the F. O., Two-way Stretch, The Adventure of Sherlock Holmes' Smarter Brother, The People that time Forgot* and *The Sign of Four* (TVM).

Hammer credits:
Don't Panic, Chaps! (1959), *The Phantom of the Opera* (1962), *Dracula - Prince of Darkness* (1966), *Frankenstein Created Woman* (1967), *Frankenstein Must be Destroyed* (1969), *Vampire Circus* (1972)

Whitaker, David
British composer/conductor/arranger/ songwriter, trained at London's Guildhall School of Music. His first film score was for the Jerry Lewis 'comedy' *Don't Raise the Bridge, Lower the River* (1967). The seventies proved to be a prolific period for him and includ-

ed many genre entries (*Blind Terror, Vampira, Dominique,* etc.). His atmospheric *Vampire Circus* score for Hammer is perhaps his best, closely followed by *Dr Jekyll and Sister Hyde.* His score for *The Sword and the Sorcerer* won him the Best Original Score Award from The Academy of Science Fiction.

Hammer credits:
Dr Jekyll and Sister Hyde (1971), *Vampire Circus* (1972)

Wicking, Christopher (1944 -)
British screenwriter, former journalist, who was also one of Hammer's story editors. Credits include *The Oblong Box* (additional dialogue), *Scream and Scream Again, Cry of the Banshee, Murders in the Rue Morgue* and *Venom* (co-w).

Hammer credits:
Blood from the Mummy's Tomb (1971 - w), *Demons of the Mind* (1972 w/ co-story), *To the Devil... A Daughter* (1976 - co-w)

Williams, Cedric
British cinematographer who worked on several of Hammer/Exclusive's early second features.

Hammer credits:
Dr Morelle - The Case of the Missing Heiress (1949), *Dick Barton Strikes Back* (1949), *Celia* (1949), *The Adventures of P. C. 49* (1949), *The Man in Black* (1950), *Meet Simon Cherry* (1950), *Room to Let* (1950)

Williamson, Malcolm (1931 -)
Australian born composer/conductor, latterly Master of the Queen's Music. Many documentary scores to his credit. His work for Hammer has been somewhat sporadic and lacklustre however, his best effort for them being 1960's *Brides of Dracula.*

Hammer credits:
The Brides of Dracula (1960), *Crescendo* (1969), *Horror of Frankenstein* (1970)

Wills, J. (Jim) Elder
British art director, a former stage designer who, for a short period, turned to direction in the thirties with such films as *Big Fella.* A company director with Hammer in the thirties,

he later returned to the company in the fifties as an art director.

Hammer credits:
The Song of Freedom (1936 - d), *Sporting Love* (1937 - d), *Mantrap* (1952 - ad), *The Gambler and the Lady* (1953 - ad), *Four-sided Triangle* (1953 - ad), *Spaceways* (1953 - ad), *The Saint's Return* (1953 - ad), *Face the Music* (1954 - ad), *Blood Orange* (1954 -ad), *The House Across the Lake* (1954 - ad), *The Stranger Came Home* (1954 - ad), *Five Days* (1954 - ad), *36 Hours* (1954 - ad), *Men of Sherwood Forest* (1954 - ad), *Mask of Dust* (1954 - ad), *Break in the Circle* (1955 - ad), *Third Party Risk* (1955 - ad), *Murder by Proxy* (1955 - ad), *The Glass Cage* (1955 - ad), *The Quatermass Experiment* (1955 - ad)

Winstone, Eric
Popular British bandleader who top-lined two of Hammer's musical featurettes in the mid to late fifties. Also scored the featurette *The Right Person* for them.

Hammer credits:
The Eric Winstone Bandshow (1955), *The Right Person* (1955 - m only), *Eric Winstone's Stagecoach* (1956)

Woodbridge, George (1907 - 1973)
Portly, gravel-voiced British character actor, best remembered for playing 'Stryker of the Yard' in a number of fifties featurettes (*The Case of the Second Shot, The Case of the Marriage Bureau, The Case of the Black Falcon,* etc.). Popped up in a number of Hammer films, usually as an inn keeper or policeman. Other credits numerous (*The October Man, Richard III, What a Carve Up, Heavens Above, Where's Jack?* etc.). Finished his career with the children's series *Pipkins.*

Hammer credits:
Cloudburst (1951), *The Flanagan Boy* (1953), *Third Party Risk* (1955), *The Revenge of Frankenstein* (1958), *Dracula* (1958), *The Mummy* (1959), *Brides of Dracula* (1960), *Curse of the Werewolf* (1960), *Dracula - Prince of Darkness* (1966), *The Reptile* (1966)

Wordsworth, Richard
British stage actor, the great-great-grandson of the poet

Wordsworth, whose first film appearance was as the mute Victor Caroon in Hammer's *The Quatermass Experiment.* Other credits include *Lock up your Daughters.*

Hammer credits:
The Quatermass Experiment (1955), *The Camp on Blood Island* (1958), *The Revenge of Frankenstein* (1958), *The Curse of the Werewolf* (1961)

Wyer, Reginald (Reg)
British cinematographer with many low budget films to his credit, including four for Hammer/Exclusive.

Hammer credits:
Never look Back (1953), *Mantrap* (1952), *Four-Sided Triangle* (1953), *Spaceways* (1953)

Young, Aida
British producer who worked her way up from third assistant and second assistant director (on *The Quatermass Experiment*). Joined Michael Carreras's Capricorn Productions in 1963 and acted as his associate producer on *What a Crazy World* and several Hammer films (*She, One Million Years B. C., Slave Girls, The Vengeance of She*). Graduated successfully to fully-fledged producer with *Dracula Has Risen from the Grave.*

Hammer credits:
Dracula Has Risen from the Grave (1968), *Taste the Blood of Dracula* (1970), *Scars of Dracula* (1970), *When Dinosaurs Ruled the Earth* (1970), *Hands of the Ripper* (1971)

Young, Robert
British director with television experience. His first feature film was Hammer's excellent *Vampire Circus* (1971). Also directed *Charlie Boy* (1980), an episode of *Hammer House of Horror.*

Younger, Henry see **Carreras, Michael**

Zenobia, Ludmilla (1808 - 1996)
Beautiful, enduringly youthful actress, of obscure Central European origins. Rumoured to be a direct descendent of Vlad the Impaler - the Transylvanian Count on whose exploits the Dracula legend is based.

Hammer credits:

UNMADE HAMMER

Like all film companies, Hammer owned a large
quantity of projects (scripts, novels, ploy synopses, story suggestions, etc), several of
which, though considered for production, finally
never made it to the screen for one reason or
another. The following is a year by year list of
unmade Hammer projects. Proposed television
projects, never realised, include:

KING CHARLES AND THE ROUNDHEADS
  (announced 1955)
FRIAR TUCK (announced 1956)
STAND AND DELIVER (announced 1956)
A HOLIDAY FOR SIMON (announced 1956)
DEER SLAYER (announced 1956)
BUILD US A DAM (announced 1957)
CHARTER TO DANGER (announced 1957)
CHORUS OF ECHOES (announced 1957)
NIGHT CREATURES (announced 1957)
NEVER LET GO (announced 1958)
THE REVENGE OF DRACULA
  (announced 1958)
AND THEN FRANKENSTEIN CREATED
  WOMAN (announced 1959)
THE BRUTAL LAND (announced 1959)
THE RAPE OF SABENA (aka *The Inquisitor*,
  (announced 1959 and 1960)
THE MAN WITH TWO SHADOWS
  (announced 1960)
THE BIG WHEEL (announced 1960)
SEE NO EVIL (announced 1960)
ONE MORE RIVER (announced 1960)
THE BLACK HOLE OF CALCUTTA
  (announced 1960)
THE AMOROUS PAWN (announced 1961,
  made in 1962 by British Lion/Covent Garden
  Films)
RUFFIANS (announced 1962)
LOVE IN SMOKY REGIONS (announced 1962)
THE CAPTIVES (announced 1963)
BRAINSTORM (announced 1963)
THE MUTATION (announced 1964)
THE PIT OF DOOM
  (aka *The Pit*, announced 1966)
DISCIPLE OF VENGEANCE (announced 1967)

THE HAUNTING OF TOBY JUGG
  (announced 1967)
THE RELUCTANT VIRGIN (aka *The Bride of
  Newgate Prison*, announced 1967 and 1971)
BLOOD OF THE FOREIGN LEGION
  (announced 1967)
THE KA OF GIFFORD HILARY
  (announced 1967)
THE FAIRY TALE MAN (announced 1968)
WOLFSHEAD: THE LEGEND OF ROBIN HOOD
  (announced 1969, filmed for television in
  1969 by LWT)
QUATERMASS 4 (fourth instalment in the
  series, announced 1969, filmed for television
  in 1978 as *Quatermass* by Euston Films)
ZEPPELIN VS PTERODACTYLS
  (announced 1969)
THE ECSTACY OF DORIAN GRAY
  (announced 1970)
IN THE SUN (announced 1970)
THE RAG TRADE GOES MOD
  (announced 1971)
KALI: DEVIL BRIDE OF DRACULA
  (announced 1971 and 1974)
KING KONG (announced 1971)
LORNA DOONE (announced 1972)
HIGH PRIEST OF VAMPIRES (announced 1972)
NEARER AND DEARER (proposed sequel to
  Nearest and Dearest, announced 1972)
THE GOLDFISH BOWL (announced 1972)
MISTRESS OF THE SEAS (announced 1972,
  filmed in 1995 as *Cutthroat Island* by another
  company)
DISASTER IN SPACE (proposed sequel to
  Moon Zero Two, announced 1970)
DANTE'S INFERNO (announced 1971)
THE MAN WHO LAUGHED (announced 1971)
DINOSAUR GIRL (proposed sequel to *When
  Dinosaurs Ruled the Earth*, announced 1971)
PAYMENT IN FEAR (announced 1972)
A GATHERING OF VULTURES
  (announced 1972)
JUST FOR KICKS (announced 1972)
SWORD OF ROBIN HOOD
  (announced 1972 and 1979)
THE GODMOTHER (announced 1972)
VAMPIRE VIRGINS (announced 1972)

THE DISCIPLE (announced 1972, filmed in
  1972 as *The Disciple of Death* by another
  company)
A SCENT OF NEW-MOWN HAY
  (announced 1972)
VAMPIRE HUNTERS (proposed sequel to *The
  Vampire Lovers*, *Lust for a Vampire* and *Twins
  of Evil*, announced 1972)
VLAD THE IMPALER (announced 1972)
SHOOT (announced 1972)
THE SAVAGE JACKBOOT (announced 1972)
VICTIM OF HIS IMAGINATION
  (announced 1972)
MURDERS IN THE MOULIN ROUGE (aka *The
  Soho Murders*, announced 1972)
STONES OF EVIL (announced 1972)
WHEN THE EARTH CRACKED OPEN
  (announced 1972)
MONSTER OF THE NIGHT (announced 1972)
ON THE BUSES 4 (proposed fourth instalment
  of the series, announced 1973)
RESTLESS (announced 1973)
VILLAGE OF VAMPIRES (announced 1973)
BURY HIM DARKLY (announced 1973)
VAULT OF BLOOD (announced 1973)
THE INSATIABLE THIRST OF DRACULA
  (announced 1974)
EYE FOR AN EYE (announced 1974)
THE EXPERIMENT (announced 1974)
THE REVENGE OF THE CHILDREN
  (announced 1974)
CALLAN (announced 1974, made in 1974 by
  EMI/Magnum Productions)
ALLAN QUATERMAIN ESQ: HIS QUEST FOR
  THE HOLY FLOWER (announced 1974)
THE SATANIST (announced 1975)
VAMPIRELLA (announced 1975)
NESSIE (announced 1976)
THE DRACULA ODYSSEY (announced 1976)
DEAD OF NIGHT (announced 1978)
DRACULA (announced 1978)
JACK THE RIPPER GOES WEST
  (announced 1978)
DEATH RATTLE (announced 1978)
DRACULA... WHO? (announced 1983)
DRACULA - THE BEGINNING (announced 1984)

filmography & reviews

The following is an A-Z critique of every Hammer film ever made. The year and country of origin, running time and colour process is listed for each entry, as are all the relevant cast and credit details. Those credits listed in capitals denote a stronger than average contribution to a film, be it in writing, direction, photography, music or performance, etc. Credit abbreviations are as follows:

p: producer
exec p: executive producer
w: writer
d: director
ph: photographer
m: music
ed: editor
ad: art director
pd: production designer
cos: costumes
sp: special effects
sound: sound recording
TVM: TV movie

The ratings are as follows:

no stars = poor
* = average
** = good
*** = excellent
**** = a classic

THE ABOMINABLE SNOWMAN **
GB 1957 91m bw Hammerscope

Explorers in the Himalayas searching for the Yeti find their numbers decreasing one by one.
Eerily effective, intelligently scripted addition to Hammer's gallery of monsters, though the Yeti themselves are only fleetingly glimpsed. Also known as THE ABOMINABLE SNOWMAN OF THE HIMALAYAS.

p: Aubrey Baring for Hammer/Clarion
exec p: Michael Carreras
w: NIGEL KNEALE from his TV play
d: VAL GUEST
ph: Arthur Grant
m: Humphrey Searle
md: John Hollingsworth
ed: Bill Lenny

pd: Bernard Robinson
cos: Beatrice Dawson
sound: Jock May
make-up: Phil Leakey
associate p: Anthony Nelson Keys

PETER CUSHING, Forrest Tucker, Maureen Connell, Richard Wattis, ARNOLD MARLE, Robert Brown

THE ABOMINABLE SNOWMAN OF THE HIMALAYAS see THE ABOMINABLE SNOWMAN

THE ADVENTURES OF P.C. 49
GB 1949 60m bw

PC 49 disguises himself as a villain in order to infiltrate a gang of thieves.
Cheaply produced programme filler from the BBC radio series. DIXON OF DOCK GREEN it ain't. A CASE FOR PC 49 followed in 1950.

p: Anthony Hinds for Exclusive
w: Alan Stranks, Vernon Harris
d: Godfrey Grayson
ph: Cedric Williams
md: Frank Spencer, Rupert Grayson
ed: Ray Pitt
ad: James Mordant
sound: Edgar Vetter

Hugh Lattimer, Patricia Cutts, John Penrose, Pat Nye, Annette Simmons, Arthur Brandler

AND THE WALL CAME TUMBLING DOWN
GB 1984 74m colour TVM

The demolition of an old church releases an evil force.
Perhaps slightly more tolerable than most of the movies in the HAMMER HOUSE OF MYSTERY AND SUSPENSE tele-series (aka FOX MYSTERY THEATRE), but even that's not saying very much.

p: Roy Skeggs for Hammer/Twentieth Century Fox
w: Dennis Spooner, John Peacock
d: Paul Annett
ph: Frank Watts
m: Anthony Page
md: Philip Martell
ed: Bob Dearberg
ad: Heather Armitage

Gareth Hunt, Barbi Benton, Brian Deacon, Peter Wyngarde, Patricia Hayes, Carol Royal, Ralph Michael, Robert James, Gary Waldhorn, Richard Hampton

THE ANNIVERSARY *
GB 1968 95m Technicolor

The one-eyed mother of a family of building contractors plays a malevolent game of cat and mouse with her sons when they gather to celebrate her anniversary.

Delightfully camp black comedy melodrama with a cherishable star performance. The adaptation is variable, however, and some of the supporting performances are wooden to say the least.

p: Jimmy Sangster for Hammer/Warner
w: Jimmy Sangster
play: BILL MCILWRAITH
d: Roy Ward Baker
ph: Harry Waxman
md: Philip Martell
ed: James Needs, Peter Weatherley
ad: Reece Pemberton
cos: Mary Gibson
sound: Les Hammond, A. W. Lumkin

BETTE DAVIS, Jack Hedley, JAMES COSSINS, SHEILA HANCOCK, Elaine Taylor, Christian Roberts, Timothy Bateson

BAD BLONDE see THE FLANAGN BOY

BIG DEADLY GAME see THIRD PARTY RISK

BLACK CARRION
GB 1984 74m colour TVM

A journalist searches for two pop stars who mysteriously disappeared in the 1960s.
One of several unwatchable tele-thrillers which formed THE HAMMER HOUSE OF MYSTERY AND SUSPENSE series (aka FOX MYSTERY THEATRE).

p: Roy Skeggs for Hammer/Twentieth Century Fox
w/d: John Hough
ph: Brian West
m: Paul Patterson
md: Philip Martell
ed: Bob Dearberg
ad: Carolyn Jones

Season Hubley, Leigh Lawson, Norman Bird, Alan Love, Diana King, Julian Littman, William Hootkins

THE BLACK GLOVE see FACE THE MUSIC
THE BLACK WIDOW
GB 1951 62m bw

When a murder plot goes wrong, a man discovers the truth about his wife.
Intriguingly plotted but otherwise routinely handled thriller out of which much more could have been made. Like much of Exclusive's product, it was based on a successful radio serial.

p: Anthony Hinds for Ecxlusive
w: Alan MacKinnon
serial: Lester Powell
d: Vernon Sewell
ph: Walter Harvey
ed: James Needs

Christine Norden, Robert Ayres, Anthony Forwood, John Longden, Joghn Harvey, Jennifer Jayne

BLACKOUT see MURDER BY PROXY

BLOOD FROM THE MUMMY'S TOMB *
GB 1971 94m Technicolor

A young woman is possessed by the spirit of a mummy discovered by her father on a secret expedition.
Competently mounted though less than wholly satisfactory transcription of one of Bram Stoker's lesser known novels, later tackled with even less success as THE AWAKENING in 1980. Studio head Michael Carreras stepped in to complete the film when director Seth Holt died during production.

p: Howard Brandy for Hammer
w: Christopher Wicking
novel: Bram Stoker
d: Seth Holt (and Michael Carreras)
ph: Arthur Grant
m: Tristam Cary
md: Philip Martell
ed: Peter Weatherly
ad: Scott MacGregor
cos: Rosemary Burrows
sp: Michael Collins
sound: Tony Dawe

Valerie Leon, Andrew Keir, James Villiers, Hugh Burden, George Coulouris, Rosalie Crutchley, Aubrey Morris, David Markham

BLOOD ORANGE
GB 1953 82m bw

Murder and theft plague a London fashion house.
Routine second feature, pretty plain

even by Exclusive's standards. Certainly not worthy of its imported star. Also known as THREE STOPS TO MURDER.

p: Michael Carreras for Exclusive
w: Jan Read
d: Terence Fisher
ph: Jimmy Harvey
md: Ivor Slaney
ed: Maurice Rootes
ad: J. Elder Wills
cos: Ben Pearson

Tom Conway (playing a character named Tom Conway), Mila Parley, Naomi Chance, Eric Pohlman, Richard Wattis, Eileen Way, Margaret Halstan, Delphi Lawrence.

BLOOD WILL HAVE BLOOD see DEMONS OF THE MIND

BREAK IN THE CIRCLE
GB 1956 91m Eastmancolor

The captain of a small fishing boat agrees to help smuggle a German scientist into Britain.
Mild location-filmed thriller, surprisingly shot in colour given its B-picture status. Better than average cast, too.

p: Michael Carreras for Exclusive
w/d: Val Guest
novel: Philip Loraine
ph: Walter Harvey
m: Doreen Corwithen
md: John Hollingsworth
ed: Bill Lenny
ad: J. Elder Wills
cos: Molly Arbuthnot
sound: H. C. Pearson, Ken Cameron
production manager: Jimmy Sangster

Forrest Tucker, Eva Bartok, Marius Goring, Guy Middleton, Arnold Marle, Eric Pohlmann, Reginald Beckwith

BRED TO STAY
GB 1947 36m bw
Long unseen documentary featurette on the breeding of French race horses.

p: A. A. Housset for Exclusive
w/d: A. A. Housset

THE BRIDES OF DRACULA **
GB 1960 85m Technicolor

A lady traveller staying at a lonely castle accidentally frees a vampire. Well mounted vampire saga in Hammer's very best tradition, with plenty of pace and atmosphere. One of the studio's key films.

p: Anthony Hinds for Hammer/Universal/Hotspur
w: Jimmy Sangster, Peter Bryan, Edward Percy
d: TERENCE FISHER
ph: JACK ASHER
m: Malcolm Williamson
md: John Hollingsworth
ed: James Needs, Alfred Cox
pd: Bernard Robinson
cos: Molly Arbuthnot
sp: Sydney Pearson
sound: Jock May
make-up: Roy Ashton

PETER CUSHING, DAVID PEEL (as Baron Meinster), MARTITA HUNT, Yvonne Molnaur, Andree Melly, Mona Washbourne, FREDA JACKSON, Henry Oscar, Miles Malleson

THE BRIGAND OF KANDAHAR
GB 1965 81m Technicolor 'Scope

In the 1850s, life at an Indian outpost is interrupted by the arrival of murderous bandits, to whom a Bengal Lancer swaps alliegence.
Stale nonsense, unimaginatively handled. Further hampered by some very obvious studio work.

p: Anthony Nelson Keys for Hammer/Columbia
w/d: John Gilling
ph: Reg Wyer
m: Don Banks
md: Philip Martell
ed: James Needs
pd: Bernard Robinson

Oliver Reed, Ronald Lewis, Duncan Lamont, Glyn Houston, Yvonne Romain, Catherine Woodville

CALL HIM MR SHATTER see SHATTER

THE CAMP ON BLOOD ISLAND
GB 1958 81m bw Megascope

An account of the attrocities suffered by British soldiers inside a Japanese prisoner of war camp, ruled by a sadistic commandant.
Predictable wartime drama with some surprisingly brutal moments, on

which count it managed to stir up a certain degree of controversy at the time. Production competent if uninspired, it was at least an antidote to the usual stiff upper lip-style war films produced during this period.

p: Anthony Hinds for Hammer/Columbia
exec p: Michael Carreras
w: Val Guest, John Manchip White
d: Val Guest
ph: Jack Asher
m: Gerard Schurmann
ed: James Needs, Bill Lenny
ad: John Stoll

Andre Morell, Carl Mohner, Edward Underdown, Michael Goodliffe, Richard Wordsworth, Michael Gwynn, Marne Maitland, Mary Merrall, Barbara Shelley, Walter Fitzgerald, Phil Brown, Ronald Radd

CANDY'S CALENDAR
GB 1946 36m bw

The adventures of Candy the cat. Tame animal featurette which did little for the reputation of the re-emerging Exclusive.

p: Exclusive
d: Horace Shepherd

CAPTAIN CLEGG *
GB 1962 82m Technicolor

A pirate disguises himself as a mild-mannered parish vicar whilst carrying on with his smuggling activities. Lively adventure thriller in the best Hammer tradition. Also known as NIGHT CREATURES.

p: John Temple Smith for Hammer/Universal
w: John Elder (Anthony Hinds), Barbara S. Harper
d: PETER GRAHAM SCOTT
ph: Arthur Grant
m: Don Banks
ed: James Needs, Eric Boyd-Perkins
ad: Bernard Robinson
cos: Molly Arbuthnot
sp: Les Bowie

Peter Cushing, Patrick Allen, Oliver Reed, Michael Ripper, Derek Francis, Milton Reid, Martin Benson, David Lodge, Jack MacGowran

CAPTAIN KRONOS: VAMPIRE HUNTER *

GB 1972 96m Technicolor

A professional vampire hunter rids a European township of life-sucking vampires.
Low budget latter day Hammer horror, quite inventively staged. Sadly none of the planned sequels materialised. Also known as KRONOS.

p: Albert Fennell, Brian Clemens for Hammer
w: Brian Clemens
d: BRIAN CLEMENS
ph: Ian Wilson
m: Laurie Johnson
md: Philip Martlell
ed: James Needs
pd: Robert Jones
cos: Dulcie Midwinter
sound: A. W. Lumkin, Jim Willis

Horst Janson, John Cater, Caroline Munro, Ian Hendry, John Carson, Shane Briant, Wanda Ventham, Lois Dane, William Hobbs

A CASE FOR P.C. 49
GB 1950 79m bw

A model's plans to murder a millionaire are uncovered by a police constable.
Poorly produced low budget programmer, based on a popular BBC radio series.

p: Anthony Hinds for Exclusive
w: Vernon Harris, Alan Stranks
d: Francis Searle
ph: Walter Harvey
md: Frank Spencer
ed: James Needs
ad: no credit given
sound: Edgar Vetter
ass d: Jimmy Sangster

Brian Reece, Joan Shelton, Christine Norden, Leslie Bradley, Gordon Mcleod, Campbell Singer

CASH ON DEMAND *
GB 1963 86m bw

A high-class bank robber posing as an insurance investigator robs a suburban bank.
Taut little low budget suspenser, very adequately put across.

p: Michael Carreras for Hammer/Columbia/Woodpecker
w: Lewis Greifer, David T. Chantler
play: Jacques Gillies

d: QUENTIN LAWRENCE
ph: Arthur Grant
m: Wilfred Josephs
md: John Hollingsworth
ed: James Needs, Eric Boyd-Perkins
ad: Don Mingaye
cos: Mary Arbuthnot
sound: Jock May

PETER CUSHING, ANDRE MORELL,
RICHARD VERNON, Norman Bird,
Edith Sharp

CELIA
GB 1949 67m bw

An actress disguises herself as her
aunt so as to expose her step-uncle,
who she suspectes of being a poisoner.
Mild comedy thriller, not quite the
worst of Exclusive's mediocre output.

p: Anthony Hinds for Exclusive
w: Francis Searle, Edward J. Mason,
A. R. Rawlinson
radio series: Edward J. Mason
d: Francis Searle
ph: Cedric Williams
m: Frank Spencer, Rupert Grayson

Hy Hazell, Bruce Lister, John Bailey,
James Raglan, Elsie Wagstaff,
Lockwood West

A CHALLENGE FOR ROBIN HOOD
GB 1967 96m Technicolor

Robin Hood thwarts the evil Sheriff of
Nottingahm - again.
Acceptable version of the oft-told
story, tolerable enough for Saturday
morning audiences.

p: Clifford Parkes for Hammer
w: Peter Bryan
d: C. Pennington-Richards
ph: Arthur Grant
m: Gary Hughes
md: Philip Martell
ed: James Needs
ad: Maurice Carter
sp: Les Bowie
sound: George Stephenson, Laurie
Barnett

Barrie Ingham, James Hayter, Leon
Greene, John Arnatt, Alfie Bass,
Donald Pickering

CHASE ME CHARLIE! *
GB 1951 46m bw

Refashioned re-release of a 1917

compilation featuring clips from a
selection of Charlie Chaplin's Essanay
shorts, including extracts from The
Champion, At the Show, The Tramp
and The Champion.

p: Exclusive
no other credits available

CHILD'S PLAY
GB 1984 74m colour TVM

A family wake up to discover that
their house is surrounded by an
impenetrable wall.
A mildly intriguing idea which might
have made an entertaining half hour
is unfortunately drawn out to undue
length in yet another almost
unwatchable entry in the disappointing HAMMER HOUSE OF MYSTERY
AND SUSPENSE tele-series (aka FOX
MYSTERY THEATRE).

p: Roy Skeggs for Hammer/Twentieth
Century Fox
w: Graham Wassell
d: Val Guest
ph: Frank Watts
m: David Bedford
md: Philip Martell
ed: Peter Weatherley
ad: Heather Armitage

Mary Crosby, Nicholas Clay, Debbie
Chsan, Suzanne Church, Joanna
Joseph

CLEAN SWEEP
GB 1958 29m bw

Comedy featurette involving a pools
win, long unseen.

p: Anthony Hinds for Hammer
exec p: Michael Carreras
w/d: Maclean Rogers
ph: Arthur Grant
ed: James Needs
ad: Ted Marshall

Eric Barker, Thora Hird, Vera Day, Ian
Whittaker, Wallas Eaton, Bill Fraser

CLOUDBURST
GB 1951 92m bw

A code expert avenges himself
against the criminals who ran down
his wife during a getaway.
Standard second feature fare helped
along by its imported star.

p: Anthony Hinds for Exclusive

w: Leo Marks, Francis Searle
story: Leo Marks
d: Francis Searle
ph: Walter Harvey
m: Frank Spencer
ed: John Ferris

Robert Preston, Elizabeth Sellars,
Colin Tapley, Harold Lang, Sheila
Burrell

COPENHAGEN
GB 1956 16m Eastmancolor
Cinemascope

A tour of the sights in Copenhagen.
Mildly engaging travelogue short,
filmed during location work for THE
RIGHT PERSON.

p: Michael Carreras for Exclusive
d: Michael Carreras
ph: Len Harris and others
m: Eric Winstone
ed: Bill Lenny
narrator: Tom Conway

CORNISH HOLIDAY
GB 1946 33m bw

A look at the tourist spots of
Cornwall.
Travelogue featurette of the kind later
churned out by the British Transport
Film unit.

p: Exclusive
d: Harry Long

THE CORVINI INHERITANCE
GB 1984 74m colour TVM

A video security expert helps a neigh-
bour to trap a man in a ski mask who
has been terrorising her.
Adequate but over-streched
tele-thriller, part of the HAMMER
HOUSE OF MYSTERY AND SUS-
PENSE series (aka FOX MYSTERY
THEATRE).

p: Roy Skeggs for Hammer/Twentieth
Century Fox
w: Davis Fisher
d: Gabrielle Beaumont
ph: Frank Watts
m: David Bedford
md: Philip Martell
ed: Peter Weatherley
ad: Carolyn Scott

David McCallum, Jan Francis, Terence
Alexander, Stephen Yardley, Paul
Bacon, Johnny Wade, Timothy Morand

COUNTESS DRACULA
GB 1971 93m Eastmancolor

An ageing countess discovers that bathing in the blood of virgins restores her youth.
Initially promising but ultimately disappointing variation on a well worn theme. A little more style would have worked wonders, though the star performs well.

p: Alexander Paal for Hammer/Rank
w: Jeremy Paul
story: Alexander Paal, Peter Sasdy, Gabriel Ronay
d: Peter Sasdy
ph: Ken Talbot
m: Harry Robinson
md: Philip Martell
ed: Henry Richardson
ad: Philip Harrison
cos: Raymond Hughes
sp: Bert Luxford
sound: Kevin Sutton, Ken Barker
make-up: Tom Smith
ch: Mia Nardi

INGRID PITT, Nigel Green, Sandor Eles, Maurice Denham, Lesley-Anne Down, Patience Collier, Peter Jeffrey, Jessie Evans

CREATURES THE WORLD FORGOT
GB 1970 95m Technicolor

The lives and battles of a prehistoric tribe.
Dull and rather silly follow-up to Hammer's various other prehistoric adventures.

p: Michael Carreras for Hammer/Columbia
w: Michael Carreras
d: Don Chaffey
ph: Vincent Cox
m: Mario Nascimbene
md: Philip Martell
ed: Chris Barnes
pd: John Stoll
cos: Rosemary Burrows
sp: Syd Pearson
sound: John Streeler
2nd unit ph: Ray Sturgess

Julie Ege, Brian O'Shaughnessy, Robert John, Marcia Fox, Rosalie Cruchley

THE CREEPING UNKNOWN see THE QUATERMASS EXPERIMENT

CRESCENDO *
GB 1969 95m Technicolor

A girl researching the life of a great composer goes to stay with his widow, only to find herself involved in a macabre plot.
Highly derivative thriller in typical Hammer style. Fair enough for those who haven't been here a hundred times before.

p: Michael Carreras for Hammer/Warner
w: Jimmy Sangster, Alfred Shaughnessy
story: Alfred Shaughnessey
d: ALAN GIBSON
ph: Paul Beeson
m: Malcolm Williamson
md: Philip Martell
ed: Chris Barnes
ad: Scott MacGregor
cos: Jackie Breed
sound: Claude Hitchcock

Stefanie Powers, James Olson, Margaretta Scott, Jane Lapotaire, Joss Ackland

CRIME REPORTER
GB 1947 36m bw

A crime reporter connects the murder of a taxi driver to a Soho gang.
One of several early featurettes from Exclusive, about which little information survives.

p: Hal Wilson for Exclusive
w: Jimmy Corbett
d: Ben R. Hart

John Blythe, Stan Paskin, Jackie Brent

THE CRIMSON BLADE see THE SCARLET BLADE

THE CURSE OF FRANKENSTEIN **
GB 1957 83m Eastmancolor

Baron Frankenstein experiments with reanimating the dead, the result being a mutant which goes on the rampage.
Generally spirited and efficient re-telling of the Frankenstein story, notable for establishing Hammer as Britain's leading purveyors of horror and for launching Cushing and Lee as stars of the genre. All in all, a film with much to answer for.

p: Anthony Hinds for Hammer/Warner
exec p: Michael Carreras
w: JIMMY SANGSTER
novel: MARY SHELLEY
d: TERENCE FISHER
ph: JACK ASHER
m: JAMES BERNARD
md: John Hollingsworth
ed: James Needs
pd: Bernard Robinson
ad: Ted Marshall
cos: no credit given
sound: no credit given
make-up: Phil Leakey
associate p: Anthony Nelson Keys

PETER CUSHING, CHRISTOPHER LEE, Hazel Court, Robert Urquhart, Melvyn Hayes, Valerie Gaunt, Noel Hood

THE CURSE OF THE MUMMY'S TOMB
GB 1964 80m Technicolor Techniscope

At the turn of the century, members of an archaeological expedition are murdered one by one by a vengeful mummy, encouraged by his twin brother, himself doomed to eternal life.
Childishly scripted and slackly directed hokum which takes forever to get nowhere in particular. The mummy's first appearance is a long time coming.

p: Michael Carreras for Hammer/Columbia/Swallow
w: Henry Younger (Michael Carreras)
d: Michael Carreras
ph: Otto Heller
m: Carlo Martelli
md: Philip Martell
ed: James Needs, Eric Boyd-Perkins
pd: Bernard Robinson
cos: Betty Adamson, John Briggs
sound: Claude Hitchcock
make-up: Roy Ashton

Ronald Howard, Terence Morgan, Fred Clark, Jeanne Roland, George Pastell, Jack Gwillim, John Paul, Dickie Owen (as The Mummy), Michael Ripper, Harold Goodwin

THE CURSE OF THE WEREWOLF *
GB 1961 92m Technicolor

Having been raped by a raving beggar, a mute servant girl gives birth to a boy who grows up to become a

werewolf.
Curiously slow and ineffective addition to the Hammer horror cycle which, despite goodish production values, becomes tedious to watch before the end, though some consider it a classic.

p: Anthony Hinds for Hammer/Universal
w: John Elder (Anthony Hinds)
novel: Guy Endore
d: Terence Fisher
ph: Arthur Grant
m: Benjamin Frankel
ed: James Needs, Alfred Cox
ad: Bernard Robinson
cos: Molly Arbuthnot
sp: Les Bowie
sound: Jock May
make-up: Roy Ashton

Oliver Reed, Clifford Evans, Catherine Feller, Yvonne Romain, Anthony Dawson, Richard Wordsworth, Warren Mitchell, Michael Ripper, Desmond Llewellyn, Peter Sallis

CYRIL STAPLETON AND THE SHOW BAND
GB 1955 30m Technicolor Cinemascope

Musical featurette with the popular bandleader.
Of interest chiefly for musical historians - and also for being filmed in Cinemascope.

p: Michael Carreras for Hammer/Exclusive
d: Michael Carreras
ph: Geoffrey Unsworth

Cyril Stapleton and the Show Band, Lita Roza, Ray Burns

CZECH MATE
GB 1984 74m colour TVM

A woman's husband disappears whilst they are in Prague and she finds herself in mortal danger.
Watchable what-on-earth-is-going-on thriller, one of the better episodes from the HAMMER HOUSE OF MYSTERY AND SUSPENSE series of tele-movies (aka FOX MYSTERY THEATRE).

p: Roy Skeggs for Hammer/Twentieth Century Fox
w: Jeremy Burnham
d: John Hough

ph: Brian West
m: John McCabe
md: Philip Martell
ed: Peter Weatherley
ad: Carolyn Scott

Susan George, Patrick Mower, Richard Heffer, Peter Vaughan, Stefan Gryff, Sandor Eles, Catherine Nielson

THE DAMNED *
GB 1963 87m bw Hammerscope

A scientist breeds radioactive children in preparation for a nuclear strike.
Sometimes striking but not entirely convincing science fiction piece, of interest chiefly for the talent involved. Also known as THESE ARE THE DAMNED.

p: Anthony Hinds for Hammer/Columbia/Swallow
exec p: Michael Carreras
w: Evan Jones
novel: H.L. Lawrence
d: Joseph Losey
ph: Arthur Grant
m: James Bernard
md: John Hollingsworth
ed: James Needs, Reginald Mills
pd: Bernard Robinson
cos: Molly Arbuthnot
sound: Jock May

Macdonald Carey, Shirley Ann Field, Oliver Reed, Viveca Lindfors, Alexander Knox, Walter Gotell, James Villiers

DANGER LIST
GB 1957 22m bw

Little seen featurette thriller.

p: Anthony Hinds for Exclusive
w: J. D. Scott
d: Leslie Arliss
ph: Arthur Grant
ed: James Needs
ad: Ted Marshall

Philip Friend, Honor Blackman, Mervyn Johns, Constance Fraser

THE DARK LIGHT
GB 1951 66m bw

A group of lighthouse workmen find themselves in danger from a gang of thieves.
Poorly made and dubbed program-

mer, one of Exclusive's shoddiest.

p: Michael Carreras for Exclusive
exec p: Anthony Hinds
w/d: Vernon Sewell

Albert Lieven, David Greene, Norman MacOwan, Martin Benson, Jack Stewart, Joan Carol, Catherine Blake

THE DARK ROAD
GB 1948 70m bw

The rise of a petty thief to underworld crimelord.
Dated crime melodrama, one of Exclusive early programme fillers.

p: Henry Halsted for Exclusive
d: Alfred Goulding

Charles Stuart, Joyce Linden, Anthony Hollies

DAY OF GRACE
GB 1957 26m Eastmancolor Hammerscope

Little seen featurette.

p: Francis Searle for Exclusive
w: Jon Manchip
d: Francis Searle
ph: Denny Densham
ed: Bill Lenny, Stanley Smith
ad: Bernard Robinson

Vincent Winter, John Laurie, Grace Arnold, George Woodbridge, Nora Gordon, David Grahame

DEADLY GAME see THIRD PARTY RISK

DEATH IN HIGH HEELS
GB 1947 47m bw

The police investigate a poisoning at a Bond Street dress shop.
Early crime featurette, long unseen, though of passing interest for the appearance of its leading man, who later played Dick Barton for Exclusive in three increasingly unwatachable programmers.

p: Henry Halsted for Exclusive
w: Christianna Brand
d: Lionel Tomlinson

Don Stannard, Bill Hodge, Veronica Rose

DEATH OF AN ANGEL
GB 1951 68m bw

Locals investigate when a
much-loved doctor's wife is found
murdered.
Unremarkable low budget filler.

p: Anthony Hinds for Exclusive
w: Reginald Long
play: Frank King
d: Charles Saunders
ph: Walter Harvey
md: Frank Spencer
ed: John Ferris
ad: no credit given
sound: Edgar Vetter
ass d: Jimmy Sangster
casting: Michael Carreras

Patrick Barr, Jane Baxter, Jean Lodge,
Raymond Young, Russell Napier, Julie
Somers, Katie Johnson

DEMONS OF THE MIND *
GB 1972 85m Technicolor

In 1830, a Bavarian count locks up his
children, believing them to be mad.
Good looking though confusingly plot-
ted psychological thriller in typical
Hammer style. Also known as
BLOOD WILL HAVE BLOOD.

p: Frank Godwin for Hammer
w: Christopher Wicking
story: Frank Godwin
d: Peter Sykes
ph: Arthur Grant
m: Harry Robinson
md: Philip Martell
ed: Chris Barnes
ad: Michael Stringer
cos: Rosemary Burrows
sound: John Purchese

Paul Jones, Patrick Magee, Yvonne
Mitchell, Robert Hardy, Michael
Hordern, Kenneth J. Warren, Shane
Briant, Virginia Wetherell, Deidre
Costello, Barry Stanton, Sidonie Bond

THE DEVIL RIDES OUT **
GB 1968 95m Technicolor

The Duke de Richleau discovers that
one of his friends is a member of a
Satanic ring and sets out to save him,
only to cross paths with the Devil
himself.
Enjoyable, full-blooded, persuasively
handled version of the Dennis
Wheatley novel, with plenty going on
to keep one watching. A genuine

Hammer classic. Also known as THE
DEVIL'S BRIDE.

p: Anthony Nelson Keys for
Hammer/Associated British
w: Richard Matheson
novel: Dennis Wheatley
d: TERENCE FISHER
ph: ARTHUR GRANT
m: JAMES BERNARD
md: Philip Martell
ed: James Needs, Spencer Reeve
ad: BERNARD ROBINSON
cos: Rosemary Burrows
sp: Michael Stalmer-Hutchins
sound: Ken Rawkins, A. W. Lumkin
cam op: Moray Grant

CHRISTOPHER LEE, CHARLES
GRAY, Leon Greene (dubbed by
Patrick Allen), Patrick Mower, Nike
Arrighi, Gwen Ffrangcon Davies, Paul
Eddington, Sarah Lawson, Rosalyn
Landor, Russell Waters

THE DEVIL'S BRIDE see THE DEVIL
RIDES OUT

THE DEVIL'S OWN see THE
WITCHES

THE DEVIL-SHIP PIRATES
GB 1963 95m Technicolor
Megascope

Spanish pirates put in at a small
Cornish fishing village to make
repairs and terrorise the locals.
Initially lively pirate adventure which
unfortunately goes on much too long.
Adequate Saturday morning fare.

p: Anthony Nelson Keys for
Hammer/Columbia
w: Jimmy Sangster
d: DON SHARP
ph: Michael Reed
m: Gary Hughes
md: John Hollingsworth
ed: James Needs
ad: Bernard Robinson
cos: Rosemary Burrows
sp: Les Bowie
sound: Ken Rawkins

Christopher Lee, Andrew Keir, John
Cairney, Barry Warren, Ernest Clark,
Duncan Lamont, Michael Ripper

DICK BARTON AT BAY
GB 1950 66m bw

Dick Barton helps the police track
down a missing scientist and the

death ray he has invented.
Third and final entry in a brief series
of tatty-looking crime thrillers from
the popular radio series.

p: Henry Halsted for
Exclusive/Marylebone
w: Jackson C. Budd, Ambrose
Grayson, Emma Trechman
story: Ambrose Grayson
d: Godfrey Grayson
ph: Stanley Clinton
m: Rupert Grayson
md: Frank Spencer
ed: Max Brenner
ad: James Merchant
sound: Charles Hasher

Don Stannard, George Ford, Tamara
Desni, Meinhart Maur, Percy Walsh,
Joyce Linden, Campbell Singer, John
Arnatt, Patrick Macnee

DICK BARTON - DETECTIVE see
DICK BARTON - SPECIAL AGENT

DICK BARTON - SPECIAL AGENT
GB 1948 72m bw

Dick Barton prevents foreign agents
from planting germ bombs in Britain's
reservoirs.
First of three low budget programme
fillers from the popular radio series.
Hard to sit through today. Also known
as DICK BARTON - DETECTIVE.

p: Henry Halsted for
Exclusive/Marylebone
w: Alan Stranks, Alfred Goulding
story: Alfred Stranks
d: Alfred Goulding
ph: Stanley Clinton
md: John Bath
ed: Etta Simpson
ad: James Merchant
sound: Charles Hasher

Don Stannard, George Ford, Jack
Shaw, Gillian Maude, Ivor Danvers,
Beatrice Kane, Geoffrey Wincott

DICK BARTON STRIKES BACK
GB 1949 76m bw

Dick Barton tracks down a gang who
have stolen vital atomic apparatus.
Second of three shoddy second features featuring the popular radio
detective.

p: Anthony Hinds, Mae Murray for
Exclusive
w: Elizabeth Baron

story: Ambrose Grayson
d: Godfrey Grayson
ph: Cedric Williams
m: Frank Spencer, Rupert Grayson
ed: Ray Pitt
ad: Ivan King
sound: no credit given

Don Stannard, Sebastian Cabot, Jean
Lodge, James Raglan

DICK TURPIN - HIGHWAYMAN *
GB 1956 30m Eastmancolor
Hammerscope

Dick Turpin steals a bride's dowry and
protects her from the schemes of her
crooked would-be husband.
Agreeable featurette, surprisingly
shot in colour and 'scope. One of the
better examples of its kind.

p: Michael Carreras for Hammer
w: Joel Murcott
d: David Paltenghi
ph: Stephen Dade
m: Eric Winstone
ed: James Needs
ad: Ted Marshall
sound: no credit given
production manager: Jimmy Sangster

Philip Friend, Diane Hart, Alan
Cuthbertson, Raymond Rollet, Hal
Osmond, Norman Mitchell

DIE! DIE! MY DARLING!
see FANATIC

A DISTANT SCREAM
GB 1984 74m colour TVM

A dying man dreams the truth about a
murder he did not commit but was
sent to prison for.
Another time filler from the HAM-
MER HOUSE OF MYSTERY AND
SUSPENSE stable (aka FOX MYS-
TERY THEATRE), most of which are
indistinguishable from each other.

p: Roy Skeggs for Hammer/Twentieth
Century Fox
w: Martin Worth
d: John Hough
ph: Brian West
m: Paul Patterson
md: Philip Martell
ed: Peter Weatherley
ad: Carolyn Scott

David Carradine, Stephanie Beacham,
Stephen Greif, Stephen Chase, Fanny
Carby, Lesley Dunlop

DR MORELLE - THE CASE OF THE
MISSING HEIRESS
GB 1949 73m bw

Dr Morelle investigates the mysterious death of a friend's sister.
Unremarkable mystery thriller derrived from a successful radio series.

p: Anthony Hinds for Exclusive
w: Ambrose Grayson, Roy Plomley
radio series: Wilfred Burr
d: Godfrey Grayson
ph: Cedric Williams
m: Frank Spencer, Rupert Grayson
ed: Ray Pitt
ad: James Marchant

Valentine Dyall, Julia Lang, Philip
Leaver, Peter Drury, Jean Lodge

DR JEKYLL AND SISTER HYDE *
GB 1971 97m Technicolor

Dr Jekyll experiments with female
hormones in the search for a
life-extending serum only to discover
himself turning into a woman.
It had to come, one supposes, yet
despite a predictable plot and some
restricted sets, the results aren't too
bad at all.

p: Brian Clemens, Albert Fennel for
Hammer/EMI
w: Brian Clemens
d: Roy Ward Baker
ph: Norman Warwick
m: David Whitaker
md: Philip Martell
ed: James Needs
ad: Robert Jones
cos: Rosemary Burrows
sound: Bill Rowe
make-up: Trevor Crole-Rees

Ralph Bates, Martine Beswick, Gerald
Sim, Lewis Fiander, Susan Brodrick,
Dorothy Alison, Ivor Dean, Tony
Calvin, Paul Whitsun-Jones, Philip
Madoc

DON'T PANIC, CHAPS!
GB 1959 85m bw

During the war, British and German
troops who have been posted to the
same Adriatic island agree with
eachother to sit the war out in peace.
A promising comic situation.
Unfortunately, the script isn't up to
the task at hand.

p: Teddy Baird for
Hammer/Columbia/ACT
w: Jack Davies
story: Michael Corston, Ronald
Holroyd
d: George Pollack
ph: Arthur Graham
m: Philip Green
md: John Hollingsworth
ed: Harry Aldous
ad: Scott MacGregor

Dennis Price, George Cole, Thorley
Walters, Nicholas Phipps, Harry
Fowler, Percy Herbert, Nadja Regin

DRACULA ****
GB 1958 82m Technicolor

Dracula is pursued to his castle in
Transylvania by his Nemesis
Professor Van Helsing.
Arguably the best of the Hammer
horrors, this pacy, richly coloured
remake of the 1930 movie sees
everyone working hard to preserve
the spirit if not the letter of the book.
Also notable for giving Cushing and
Lee the roles for which they became
synonymous, and for its imaginative
use of limited sets. Also known as
THE HORROR OF DRACULA.

p: Anthony Hinds for Hammer
exec p: Michael Carreras
w: JIMMY SANGSTER
novel: BRAM STOKER
d: TERENCE FISHER
ph: JACK ASHER
m: JAMES BERNARD
md: John Hollingsworth
ed: James Needs, Bill Lenny
ad: BERNARD ROBINSON
cos: Molly Arbuthnot
sp: Sydney Pearson
sound: Jock May
make-up: Phil Leakey
associate p: Anthony Nelson Keys

PETER CUSHING, CHRISTOPHER
LEE, Melissa Stribling, Michael
Gough, Carol Marsh, Miles Malleson,
Geoffrey Bayldon, John Van Eyssen,
Valerie Gaunt

DRACULA A.D. 1972
GB 1972 95m Eastmancolor

A Satanist revives Dracula in a
desanctified church in modern day
Chelsea.
Abysmal fang and cross flick without
even the saving grace of humour. The
worst of the Hammer Draculas, its

would-be hip dialogue has to be heard to be believed.

p: Josephine Douglas for Hammer/Warner
w: Don Houghton
d: Alan Gibson
ph: Dick Bush
m: Mike Vickers
md: Philip Martell
ed: James Needs
ad: Don Mingaye
cos: Rosemary Burrows
sp: Les Bowie
sound: A. W. Lumkin, Claude Hitchcock, Bill Rowe

Christopher Lee, Peter Cushing, Christopher Neame (as Johnny Alucard), Stephanie Beecham, Michael Coles, William Ellis, Caroline Munro, Lally Bowers, Michael Kitchen, Marsha Hunt, Janet Key, Philip Muller, David Andrews

DRACULA HAS RISEN FROM THE GRAVE
GB 1968 92m Technicolor

Resuscitated by the blood of a priest, Dracula again terrorises the country-side near his castle.
Lame addition to the on-going series, lacking both excitement and invention, with script and performances of the lowest order. It did pretty well at the box office, though.

p: Aida Young for Hammer/Warner
w: John Elder (Anthony Hinds)
d: Freddie Francis
ph: Arthur Grant
m: James Bernard
md: Philip Martell
ed: James Needs, Spencer Reeve
ad: Bernard Robinson
cos: Jill Thompson
sp: Frank George, Peter Melrose
sound: Ken Rawkins

Christopher Lee, Rupert Davies, Veronica Carlson, Barbara Ewing, Barry Andrews, Michael Ripper

DRACULA - PRINCE OF DARKNESS **
GB 1966 90m Technicolor Techniscope

Four stranded travellers unwittingly spend the night at Castle Dracula. The first and best of the direct sequels to Hammer's DRACULA, though the script itself is little more than a clever re-working of the origi-

nal. Made back to back with RASPUTIN - THE MAD MONK.

p: Anthony Nelson Keys for Hammer/Warner
w: John Sansom (Jimmy Sangster)
story: John Elder (Anthony Hinds)
d: Terence Fisher
ph: Michael Reed
m: JAMES BERNARD
md: Philip Martell
ed: James Needs, Chris Barnes
ad: Bernard Robinson
cos: Rosemary Burrows
sp: Les Bowie
sound: Ken Rawkins

Christopher Lee, Francis Matthews, BARBARA SHELLEY, Charles Tingwell, Suzan Farmer, PHILIP LATH-AM, Andrew Keir, Thorley Walters

THE ERIC WINSTONE BAND SHOW
GB 1955 30m Eastmancolor Cinemascope

Musical featurette with the popular band leader and guests.

p: Michael Carreras for Exclusive
d: Michael Carreras
ph: Geoffrey Unsworth

Eric Winstone and his Orchestra, Alma Cogan, Kenny Baker, The George Mitchell Singers

ERIC WINSTONE'S STAGECOACH
GB 1956 30m Eastmancolor Cinemascope

More musical moments with Eric Winstone and his guests.

p: Michael Carreras for Exclusive
d: Michael Carreras
ph: Geoffrey Unsworth

Eric Winstone and his Orchestra, Alma Cogan, Marion Ryan, The Ray Ellington Quartet

THE EDMUNDO ROS HALF HOUR
GB 1957 30m Eastmancolor Cinemascope

Musical featurette in the by now familiar mould.

p: Michael Carreras for Exclusive
d: Michael Carreras
ph: Geoffrey Unsworth
ed: James Needs
ad: Ted Marshall

The Edmundo Ros Latin American Orchestra, Ines Del Carmen, The Buddy Bradley Dancers, Elizabeth Shelley, Morton Fraser's Harmonica Gang.

THE ENEMY FROM SPACE see QUATERMASS II

THE EVIL OF FRANKENSTEIN *
GB 1964 94m Technicolor

Frankenstein revives one of his previous creations, found preserved in a glacier.
Variably handled third entry in the studio's on-going Frankenstein series in which the Monster's make-up verges on the ludicrous. Good sequences along the way, however.

p: Anthony Hinds for Hammer/Universal
w: John Elder (Anthony Hinds)
d: Freddie Francis
ph: John Wilcox
m: DON BANKS
md: Philip Martlell
ed: James Needs
ad: Don Mingaye
cos: Rosemary Burrows
sp: Les Bowie
sound: Ken Rawkins
make-up: Roy Ashton

Peter Cushing, Sandor Eles, Peter Woodthorpe, Duncan Lamont, David Hutcheson, Katy Wild, Kiwi Kingsaton (as the Monster)

FACE THE MUSIC
GB 1954 84m bw

A trumpeter finds himself wrongly accused of a singer's murder. Standard second feature thriller, slightly better than the Exclusive norm. Also known as THE BLACK GLOVE.

p: Michael Carreras for Exclusive/Hammer
w: Ernest Bornemann from his novel
d: Terence Fisher
ph: Jimmy Harvey
m: Ivor Slaney, Kenny Baker
ed: Maurice Rootes
ad: J. Elder Wills

Alex Nicol, Eleanor Summerfield, John Salew, Geoffrey Keen, Paul Carpenter, Ann Hanslip

A FAMILY AFFAIR see LIFE WITH
THE LYONS

FANATIC *
GB 1965 96m Technicolor

Visiting her dead fiance's mother, a
young American woman finds herself
the prisoner of a religious fanatic.
Not quite as much fun as it could
have been, this over the top melodrama benefits chiefly from the presence of its star, who is in fighting
form. Also known as DIE! DIE! MY
DARLING!

p: Anthony Hinds for Hammer/Seven
Arts
w: Richard Matheson
novel: Anne Blaisdel
d: Silvio Narizzano
ph: Arthur Ibbetson
m: Wilfred Josephs
md: Philip Martell
ed: James Needs, John Dunsford
pd: Peter Proud
cos: Mary Gibson
sound: Ken Rawkins

TALLULAH BANKHEAD, Stefanie
Powers, Peter Vaughan, Donald
Sutherland, Yootha Joyce

FEAR IN THE NIGHT *
GB 1972 85m Technicolor

After a nervous breakdown, a young
woman and her husband move to the
country where he has a new teaching
job. When a prowler starts to threat-
en her she begins to suspect foul
play, however.
Routine variation on an oft-used
theme, just about watchable for
those who haven't seen all the other
Hammer versions.

p: Jimmy Sangster for Hammer
exec p: Michael Carreras
w: Jimmy Sangster, Michael Syson
d: Jimmy Sangster
ph: Arthur Grant
m: John McCabe
md: Philip Martell
ed: Peter Weatherley
ad: Don Picton
cos: Rosemary Burrows

Peter Cushing, Ralph Bates, Joan
Collins, Judy Geeson, Gillian Lind,
James Cossins

FIVE DAYS
GB 1954 72m bw

The death of a young businessman
has differing consequences for his
various friends and associates.
So-so drama, not different enough to
be of any real note. Also known as
PAID TO KILL.

p: Anthony Hinds for
Hammer/Exclusive
w: Paul Tabori
d: Montgomery Tully
ph: Jimmy Harvey
m: Ivor Slaney
ed: James Needs
ad: J. Elder Wills

Dane Clark, Paul Carpenter, Thea
Gregory, Cecile Chevreau, Anthony
Forwood, Howard Marion Crawford

FIVE MILLION YEARS TO EARTH see
QUATERMASS AND THE PIT

THE FLANAGAN BOY
GB 1953 81m bw

A merchant seaman is groomed for
boxing stardom.
Occasionally lively but mostly quite
unremarkable low budget ringside
melodrama. Also known as BAD
BLONDE.

p: Anthony Hinds for Exclusive
w: Guy Elmes, Richard Landau
novel: Max Catto
d: Reginald Le Borg
ph: Walter Harvey
m: Ivor Slaney
ed: James Needs
ad: Wilfred Arnold
sound: Bill Salter
ass d: Jimmy Sangster

Tony Wright, Barbara Payton, Sid
James, John Slater, Frederick Valk,
Sidney Burke, Marie Burke

FOUR-SIDED TRIANGLE
GB 1953 81m bw

A scientist clones his girlfriend when
she rejects him. But so does the
clone...
So-so science fiction piece, of interest chiefly for being tried at this time
by this director.

p: Michael Carreras, Alexander Paal
for Hammer/Exclusive
w: Paul Tabori, Terence Fisher
novel: William F. Temple
d: Terence Fisher
ph: Reg Wyer

m: Malcolm Arnold
ed: Maurice Rootes
ad: J. Elder Wills

Stephen Murray, Barbara Payton,
James Hayter, Percy Marmont,
Kynaston Reeves, John Van Eyssen

FRANKENSTEIN AND THE MON-
STER FROM HELL *
GB 1973 99m Technicolor

Baron Frankenstein continues his
experiments within the confines of a
lunatic asylum.
Silly but quite lively final entry in
Hammer's on-going Frankenstein
series, with slightly more style than
had been seen in some of the previous episodes.

p: Roy Skeggs for Hammer
w: John Elder (Anthony Hinds)
d: TERENCE FISHER (his last film)
ph: Brian Probyn
m: JAMES BERNARD
md: Philip Martell
ed: James Needs
ad: SCOTT MACGREGOR
cos: Dulcie Midwinter
sound: Les Hammond
make-up: Eddie Knight

PETER CUSHING, Shane Briant,
Madeleine Smith, Dave Prowse (as
the Monster), Bernard Lee, John
Stratton, Patrick Troughton, Clifford
Mollinson, Charles Lloyd Pack

FRANKENSTEIN CREATED WOMAN *
GB 1966 86m Technicolor

The Baron restores the soul of a
wrongly executed man into the body
of his dead fiancee.
Comparatively mild addition to the
studio's Frankenstein cycle, perhaps
because this time there wasn't an
actual marauding monster. The cutting of the central laboratory scene
doesn't help matters, either, especially as it wrecks the narrative. Still
there are spirited moments.

p: Anthony Nelson Keys for
Hammer/Warner Seven Arts
w: John Elder (Anthony Hinds)
d: Terence Fisher
ph: Arthur Grant
m: James Bernard
md: Philip Martell
ed: James Needs, Spencer Reeve
pd: Bernard Robinson
ad: Don Mingaye

sp: Les Bowie
make-up: George Partleton
sound: Ken Rawkins

Peter Cushing, Susan Denberg,
THORLEY WALTERS, Robert Morris,
Duncan Lamont, Peter Blythe, Barry
Warren, Stuart Middleton, Robert
Morris, Derek Fowlds

FRANKENSTEIN MUST BE
DESTROYED *
GB 1969 96m Technicolor

Frankenstein transplants the brain of
an old associate into a new body so
as to save the secrets it holds there-
in.
Full-blooded Hammer horror, perhaps
the liveliest of their numerous
Frankenstein sequels. Worth a look
for the throat-grabbing pre-credits
sequence alone.

p: Anthony Nelson Keys for
Hammer/Columbia
w: Bert Batt
story: Bert Batt, Anthony Nelson
Keys
d: TERENCE FISHER
ph: Arthur Grant
m: James Bernard
md: Philip Martell
ed: Gordon Hales
ad: Bernard Robinson
cos: Rosemary Burrows
sp: Studio Locations Ltd
sound: Tony Lumkin, Ken Rawkins
make-up: Eddie Knight
ass d: Bert Batt

PETER CUSHING, Simon Ward,
Veronica Carlson, Freddie Jones (as
the Monster), Thorley Walters,
Geoffrey Bayldon, Maxine Audley,
Frank Middlemass, Harold Goodwin,
Peter Copley, Colette O'Neil, Windsor
Davies

THE FULL TREATMENT
GB 1960 109m bw Megascope

A psychiatrist tries to convince a racing driver that he has murdered his
wife.
Overstretched thriller which makes
too little of its various twists and
turns. Also known as STOP ME
BEFORE I KILL.

p: Val Guest for
Hammer/Columbia/Hilary/Falcon
w: Val Guest, Ronald Scott Thorn
novel: Ronald Scott Thorn

d: Val Guest
ph: Gilbert Taylor
m: Stanley Black
ed: Billy Lenny
ad: Tony Masters

Ronald Lewis, Diane Cilento, Claude
Dauphin, Bernard Braden, Francoise
Rosay

FURTHER UP THE CREEK
GB 1958 94m bw Megascope

The crew of an out-of-date frigate
decide to make as much money as
they can out of her last voyage by
taking on passengers.
Innocuous comedy, a follow-up to the
not much funnier UP THE CREEK.

p: Henry Halsted for
Hammer/Byron/Columbia
w: Val Guest, John Warren, Len
Heath
d: Val Guest
ph: Gerald Gibbs
m: Stanley Black
ed: Bill Lenny
ad: George Provis
cos: Molly Arbuthnot
sound: Jock May

David Tomlinson, Frankie Howerd,
Thora Hird, Shirley Eaton, Eric
Pohlmann, Lionel Jeffries, Lionel
Murton, Sam Kydd, John Warren,
David Lodge, Esma Cannon, Michael
Ripper, Stanley Unwin

THE GAMBLER AND THE LADY
GB 1953 74m bw

An American gambler in England
finds himself involved in gang warfare.
Unremarkable second feature filler.
Some sources indicate that Terence
Fisher and Sam Newfield were
involved in its direction.

p: Anthony Hinds for Exclusive
d: Pat Jenkins
ph: Walter Harvey
m: Ivor Slaney
ed: Maurice Rootes
ad: J. Elder Wills

Dane Clark, Naomi Chance, Kathleen
Byron, Meredith Edwards, Anthony
Forwood, Eric Pohlmann

THE GLASS CAGE
GB 1955 59m bw

Investigations follow when a circus
performer is killed after witnessing a
murder.
Standard bottom-of-the-bill thriller
with a slightly better cast than usual.
Also known as THE GLASS TOMB.

p: Anthony Hinds for Exclusive
w: Richard Landau
novel: A. E. Marti
d: Montogomery Tully
ph: Walter Harvey
m: Leonard Salzedo
ed: James Needs
ad: J. Elder Wills

John Ireland, Honor Blackman,
Geoffrey Keen, Eric Pohlmann, Sid
James, Liam Redmond

THE GLASS TOMB see THE GLASS
CAGE

THE GORGON *
GB 1964 83m Technicolor

A small European village is terrorised
by Magera, a Gorgon who can turn
those who dare look into her eyes
into stone.
Slow moving and rather talkative horror story, with the studio obviously
looking for a new monster to exploit.
A few moments of suspense, but
otherwise nothing at all new.

p: Anthony Nelson Keys for Hammer
w: John Gilling
d: Terence Fisher
ph: Michael Reed
m: James Bernard
md: Marcus Dods
ed: James Needs, Eric Boyd-Perkins
pd: Bernard Robinson
cos: Rosemary Burrows
sp: Syd Pearson
sound: Ken Rawkins

Peter Cushing, Christopher Lee,
Barbara Shelley, Richard Pasco,
Patrick Troughton

HANDS OF THE RIPPER *
GB 1971 85m Technicolor

Jack the Ripper's daughter shows
signs of following in her father's footsteps after a nasty childhood experience.
Nicely detailed latter day Hammer
horror with a climax taking place in
the Whispering Gallery of St Paul's.

Production values well above average.

p: Aida Young for Hammer
w: L. W. Davidson
d: PETER SASDY
ph: Kenneth Talbot
m: CHRISTOPHER GUNNING
md: Philip Martell
ed: Chris Barnes
ad: ROY STANNDARD
cos: Rosemary Burrows
sp: Cliff Culley
sound: Kevin Sutton

Eric Porter, Angharad Rees, Dora Bryan, Jane Merrow, Derek Godfrey, Keith Bell, Marjorie Rhodes, Linda Baron, Norman Bird

HEAT WAVE see THE HOUSE ACROSS THE LAKE

HELL IS A CITY *
GB 1959 93m bw Hammerscope

A harrassed police detective tracks down an escaped prisoner who has murdered a man.
Pacy docu-thriller which makes the most of its Manchester locations.

p: Michael Carreras for Hammer/Associated British
w/d: Val Guest
novel: Maurice Proctor
ph: Arthur Grant
m: Stanley Black
ed: James Needs
ad: Robert Jones
cos: Jacky Jackson
sound: Leslie Hammond, Len Shilton, A. W. Lumkin
cam op: Moray Grant

Stanley Baker, John Crawford, DONALD PLEASENCE, Billie Whitelaw, Maxine Audley, George A. Cooper, Joseph Tomelty, Vanda Godsell

HIGHWAY HOLIDAY
GB 1962 15m Eastmancolor

Highlights of a motor holiday through Europe.

p: Ian Lewis for Hammer/Total Oil
d: Ian Lewis

HOLIDAY ON THE BUSES
GB 1973 82m Technicolor

Stan, Jack and Inspector Blake go to work at a summer camp.

Last in a series of three artless big screen comedies derrived from the popular TV sit-com.

p: Ronald Wolfe, Ronald Chesney for Hammer
w: Ronald Wolfe, Ronald Chesney
d: Bryan Izzard
ph: Brian Probyn
m: Dennis King
md: Philip Martell
ed: James Needs
ad: Don Picton
sp: Les Bowie

Reg Varney, Bob Grant, Stephen Lewis, Doris Hare, Michael Robbins, Anna Karen, Wilfred Brambell, Kate Williams, Arthur Mullard, Henry McGee, Adam Rhodes, Gigi Gatti

HORROR OF DRACULA
see DRACULA

HORROR OF FRANKENSTEIN
GB 1970 95m Technicolor

Victor Frankenstein's experiments produce a murderous mutant.
Misguided and wholly unsuccessful rehash of Hammer's own THE CURSE OF FRANKENSTEIN. Wooden acting and a few unwise attempts at humour only make matters worse. Something of an embarrassment for all concerned.

p: Jimmy Sangster for Hammer
w: Jimmy Sangster, Jeremy Burnham
d: Jimmy Sangster
ph: Moray Grant
m: Malcolm Williamson
md: Philip Martell
ed: Chris Barnes
ad: Scott MacGregor
cos: Laura Nightingale
sound: Claude Hitchcock, Terry Lumkin
make-up: Tom Smith

Ralph Bates, Kate O'Mara, Graham Jones, Veronica Carlson, James Hayter, Joan Rice, Dennis Price, Bernard Archand, Dave Prowse (as the Monster), James Cossins, Jon Finch, Terry Duggan

THE HOUND OF THE BASKERVILLES **
GB 1958 86m Technicolor

Sherlock Holmes discovers the truth about a legendary hound from hell.
Well-mounted version of the Conan

Doyle classic with strong production values and performances, let down only by the familiarity of the story itself.

p: Anthony Hinds for Hammer
exec p: Michael Carreras
w: Peter Bryan
novel: Arthur Conan Doyle
d: TERENCE FISHER
ph: JACK ASHER
m: JAMES BERNARD
md: John Hollingsworth
ed: James Needs, Alfred Cox
pd: BERNARD ROBINSON
cos: Molly Arbuthnot
sp: Sydney Pearson
sound: Jock May

PETER CUSHING, ANDRE MORELL, CHRISTOPHER LEE, Francis de Wolff, Marla Landi, Ewen Solon, Miles Malleson, Sam Kydd, John le Mesurier

THE HOUSE ACROSS THE LAKE
GB 1953 68m bw

An author becomes involved with a married woman, whose husband is later found murdered.
Straightforward second feature with predictable plot developments. Also known as HEAT WAVE.

p: Anthony Hinds for Exclusive
w/d: Ken Hughes from his novel
ph: James Harvey
m: Ivor Slaney
ed: James Needs
ad: J. Elder Wills

Alex Nichol, Hillary Brook, Susan Stephen, Sid James, Paul Carpenter, Alan Wheatley
HOUSE OF FRIGHT see THE TWO FACES OF DR JEKYLL

HYSTERIA
GB 1965 85m bw

An amnesiac finds himself involved in a bizarre murder plot.
Yet another variation on TASTE OF FEAR by way of PSYCHO and LES DIABOLIQUES. Mildly diverting for those who haven't been here before, though by no means the best example of its familiar kind.

p: Jimmy Sangster for Hammer/Columbia
w: Jimmy Sangster
d: Freddie Francis

ph: John Wilcox
m: Don Banks
md: Philip Martell
ed: James Needs
pd: Edward Carrick
sound: Cyril Swern

Robert Webber, Lelia Goldoni,
Maurice Denham, Peter Woodthorpe,
Anthony Newlands, Jennifer Jayne

I ONLY ARSKED
GB 1959 82m bw

Misadventures of a group of army
misfits.
Mildly amusing big screen version of
the popular TV sit-com THE ARMY
GAME.

p: Anthony Hinds for
Hammer/Granada
w: Sid Colin, Jack Davies
d: Montgomery Tully
ph: Lionel Banes
m: Benjamin Frankel
md: John Hollingsworth
ed: James Needs, Alfred Cox
ad: John Stoll

Bernard Bresslaw, Michael Medwin,
Alfie Bass, Geoffrey Summer, Charles
Hawtrey, Norman Rossington, David
Lodge

IN POSSESSION
GB 1984 74m colour TVM

A married couple find themselves
experiencing a series of strange
visions.
Perhaps the most tolerable of the
HAMMER HOUSE OF MYSTERY
AND SUSPENSE tele-movies (aka
FOX MYSTERY THEATRE).

p: Roy Skeggs for Hammer/Twentieth
Century Fox
w: Michael J. Bird
d: Val Guest
ph: Brian West
m: Paul Patterson
md: Philip Martell
ed: Peter Weatherley
ad: Carolyn Scott

Carol Lynley, Christopher Cazenove,
Bernard Kay, Vivienne Burgess, Judy
Loe, David Healey

ITALIAN HOLIDAY
GB 1957 10m Eastmancolor

Location filmed travelogue short.

p: Hammer
d: Peter Bryan
ph: Harry Oakes

IT'S A DOG'S LIFE
GB 1949 36m bw

Documentary featurette on the
breeding of greyhounds for racing.

p: Exclusive
d: Leslie Lawrence

THE JACK OF DIAMONDS
GB 1949 69m bw

Whilst on a yachting holiday, a young
couple agree to help an adventurer
track down a treasure chest.
An outdsoor adventure, somewhat
typical of Exclusive early programmer
output.

p: Vernon Sewell for Exclusive
w: Nigel Patrick, Cyril Raymond
d: Vernon Sewell

Nigel Patrick, Cyril Raymond, Joan
Carol

JEKYLL'S INFERNO see THE TWO
FACES OF DR JEKYLL

JUST FOR YOU
GB 1956 30m Eastmancolor
Cinemascope

Musical featurette with Cyril
Stapleton and the Show Band.

p: Michael Carreras for Exclusive
d: Michael Carreras
ph: Geoffrey Unsworth

Cyril Stapleton and the Show Band,
The Show Band Singers, Joan Regan,
Ronnie Harris

KEEP FIT WITH YOGA
GB 1951 30m bw

A follow up to *Yoga and You*, which
further explores the benefits of yoga.
Also see *Yoga and You* and *Keep Fit
with Yoga*.

p: Exclusive
no other credits available

KISS OF EVIL see KISS OF THE VAM-
PIRE

KISS OF THE VAMPIRE **
GB 1962 88m Eastmancolor

In turn-of-the-century Bavaria, a honeymooning couple inadvertantly
become involved with a sect of vampires.
Lively vampire saga which makes
good use of its budget and settings.
One of Hammer's better Dracula
spin-offs, it is perhaps best remembered for its finale in which a swarm
of bats destroy the sect. Also known
as KISS OF EVIL.

p: Anthony Hinds for
Hammer/Universal
w: John Elder (Anthony Hinds)
d: DON SHARP
ph: Alan Hume
m: James Bernard
md: John Hollingsworth
ed: James Needs
pd: Bernard Robinson
ad: Don Mingaye
cos: Molly Arbuthnot
sp: Les Bowie
sound: Ken Rawkins
make-up: Roy Ashton
cam op: Moray Grant

NOEL WILLMAN, Edward de Souza,
Clifford Evans, Jennifer Daniel, Isobel
Black, Peter Madden, Barry Warren,
Brian Oulton, Noel Howelett, Jacquie
Wallis

KRONOS see CAPTAIN KRONOS:
VAMPIRE HUNTER

THE LADY CRAVED EXCITEMENT
GB 1950 69m bw

A pair of cabaret artists uncover an
art smuggling racket.
Dim romp based on a popular BBC
radio serial. Barely watchable by
today's standards, and probably not
much more bearable at the time.

p: Anthony Hinds for Exclusive
w: John Gilling, Edward J. Mason,
Francis Searle
radio series: Edward J. Mason
d: Francis Searle
ph: Walter Harvey
m: Frank Spencer
songs: James Dyrenforth, George
Melachrino
ed: John Ferris
ad: no credit given
sound: Edgar Vetter
ch: Leslie Roberts
ass d: Jimmy Sangster
Hy Hazell, Michael Medwin, Sid
James, Danny Green, Andrew Keir,
Thelma Grigg

LADY IN THE FOG
GB 1952 80m bw

An American journalist in London
helps a young woman track down the
murderer of her brother.
Undistinguished programmer, somewhat typical of Exclusive's output.
Also known as SCOTLAND YARD
INSPECTOR.

p: Anthony Hinds for Exclusive
w: Orville Hampton
radio series: Lester Powell
d: Sam Newfield
ph: Walter Harvey
m: Ivor Slaney
md: Muir Mathieson
ed: James Needs
ad: Wilfred Arnold
sound: Bill Salter
cam op: Moray Grant

Cesar Romero, Lois Maxwell,
Bernadette O'Farrell, Campbell
Singer, Geoffrey Keen, Alister Hunter,
Frank Birch, Lisa Lee

THE LADY VANISHES *
GB 1979 97m Eastmancolor
Panavision

Just before the outbreak of World War
Two, a madcap socialite befriends an
apparently mild-mannered British
nanny on a European train and
engages the help of a fellow American
to search for her when she suddenly
disappears.
Harmless remake of the Hitchcock
classic in which everyone tries their
best. Quite tolerable on its own count,
especially for those who haven't seen
the original, this is an underrated film
waiting to be re-discovered. It was,
however, greeted with box office disdain at the time and turned out to be
Hammer's last theatrical feature.

p: Tom Sachs for Hammer/Rank
exec p: Michael Carreras
w: George Axelrod
novel: Ethel Lina White
d: Anthony Page
ph: Douglas Slocombe
m: Richard Hartley, Les Reed (theme)
md: Philip Martell
ed: Russell Lloyd
pd: Wilfred Shingleton
cos: Emma Porteous
sp: Don Hangard
sound: Peter Handford
2nd unit ph: John Harris
cam op: Chick Waterson

CYBILL SHEPHERD, ELLIOTT
GOULD, Angela Lansbury (as Miss
Froy), Herbert Lom, Ian Carmichael,
Arthur Lowe (as Charters and
Caldicott), Gerald Harper, Vladek
Sheybal, Jenny Runacre, Jean
Anderson

THE LAST PAGE
GB 1952 84m bw

A small book shop becomes the
focus of blackmail and murder.
So-so supporting feature, of no outstanding interest or merit, despite the
script credit and a better than average cast. Also known as MAN BAIT

p: Anthony Hinds for Exclusive
w: Frederick Knott
play: James Hadley Chase
d: Terence Fisher
ph: Walter Harvey
m: Frank Spencer
ed: Maurice Rootes
ad: no credit given
sound: Bill Salter
ass d: Jimmy Sangster
casting: Michael Carreras

George Brent, Margueritte Chapman,
Diana Dors, Raymond Huntley,
Eleanor Summerfield, Peter
Reynolds, Harry Fowler

LAST VIDEO AND TESTAMENT
GB 1984 74m colour TVM

An electronics expert fakes his own
death after discovering his wife's infi-
delities and extracts an elaborate
revenge.
Mild entry in the disappointing HAM-
MER HOUSE OF MYSTERY AND
SUSPENSE series of tele-films (aka
FOX MYSTERY THEATRE).

p: Roy Skeggs for Hammer/Twentieth
Century Fox
w: Roy Russell
d: Peter Sasdy
ph: Frank Watts
md: Philip Martell
ed: Bob Dearberg
ad: Carolyn Scott
cos: Laura Nightingale
sound: John Bramall, Ernie Marsh

Deborah Raffin, David Langton, Oliver
Tobias, Christopher Scoular, Clifford
Rose, Shane Rimmer

THE LATE NANCY IRVING
GB 1984 74m colour TVM

A lady golfer is kidnapped by an
exclusive clinic because of her rare
blood type.
Another over-padded tele-film from
the HAMMER HOUSE OF MYSTERY
AND SUSPENSE series (aka FOX
MYSTERY THEATRE).

p: Roy Skeggs for Hammer/Twentieth
Century Fox
w: David Fisher
d: Peter Sasdy
ph: Brian West
m: Paul Glass
md: Philip Martell
ed: Bob Dearberg
ad: Carolyn Scott

Christina Raines, Marius Goring, Mick
Ford, Simon Williams, Tony Anhalt,
Zienia Merton

THE LEGEND OF THE SEVEN GOLD-
EN VAMPIRES
GB/Hong Kong 1974 88m
Eastmancolor Panavision

In 1904, Professor Van Helsing tracks
down the six surviving members of a
vampire cult in Chungking.
Dismal amalgam of poorly staged
thrills and chop-sockey. The nadir of
the Hammer horror cycle. Also
known as THE SEVEN BROTHERS
MEET DRACULA.

p: Vee King Shaw, Don Houghton for
Hammer
exec p: Michael Carreras
w: Don Houghton
d: Roy Ward Baker
ph: John Wilcox, Roy Ford
m: James Bernard
md: Philip Martell
ed: Chris Barnes, Larry Richardson
ad: Johnson Tsau
cos: Lui Chi-Yu
sp: Les Bowie
sound: Les Hammond
fight ch: Tang Chia, Liu Chia-Liang

Peter Cushing, David Chiang, Julie
Ege, John Forbes Robertson (as
Dracula), Robin Stewart

LIFE WITH THE LYONS *
GB 1954 81m bw

Domestic travails as the Lyons family
move into a new house and have
trouble with the lease.
Lively domestic comedy from the
popular BBC radio series, helped
along by its personable stars, whose

own children also appear. Also known as A FAMILY AFFAIR.

p: Robert Dunbar for Exclusive
w: Val Guest, Robert Dunbar
d: Val Guest
ph: Walter Harvey
m: Arthur Wilkinson
ed: Doug Myers
ad: Wilfred Arnold

Ben Lyon, Bebe Daniels, Barbara Lyon, Richard Lyon, Hugh Morton, Horace Percival, Gwen Lewis, Doris Rogers, Belinda Lee, Arthur Hill

THE LOST CONTINENT
GB 1968 98m Technicolor

Passengers on a tramp steamer come across a strange island governed by the Spanish Inquisition. Preposterous adventure yarn with some rather silly looking monsters thrown in for good measure. A few lively moments, but on the whole the results are fairly tedious.

p: Michael Carreras for Hammer
w: Michael Nash (Michael Carreras)
novel: Dennis Wheatley
d: Michael Carreras
ph: Paul Beeson
m: Gerard Schurmann
md: Philip Martell
ed: James Needs, Chris Barnes
ad: ARTHUR LAWSON
cos: Carl Toms
sp: Robert A. Mattey, Cliff Richardson
sound: Denis Whitlock

Eric Porter, Hildegarde Neff, Suzanna Leigh, Tony Beckley, Nigel Stock, Jimmy Hanley, Michael Ripper

LOVE THY NEIGHBOUR
GB 1973 85m Technicolor

A bigotted white man has to come to terms with the fact that his neighbours are black.
Uncomfortable, not to mention artless, big screen version of the popular TV sit-com, whose humour is probably now no longer deemed politically correct.

p: Roy Skeggs for Hammer
w: Vince Powell, Harry Driver
d: John Robins
ph: Moray Grant
m: Albert Elms
ed: James Needs
ad: Lionel Couch

Jack Smethurst, Kate Williams, Rudolph Walker, Nina Baden-Semper, Bill Fraser, Keith Marsh, Charles Hyatt, Patricia Hayes, Arthur English

LUST FOR A VAMPIRE
GB 1970 95m Technicolor

In 1830, an English writer falls foul of the Karnstein family while teaching at a girls' school.
Somewhat typical of Hammer's later output, this rather routine brew also contains elements of lesbianism in a bid to spice things up. Part two of the studio's Karnstein trilogy; also see THE VAMPIRE LOVERS and TWINS OF EVIL.

p: Harry Fine, Michael Style for Hammer
w: Tudor Gates
d: Jimmy Sangster
ph: David Muir
m: Harry Robinson
md: Philip Martell
ed: Spencer Reeve
ad: Don Mingaye
cos: Laura Nightingale
sound: Ron Barron, Tony Lumkin

Ralph Bates, Michael Johnson, Barbara Jefford, Yutte Stensgaard, Suzanna Leigh, Helen Christie, Mike Raven, Eric Chitty, Christopher Neame, Pippa Steele

THE LYONS IN PARIS *
GB 1955 81m bw

Whilst holidaying in Paris, Ben Lyon is accused of having a dalliance with a French girl, whose boyfriend subsequently challenges him to a duel. Harmless location-filmed comedy romp, a follow up to LIFE WITH THE LYONS.

p: Robert Dunbar for Exclusive
w/d: Val Guest
ph: Jimmy Harvey
m: Bruce Campbell
ed: Doug Myers
ad: Wilfred Arnold

Ben Lyon, Bebe Daniels, Barbara Lyon, Richard Lyon, Horace Percival, Molly Weir, Doris Rogers, Gwen Lewis, Martine Alexis, Reginald Beckwith, Hugh Morton

MAN ABOUT THE HOUSE
GB 1974 91m Technicolor

The owners and tennants of a run-down rooming house attempt to prevent their building from being demolished.
Lame big screen version of an enjoyable TV sit-com. Here, however, the familiar jokes just lie there and die there.

p: Roy Skeggs for Hammer/EMI
w: Johnnie Mortimer, Briane Cooke from their TV series
d: John Robbins
ph: Jimmy Allen
m: Christopher Gunning
ed: Archie Marshek

Richard O'Sullivan, Paula Wilcox, Sally Thomsett, Yootha Joyce, Brian Murphy, Peter Cellier, Patrick Newell, Spike Milligan, Arthur Lowe, Julian Orchard, Ami McDonald, Melvin Hayes, Jack Smethurst, Bill Grundy, Michael Robbins, Johnnie Briggs, Bill Pertwee, Rudolph Walker

MAN AT THE TOP *
GB 1973 87m Technicolor

A rough and ready company executive from a working class background discovers that his firm is marketing an unsafe drug.
Film version of a TV series, itself inspired by the 1958 film ROOM AT THE TOP. Quite watchable, with plenty of sex and violence to hold one's interest.

p: Peter Charlesworth for Hammer/Dufton
w: Hugh Whitemore, John Junkin
d: Mike Vardy
ph: Bryan Probyn
m: Roy Budd
ed: Christopher Barnes
ad: Don Picton

Kenneth Haig (as Joe Lampton), Nanette Newman, Harry Andrews, John Quentin, Charlie Williams

MAN BAIT see THE LAST PAGE

THE MAN IN BLACK
GB 1950 75m bw

A storyteller relates how two women came to commit murder.
Unremarkable second feature thriller from yet another radio series, no better for being told by a storyteller.

p: Anthony Hinds for Exclusive

w: John Gilling
d: Francis Searle
ph: Cedric Williams
m: Frank Spencer
ed: Ray Pitt
ad: Denis Wreford

Betty Anne Davies, Sheila Burrell, Valentine Dyall (as the storyteller), Sid James, Hazel Penwarden, Anthony Forwood

MAN IN HIDING see MANTRAP

A MAN ON THE BEACH *
GB 1955 29m Eastmancolor

After robbing a casino disguised as a duchess, a crook on the run is forced to hide out with a blind recluse. Mildly diverting but flatly handled featurette which could have been a little gem. Interesting credits, though.

p: Anthony Hinds for Exclusive
w: Jimmy Sangster
novel: Victor Canning
d: Joseph Losey
ph: Wilkie Cooper
m: John Hotchkiss
ed: Henry Richardson
ad: Edward Marshall
sound: W. H. May
make-up: Phil Leakey

Donald Wolfit, Michael Medwin, Michael Ripper

THE MAN WHO COULD CHEAT DEATH
GB 1959 83m Technicolor

A Parisian sculptor keeps his youth by undergoing a series of gland replacement operations, his real age being 104.
Talkative and somewhat lethargically handled horror story with memories of THE PICTURE OF DORIAN GRAY, based on a play originally filmed as THE MAN IN HALF MOON STREET in 1944. Of little interest, even for staunch Hammer fans, despite the talent involved.

p: Anthony Hinds for Hammer
w: Jimmy Sangster
play: Barre Lyndon
d: Terence Fisher
ph: Jack Asher
m: Richard Rodney Bennett
md: John Hollingsworth
ed: James Needs, John Dunstead
ad: Bernard Robinson

cos: Molly Arbuthnot
sound: Jock May
make-up: Roy Ashton

Anton Diffring, Hazel Court, Christopher Lee, Arnold Marle, Delphi Lawrence, Francis de Wolff

MAN WITH A DOG
GB 1958 20m bw

Little seen short.

p: Anthony Hinds for Hammer
exec p: Michael Carreras
d: Leslie Arliss
ph: Arthur Grant
ed: James Needs
ad: Ted Marshall

Maurice Denham, Sarah Lawson, John Van Eyssen, Marianne Stone, Clifford Evans

MANIAC
GB 1963 86m bw Hammerscope

Madness and mayhem in the Camargue, where murder by oxy-acetylene torch is the order of the day.
Derivative shocker with remembrances of TASTE OF FEAR and Sangster's other convoluted psychological plot-twisters.

p: Jimmy Sangster for Hammer/Columbia
w: Jimmy Sangster
d: Michael Carreras
ph: Wilkie Cooper
m: Stanley Black
md: John Hollingsworth
ed: James Needs
ad: Edward Carrick

Kerwin Mathews, Nadia Gray, Donald Houston, Liliane Brousse

MANTRAP
GB 1952 79m bw

A man escapes a mental institution to prove that he was not responsible for the murder that put him there.
Mildly intrigueing thriller, adequately mounted and performed. Also known as MAN IN HIDING.

p: Michael Carreras, Alexander Paal for Exclusive
w: Paul Tabori, Terence Fisher
novel: Elleston Trevor
d: Terence Fisher

ph: Reginald Wyer
m: Doreen Corwithen
ed: James Needs
ad: J. Elder Wills

Paul Henried, Lois Maxwell, Kieron Moore, Hugh Sinclair, Lloyd Lamble, Bill Travers, Kay Kendall

MARK OF THE DEVIL
GB 1984 74m colour TVM

A tattooist wreaks revenge from beyond the grave on the man who killed him.
More padded nonsense from the disappointing HAMMER HOUSE OF MYSTERY AND SUSPENSE series (aka FOX MYSTERY THEATRE).

p: Roy Skeggs for Hammer/Twentieth Century Fox
w: Brian Clemens
d: Val Guest
ph: David Bedford
md: Philip Martel
ed: Bob Dearberg
ad: Carolyn Scott
cos: Laura Nightingale
sound: John Bramall, Ernie Marsh

Dirk Benedict, Jenny Seagrove, George Sewell, John Paul, Tom Adams, Burt Kwouk, Reginald Marsh, James Ellis

MASK OF DUST
GB 1954 79m bw

After losing his nerve in the RAF, a former racing star attempts a comeback.
Adequate racetrack drama, at its best when the engines are running. Also known as RACE FOR LIFE.

p: Mickey Delamar for Exclusive
exec p: Michael Carreras
w: Richard Landau
novel: John Manchip White
d: Terence Fisher
ph: Jimmy Harvey
m: Leonard Salzedo
ed: Bill Lenny
ad: J. Elder Wills

Richard Conte, Mari Aldon, George Coulouris, Peter Illing

MEET SIMON CHERRY
GB 1949 67m bw

A clergyman investigates an apparent murder whilst on holiday.

Mild but surprisingly tolerable programmer.

p: Anthony Hinds for Exclusive
w: Gale Pedrick, A. R. Rawlinson, Godfrey Grayson
story: Godfrey Grayson
radio series: Gale Pedrick
d: Godfrey Grayson
ph: Cedric Williams
md: Frank Spencer, Rupert Grayson
ed: Ray Pitt
ad: Denis Wreford
sound: Edgar Vetter

Hugh Moxey, Zena Marshall, Anthony Forwood, John Bailey, Ernest Butcher, Courtney Hope

MEN OF SHERWOOD FOREST
GB 1954 77m Eastmancolor

Robin Hood helps to return King Richard to his rightful place on the throne.
Occasionally lively low budget romp, better than the average Exclusive feature.

p: Michael Carreras for Exclusive
w: Allan MacKinnon
d: Val Guest
ph: Jimmy Harvey
m: Doreen Corwithen
md: John Hollingsworth
ed: James Needs
ad: J. Edler Wills
cos: Michael Whitaker
sound: Sid Wiles, Ken Cameron

Don Taylor, Reginald Beckwith, Patrick Holt, Eileen Moore, David King Wood, John Van Eyssen

MONKEY MANNERS
GB 1950 27m by

Teatime for the monkeys at London Zoo.
Documentary programme filler - the PG Tips monkeys need have no fear about being upstaged.

p: Exclusive
no other credits available

MOON ZERO TWO
GB 1969 100m Technicolor

On the moon, a crook hires a salvage operator to gain control of an asteroid made of sapphire.
Dimly-conceived, over-talkative 'space western', unimaginatively han-

dled to boot. One of the studio's least wise follies.

p: Michael Carreras for Hammer
w: Michael Carreras
story: Gavin Lyall, Frank Hardman, Martin Davidson
d: Roy Ward Baker
ph: Paul Beeson
m: Don Ellis
md: Philip Martell
ed: Spencer Reeve
ad: Scott MacGregor
sp: Les Bowie, Colin Chilvers
sound: Roy Hyde
ch: Jo Cook

James Olson, Catherina von Schell (later Catherine Schell), Warren Mitchell, Adrienne Corri, Ori Levy, Bernard Bresslaw, Michael Ripper, Dudley Foster, Neil McCallum

THE MUMMY **
GB 1959 88m Technicolor

A 4000-year-old mummy returns to life to kill the archaeologists responsible for desecrating the tomb of an Egyptian queen.
Very competent Hammer rehash of the Boris Karloff classic, with a number of scenes in the studio's very best style. Enjoyable nonsense for afficionados.

p: Michael Carreras for Hammer/Universal
w: JIMMY SANGSTER
d: Terence Fisher
ph: Jack Asher
m: FRANK REIZENSTEIN
md: John Hollingsworth
ed: James Needs, Alfred Cox
ad: Bernard Robinson
cos: Molly Arbuthnot
sp: Bill Warrington
sound: Jock May
make-up: Roy Ashton

Peter Cushing, CHRISTOPHER LEE, Yvonne Furneaux, Felix Aylmer, Raymond Huntley, Michael Ripper, John Stuart, Eddie Byrne, George Woodbridge

THE MUMMY'S SHROUD
GB 1966 84m Technicolor

In the 1920s, a mummy returns to life and kills those who disturbed the grave of its young master.
Worse even than THE CURSE OF THE MUMMY'S TOMB. An archetyp-

al mummy farrago.

p: Anthony Nelson Keys for Hammer
w/d: John Gilling
story: John Elder (Anthony Hinds)
ph: Arthur Grant
m: Don Banks
md: Philip Martell
ed: James Needs, Chris Barnes
pd: Bernard Robinson
cos: Molly Arbuthnot
sp: Les Bowie
sound: Ken Rawkins
narrator: Peter Cushing
cam op: Moray Grant

John Phillips, Andre Morell, David Buck, Elizabeth Sellars, Michael Ripper, Maggie Kimberley, Catherine Lacey, Eddie Powell (as the Mummy), Dickie Owen, Bruno Barnabe, Toni Gilpin

MURDER BY PROXY
GB 1955 88m bw

A drunk wakes up one morning to find himself suspected of murder. Artless thriller, a filler for all concerned. Also known as BLACKOUT

p: Michael Carreras for Exclusive
w: Richard Landau
novel: Helen Nielsen
d: Terence Fisher
ph: Jimmy Harvey
m: Ivor Slaney
ed: no credit given
ad: J. Elder Wills
cos: Molly Arbuthnot
sound: Bill Salter, George Burgess

Dane Clark, Belinda Lee, Eleanor Summerfield, Andrew Osborn, Betty Ann Davies, Alfie Bass, Cleo Laine

MUTINY ON THE BUSES
GB 1972 89m Technicolor

London bus drivers have trouble with their new supervisor.
Second spin-off from the popular TV series ON THE BUSES. All very cheap-looking, it makes the Carry Ons look like GONE WITH THE WIND.

p: Ronald Woolfe, Ronald Chesney for Hammer/EMI
w: Ronald Woolfe, Ronald Chesney
d: Harry Booth
ph: Mark McDonald
m: Ron Grainer
ed: Archie Ludski

ad: Scott MacGregor

Reg Varney, Doris Hare, Bob Grant, Anna Karen, Michael Robbins, Stephen Lewis, Pat Ashton, Bob Todd, David Lodge

THE MYSTERY OF THE MARIE CELESTE
GB 1935 80m bw

An account of the great sea-faring mystery, here attributed to a vengeful sailor who murders all the crew then jumps ship.
Of passing interest for its cast and subject matter, this rather creaky early Hammer film is all too infrequently revived. Also known as PHANTOM SHIP.

p: Hammer
w/d: Denison Clift
ph: Geoffrey Faithful

Bela Lugosi, Shirley Grey, Arthur Margetson, Dennis Hoey, Edmund Willard, George Mozart, Ben Welden, Cliff McLaglen

THE NANNY **
GB 1965 93m bw

A malicious young boy continually accuses his nanny of being a psychopath... and she is.
Enjoyable nut-house melodrama, smartly handled and containing one of its star's best crazy old lady performances. Certainly worthy of comparison to a Hitchcock picture.

p: Jimmy Sangster for Hammer/Associated British
w: Jimmy Sangster
novel: Evelyn Piper
d: SETH HOLT
ph: HARRY WAXMAN
m: Richard Rodney Bennett
md: Philip Martell
ed: James Needs, Tom Simpson
pd: Edward Carrick
cos: Mary Gibson
sound: Norman Coggs, Charles Crafford

BETTE DAVIS, WILLIAM DIX, JAMES VILLIERS, WENDY CRAIG, JILL BENNETT, Pamela Franklyn, Maurice Denham, Harry Fowler, Jack Watling

NEAREST AND DEAREST
GB 1973 89m Technicolor

The owner of a pickle factory goes on holiday to Blackpool with her layabout brother and is pursued by one of his friends for her money.
Witless and vulgar comedy based on the popular TV sit-com. One of several TV spin-offs produced by Hammer and the rest of the British film industry (or what was left of it) during this period.

p: Michael Carreras for Hammer/Granada
w: Tom Brennand, Roy Bottomley
d: John Robbins
ph: David Holmes
m: Derek Hilton
ed: Chris Barnes
ad: Scott MacGregor

Hylda Baker, Jimmy Jewell, Joe Gladwyn, Eddie Malin, Madge Hindle, Yootha Joyce

NEVER LOOK BACK
GB 1952 73m bw

A lady lawyer provides an old flame with an alibi when he is accused of murder, but did she do right?
Straightforward second feature.

p: Michael Carreras for Exclusive
w: John Hunter, Guy Morgan, Francis Searle
d: Francis Searle
ph: Reginald Wyer
m: Temple Abady
ed: John Ferris
ad: Alec Gray

Rosamund John, Hugh Sinclair, Guy Middleton, Terence Longdon, John Warwick, Brenda de Banzie, Henry Edwards

NEVER TAKE SWEETS FROM A STRANGER
GB 1960 81m bw Megascope

In a small Canadian town, an elderly gentleman is accused of molesting children.
Adequately made and acted drama which nevertheless came in for a certain amount of criticism, not simply because of its subject matter, but because Hammer were accused of exploiting it (which they weren't).

p: Anthony Hinds for Hammer/Columbia
exec p: Michael Carreras

w: John Hunter
play: Roger Garis
d: Cyril Frankel
ph: Freddie Francis
m: Elisabeth Lutyens
ed: James Needs, Alfred Cox
ad: Bernard Robinson, Don Mingaye

Gwen Watford, Patrick Allen, Felix Aylmer, Niall MacGinnis, Alison Leggatt, Bill Nagy

NIGHT CREATURES see CAPTAIN CLEGG

NIGHTMARE *
GB 1964 82m bw Hammerscope

A teenage girl fears for her sanity after witnessing her mother kill her father.
Another variation on TASTE OF FEAR - and a good one, which makes the most of all the expected twists and turns.

p: Jimmy Sangster for Hammer/Universal
w: JIMMY SANGSTER
d: FREDDIE FRANCIS
ph: John Wilcox
m: Don Banks
md: John Hollingsworth
ed: James Needs
pd: Bernard Robinson
cos: Rosemary Burrows
sound: Ken Rawkins

Moira Redmond, JENNIE LINDEN, David Knight, Brenda Bruce, John Welsh

THE OLD DARK HOUSE
GB/US 1963 86m Eastmancolor

An American travels to England to visit his distant relatives, the Femms, at their spooky manor house, where all manner of gruesome incidents occur.
Would-be comic remake of the 1932 classic. A dismal failure, even by Hammer's very lowest standards.

p: William Castle, Anthony Hinds for Hammer/Columbia
w: Robert Dillon
novel: J. B. Priestley
d: William Castel
ph: Arthur Grant
m: Benjamin Frankel
md: John Hollingsworth
ed: James Needs
ad: Bernard Robinson

cos: Molly Arbuthnot
sp: Les Bowie
sound: Jock May
titles: Charles Addams

Tom Poston, Janette Scott, Mervyn Johns, Joyce Grenfell, Robert Morley, Fenella Fielding, Peter Bull, Danny Green, Amy Dalby, John Harvey.

OLD FATHER THAMES
GB 1946 33m bw

Documentary charting the flow of the Thames.
Long unseen, this was one of the first productions of the resuscitated Exclusive.

p: Exclusive
d: Hal Wilson, Ben R. Hart

ON THE BUSES
GB 1971 88m Technicolor

Women drivers threaten jobs at a London bus depot.
Cheap and cheerful spin-off from the long-running TV sit-com which proved to be Hammer's biggest commercial hit. Despite its unexpected popularity, it's really not all that good.

p: Ronald Woolfe, Ronald Chesney for Hammer/EMI
w: Ronald Woolfe, Ronald Chesney
d: Harry Booth
ph: Mark MacDonald
m: Max Harris
md: Philip Martell
ed: Archie Marshek
ad: Scott MacGregor

Reg Varney, Doris Hare, Michael Robbins, Anna Karen, Stephen Lewis, Bob Grant, Pat Coombs, Wendy Richard

ONE MILLION YEARS B.C. **
GB 1966 100m Technicolor

In prehistoric times, a cave girl abandons her tribe to look for a mate.
Lively remake of the 1940 Hal Roach film ONE MILLION B.C., here benefitting from lively action sequences and excellent effects work.

p: Michael Carreras for Hammer
w: Michael Carreras
d: DON CHAFFEY
ph: Wilkie Cooper
m: MARIO NASCIMBENE
md: Philip Martell

ed: James Needs, Tom Simpson
ad: Robert Jones
cos: Carl Toms
sp: RAY HARRYHAUSEN, Les Bowie
sound: Bill Rowe, Len Shilton
2nd unit ph: Jack Mills

Raquel Welch, John Richardson, Robert Brown, Martine Beswick, Percy Herbert, Lisa Thomas, Malya Nappil

OPERATION UNIVERSE
GB 1959 28m Technicolor
Hammerscope

Little seen documentary.

p: Peter Bryan for Hammer
w/d: Peter Bryan
ph: Len Harris
ed: Bill Lenny

PAID TO KILL see FIVE DAYS

PAINT ME A MURDER
GB 1984 74m colour TVM

An artist and his wife fake his death so that the market value of his paintings will soar, but she falls in love with someone else and decides to really kill him.
A good idea, but unfortunately the treatment resolutely fails to make the most of it. Another clinker from the HAMMER HOUSE OF MYSTERY AND SUSPENSE series of tele-movies (aka FOX MYSTERY THEATRE).

p: Roy Skeggs for Hammer/Twentieth Century Fox
w: Jesse Lasky, Jr., Pat Silver
d: Alan Cooke
ph: Frank Watts
m: Francis Shaw
md: Philip Martell
ed: Bob Dearberg
ad: Carolyn Scott

Michelle Phillips, James Laurenson, David Robb, Morgan Sheppard, Tony Sheedman, Indira Joshi, Mark Heath

PARADE OF THE BANDS
GB 1956 30m Eastmancolor
Cinemascope

Musical featurette featuring top musical talent of the day.
p: Michael Carreras for Exclusive
d: Michael Carreras
ph: Geoffrey Unsworth

Malcolm Mitchell and his Orchestra, Eric Jupp and his Players, Freddy Ranmdall and his Band, Frank Weir and his Orchestra, Liza Ashwood, Rusty Hurran, Cleo Laine, Johnny Dankworth and his Orchestra, Francisco Cavez and his Latin American Orchestra

PARANOIAC *
GB 1963 80m bw Cinemascope

The apparently dead brother of an heiress turns up to claim his inheritance - but is he really who he claims to be?
Commendably brief shocker in the TASTE OF FEAR manner, with enough twists and revelations to keep one watching.

p: Anthony Hinds for Hammer/Universal
w: JIMMY SANGSTER
d: FREDDIE FRANCIS
ph: Arthur Grant
m: Elisabeth Lutyens
md: John Hollingsworth
ed: James Needs
ad: Bernard Robinson
cos: Molly Arbuthnot
sp: Les Bowie
sound: Ken Rawkins

OLIVER REED, JANETTE SCOTT, Alexander Davion, Sheila Burrell, Liliane Brouse, Maurice Denham, John Bonney

PASSPORT TO CHINA see VISA TO CANTON

THE PHANTOM OF THE OPERA *
GB 1962 90m Technnicolor

A disfigured composer abducts a prima donna and coaches her in his lair under the opera house.
Reasonable Hammer remake of the oft-filmed story, well enough mounted, but a box office disappointment.

p: Anthony Hinds for Hammer/Universal
w: John Elder (Anthony Hinds)
d: TERENCE FISHER
ph: Arthur Grant
m: Edwin Astley
md: John Hollingsworth
ed: Alfred Cox
ad: Bernard Robinson, Don Mingaye
cos: Molly Arbutnot
sound: Jock May

make-up: Roy Ashton

Herbert Lom, Edward de Souza, Heather Sears, Thorley Walters, Michael Gough, Ian Wilson, Martin Miller, John Harvey, Miriam Karlin, Michael Ripper, Patrick Troughton, Renee Houston, Miles Malleson.

THE PIRATES OF BLOOD RIVER *
GB 1962 84m Technicolor
Hammerscope

A pirate captain forces one of his crew members to lead him back to his home town, a Puritan community where treasure is apparently hidden. Reasonably lively pirate yarn with good moments between the longeurs and better than average production values.

p: Anthony Nelson Keys for Hammer
exec p: Michael Carreras
w: John Hunter, John Gilling
story: Jimmy Sangster
d: John Gilling
ph: Arthur Grant
md: John Hollingsworth
ed: James Needs, Eric Boyd-Perkins
ad: Bernard Robinson, Don Mingaye

Andrew Keir, Christopher Lee, Kerwin Mathews, Peter Arne, Oliver Reed, Michael Ripper, Marla Landi, Glenn Corbett

PLAGUE OF THE ZOMBIES **
GB 1966 91m Technicolor

In a small Cornish village, the local squire resurrects the dead to work in his tin mine.
Spirited Hammer horror with a strong central performance, plenty of atmosphere and several standout sequences, including a mass rising of the dead. It was filmed back to back with THE REPTILE.

p: Anthony Nelson Keys for Hammer
w: John Bryan
d: JOHN GILLING
ph: ARTHUR GRANT
m: James Bernard
md: Philip Martell
ed: James Needs, Chris Barnes
pd: Bernard Robinson
ad: Don Mingaye
cos: Rosemary Burrows
sp: Les Bowie
sound: Ken Rawkins
make-up: Roy Ashton

ANDRE MORELL, John Carson, Diana Clare, Jacqueline Pearce, Alex Davison, Brook Williams, Michael Ripper, Marcus Hammond

PREHISTORIC WOMEN see SLAVE GIRLS

THE PUBLIC LIFE OF HENRY THE NINTH
GB 1935 60m bw

A street performer steps up the showbiz ladder after performing in a pub.
Hammer's first ever film - a long unseen comedy.

p: Hammer
d: Bernard Mainwaring

Leonard Henry, Betty Frankiss, Wally Patch, George Mozart

QUATERMASS AND THE PIT **
GB 1967 87m Technicolor

During extension work on London's underground, an impentetrable spacecraft and a series of strange skulls are unearthed, and a mysterious force makes itself felt.
Intellectually exciting and compulsively watchable science fiction thriller with many gripping moments, only occasionally let down by dated terminology and unconvincing effects. Certainly the best episode in Hammer's Quatermass series. Also known as FIVE MILLION YEARS TO EARTH.

p: Anthony Nelson Keys for Hammer/Associated British
w: NIGEL KNEALE, from his TV series
d: ROY WARD BAKER
ph: Arthur Grant
m: Tristam Carey
md: Philip Martell
ed: James Needs, Spencer Reeve
ad: Bernard Robinson
cos: Rosemary Burrows
sp: Les Bowie
sound: Sash Fisher

ANDREW KEIR, JAMES DONALD, BARBARA SHELLEY, Julian Glover, Duncan Lamont, Edwin Richafield, Peter Copley, Sheila Steafel, Brian Marshall

THE QUATERMASS
EXPERIMENT ***

GB 1955 82m bw

The only surviving member of a space expedition begins to mutate once back on earth and is finally cornered in Westminster Abbey after going on the rampage.
Though some aspects of this science fiction thriller have now dated, it nevertheless remains an eerily effective and sometimes quite frightening film whose success in both Britain and America helped to put Hammer on the map. Required viewing for genre addicts. Also known as THE QUATERMASS XPERIMENT and THE CREEPING UNKNOWN.

p: Anthony Hinds for Hammer/Exclusive
w: Richard Landau, Val Guest
TV series: NIGEL KNEALE
d: VAL GUEST
ph: Jimmy Harvey
m: JAMES BERNARD
md: John Hollingsworth
ed: James Needs
ad: J. Elder Wills
cos: Molly Arbuthnot
sp: Les Bowie
sound: H. C. Pearson
make-up: Phil Leakey

Brian Donlevy, Jack Warner, Margia Dean, RICHARD WORDSWORTH, David Wood King, THORA HIRD, Gordon Jackson, Lionel Jeffries, Harold Lang, Maurice Kauffmann, Sam Kydd, Jane Asher

THE QUATERMASS XPERIMENT see THE QUATERMASS EXPERIMENT

QUATERMASS II **
GB 1957 85m bw

Professor Quatermass discovers that an industrial plant allegedly making synthetic food is in fact harbouring aliens from outer space.
Imaginatively plotted follow up to THE QUATERMASS EXPERIMENT, betrayed chiefly by its low budget, general scientific naivite and a monster that looks like a walking mud pie. Plenty of interest for genre addicts, though. Also known as THE ENEMY FROM SPACE.

p: Anthony Hinds for Hammer
w: Nigel Kneale, Val Guest
TV series: NIGEL KNEALE
d: Val Guest
ph: Gerald Gibbs

m: James Bernard
md: John Hollingsworth
ed: James Needs
ad: Bernard Robinson
cos: Rene Coke
sp: Bill Warrington, Henry Harris, Frank George
sound: Cliff Sandell

Brian Donlevy, John Longden, Sid James, Bryan Forbes, William Franklyn, Michael Ripper, Charles Lloyd Pack, Percy Herbert, Tom Chatto

QUEER FISH
GB 1952 28m bw

Despite the provocative title, this documentary short is just a tour of the aquarium at London Zoo.

p: Exclusive
no other credits available

A RACE FOR LIFE see MASK OF DUST

RASPUTIN - THE MAD MONK
GB 1966 92m Technicolor
Cinemascope

Rasputin insinuates himself into the court of Tsar Nicholas II.
A coloured view of history, chiefly played for shocks in the tried and tested Hammer vein. A little on the tired side, despite a wide-eyed star performance. Made back to back with DRACULA - PRINCE OF DARKNESS.

p: Anthony Nelson Keys for Hammer/Associated British
w: John Elder (Anthony Hinds)
d: Don Sharp
ph: Michael Reed
m: Don Banks
md: Philip Martell
ed: James Needs, Roy Hyde
ad: Bernard Robinson
cos: Rosemary Burrows
sound: Ken Rawkins
make-up: Roy Ashton

Christopher Lee, Barbara Shelley, Richard Pasco, Francis Matthews, Suzan Farmer, Dinsdale Landen, Renee Asherton, Derek Francis, Joss Ackland, Robert Duncan, John Welsh

THE REPTILE *
GB 1966 90m Technicolor

The daughter of a Cornish doctor

periodically turns into a murderous reptile.
Predictable horror hokum with the usual veiled warnings and something horrible up at the manor house. Lively moments for all that. Made back to back with THE PLAGUE OF THE ZOMBIES.

p: Anthony Nelson Keys for Hammer
w: John Elder (Anthony Hinds)
d: John Gilling
ph: Arthur Grant
m: Don Banks
md: Philip Martell
ed: James Needs
ad: Bernard Robinson
sp: Les Bowie
sound: William Buckley
make-up: Roy Ashton

Noel Willman, Ray Barrett, Jennifer Daniel, Jacqueline Pearce (as the Reptile), Michael Ripper, John Laurie, Marne Maitland, George Woodbridge, Charles Lloyd Pack

THE REVENGE OF FRANKENSTEIN *
GB 1958 89m Technicolor

The good Baron continues his experiments within the confines of a poor hospital - with the expected results. Rather tame follow up to THE CURSE OF FRANKENSTEIN, with a few unwise attempts at humour and a dull monster.

p: Anthony Hinds for Hammer/Columbia
exec p: Michael Carreras
w: Jimmy Sangster, Hurford Janes
d: Terence Fisher
ph: Jack Asher
m: Leonard Salzedo
ed: James Needs, Alfred Cox
pd: BERNARD ROBINSON
cos: Rosemary Burrows
sound: Jock May
make-up: Phil Leakey
associate p: Anthony Nelson Keys

PETER CUSHING, Michael Gwynne (as the Monster), Francis Matthews, Eunice Gayson, Oscar Quitak, John Welsh, Lionel Jeffries, Richard Wordsworth, Charles Lloyd Pack, Arnold Diamond, Michael Ripper, John Stuart

RIVER PATROL
GB 1948 46m bw

Adventures of a customs officer up

and down the Thames.
Mild featurette, one of the first films to be produced by the revified Hammer/Exclusive company.

p: Hal Wilson for Hammer/Knightbridge
d: Ben R. Hart
ph: Brooks Carrington

John Blythe, Wally Patch, Lorna Dean, Stan Paskin

RIVER SHIPS
GB 1951 27m bw

A look at the various types of craft which make use of the River Thames. Documentary programmer filler, of interest for its views of the Thames, many of which have since been redeveloped.

p: Exclsuive
no other credits available

ROOM TO LET
GB 1950 68m bw

A reporter is led to believe that a fellow lodger is in fact Jack the Ripper. Not quite in the same league as Hitchcock's THE LODGER, to which this is a distant cousin. Passable enough, though.

p: Anthony Hinds for Exclusive
w: John Gilling, Godfrey Grayson
radio play: Margery Allingham
d: Godfrey Grayson
ph: Cedric Williams
m: Frank Spencer
ed: James Needs

Jimmy Hanley, Valentine Dyall, Christine Silver, Charles Hawtrey (in a serious role), Merle Tottenham, Constance Smith

THE ROSSITER CASE
GB 1950 75m Exclusive

A man is accused of murdering his mistress - or was the culprit his disabled wife?
Unremarkable murder mystery with a by numbers plot.

p: Anthony Hinds for Exclusive
w: Kenneth Hyde, John Gilling, Francis Searle
play: Kenneth Hyde
d: Francis Searle

ph: Jimmy Harvey
m: Frank Spencer
ed: John Ferris

Clement McCallin, Helen Shingler,
Frederick Leister, Henry Edwards,
Ann Codrington, Sheila Burrell,
Stanley Baker

THE SAINT RETURNS
GB 1953 68m bw

The Saint tracks down a gang of
blackmailers responsible for the
death of an old girlfriend.
Uninspired attempt to continue the
series in Britain with Hayward returning to the role of Simon Templar for
the first (and only) time since 1938's
THE SAINT IN NEW YORK. Also
known as THE SAINT'S GIRL FRIDAY.

p: Anthony Hinds, Julian Lesser for
Exclusive
w: Allan MacKinnon
d: Seymour Friedman
ph: Walter Harvey
m: Ivor Slaney
ed: James Needs
ad: J. Elder Wills
Louis Hayward, Sydney Tafler, Diana
Dors, Harold Lang, Naomi Chance,
Charles Victor

THE SAINT'S GIRL FRIDAY see THE
SAINT RETURNS

THE SATANIC RITES OF DRACULA *
GB 1973 88m Technicolor

Professor Van Helsing discovers that
Dracula is at the head of a business
empire intent on destroying the world
by plague.
Avengers-style finish to the Hammer
Dracula series. A few marks up on
DRACULA A.D. 1972, though vampires and motorcycles don't really
make good bedmates.

p: Roy Skeggs for Hammer/Warner
w: Don Houghton
d: ALAN GIBSON
ph: Brian Probyn
m: John Cacavas
md: Philip Martell
ed: Chris Barnes
ad: Lionel Couch
sp: Les Bowie
cos: Rebecca Reed
sound: Claude Hitchcock, Dennis
Whitlock

Christopher Lee, Peter Cushing,
Michael Coles, Joanna Lumley,
William Franklyn, Freddie Jones,
Patrick Barr, Richard Vernon,
Lockwood West, Barbara Yu Ling,
Valerie Van Ost

THE SCARLET BLADE *
GB 1963 82m Technicolor
Hammerscope

In 1648, Cromwell's troops pursue
the king across the country, hanging
royalist rebels along the way.
However, they reckon without the
intervention of The Scarlet Blade.
Modest swashbuckler in the Saturday
morning tradition, a typical filler
between the studio's horror ouptput.
Also known as THE CRIMSON
BLADE.

p: Anthony Nelson Keys for Hammer
w/d: John Gilling
ph: Jack Asher
m: Gary Hughes
md: John Hollingsworth
ed: James Needs, John Dunsford
ad: Don Mingaye
cos: Rosemary Burrows
sp: Les Bowie
sound: Ken Rawkins

Lionel Jeffries, Oliver Reed, Jack
Hedley, June Thorburn, Duncan
Lamont, Suzan Farmer, Michael
Ripper, Charles Houston, Harold
Goldblatt, Clifford Elkin

SCARS OF DRACULA
GB 1970 96m Technicolor

A young man and his fiancée trace
his missing brother to Castle Dracula.
Unimaginative variation on the original story, with too little invention in
the script to sustain the length,
though certain scenes have their
moments.

p: Aida Young for Hammer
w: John Elder (Anthony Hinds)
d: Roy Ward Baker
ph: Moray Grant
m: James Bernard
md: Philip Martell
ed: James Needs
ad: Scott MacGregor
cos: Laura Nightingale
sp: Roger Dicken
sound: Ron Barron, Tony Lumkin

Christopher Lee, Dennis Waterman,
Jenny Hanley, Christopher Matthews,

Patrick Troughton, Michael Gwynne,
Bob Todd, Michael Ripper

SCOTLAND YARD INSPECTOR see
LADY IN THE FOG

SCREAM OF FEAR see TASTE OF
FEAR

THE SECRET OF BLOOD ISLAND
GB 1964 84m Technicolor

A lady agent is smuggled in and out
of a Japanese prisoner of war camp
so as to report on conditions there.
Lively if somewhat absurd wartime
action drama.

p: Anthony Nelson Keys for Hammer
w: John Gilling
d: Quentin Lawrence
ph: Jack Asher
m: James Bernard
ed: James Needs, Tom Simpson
pd: Bernard Robinson

Barbara Shelley, Jack Hedley, Charles
Tingwell, Lee Montague, Bill Owen,
Michael Ripper

THE SEVEN BROTHERS MEET
DRACULA see THE SEVEN GOLDEN
VAMPIRES

THE SEVEN WONDERS OF IRELAND
GB 1957 10m Eastmancolor

Travelogue short extolling the beau-
ties of Ireland.
p: Hammer
d: Peter Bryan
ph: Harry Oakes, Len Harris

SHADOW OF THE CAT *
GB 1961 79m bw

A cat takes revenge on those relatives responsible for murdering its
mistress.
Well mounted if somewhat silly horror hokum with an insufficiently
frightening monster. (Production company BHP was a subsidiary of
Hammer Films.)

p: Jon Penington for BHP
w: George Baxt
d: JOHN GILLING
ph: Arthur Grant
m: Mikis Theodorakis
ed: James Needs, John Pomeroy
ad: Bernard Robinson, Don Mingaye
cos: Molly Arbuthnot
sp: Les Bowie

sound: Ken Cameron

Barbara Shelley, Andre Morell, William Lucas, Freda Jackson, Conrad Phillips, Alan Wheatley, Vanda Godsell, Richard Warner, Catherine Lacey

SHATTER
GB/Hong Kong 1974 93m colour

A professional assassin finds himself a target after being tricked into an assignment in Hong Kong.
Routine thick ear for the tail end of the exploitation market. Not a success, even by Hammer's rapidly declining standards, it failed to obtain a theatrical release. Also known as CALL HIM MR. SHATTER.

p: Michael Carreras, Vee King Shaw for Hammer/Run Run Shaw
w: Don Houghton
d: Michael Carreras
ph: Brian Probyn, John Wilcox, Roy Ford
m: David Lindup
md: Philip Martell
ed: Eric Boyd-Perkins
ad: Johnson Tsau
sp: Les Bowie
sound: Les Hammond

Stuart Whitman, Peter Cushing, Ti Lung, Lily Li, Anton Diffring, Yemi Ajibade, Lo Wei, James Ma, Chaing Han

SHE*
GB 1965 105m Technicolor
Hammerscope

Explorers in Africa discover a lost city ruled by a queen who cannot die unless she falls in love.
Claustrophobic Hammer remake of the 1935 classic, with neither the style nor sense of mystery of its predecessor. It was followed by THE VENGEANCE OF SHE in 1968.

p: Aida Young, Michael Carreras for Hammer/Associated British
w: David T. Chantler
novel: H. Rider Haggard
d: Robert Day
ph: Harry Waxman
m: JAMES BERNARD
md: Philip Martell
ed: James Needs, Eric Boyd-Perkins
ad: Robert Jones, Don Mingaye
cos: Carl Toms
sp: George Blackwell, Les Bowie

sound: Claude Hitchcock
make-up: Roy Ashton

Ursula Andress (as Ayesha), John Richardson, Peter Cushing, Bernard Cribbins, Christopher Lee, Andre Morell, Rosenda Monteros

SKIFFY GOES TO SEA
GB 1947 34m bw

A Thames ferryman has asipirations to be a sailor, but discovers the occupation to be harder-going than he'd imagined.
Long unseen featurette about which little information survives.

p: Exclusive
w: Bill Curry
d: Harry May

SKY TRADERS
GB 1953 21m bw

Documentary featurette on the air freight industry.

p: Exclusive
no other credits available

SLAVE GIRLS
GB 1968 74m Technicolor
Cinemascope

A hunter discovers a hidden valley ruled entirely by women.
More prehistoric nonsense, though by no means in the same league as ONE MILLION YEARS B.C. Also known as PREHISTORIC WOMEN.

p: Aida Young for Hammer
w: Henry Younger (Michael Carreras)
d: Michael Carreras
ph: Michael Reed
m: Carlo Martelli
md: Philip Martell
ed: James Needs, Roy Hyde
ad: Robert Jones
cos: Carl Toms
sound: Sash Fisher, Len Shulton
ch: Denys Palmer

Michael Latimer, Martine Beswick, Carol White, Edina Ronay, Shelley Birmingham, Stephanie Randall, Alexandra Stevenson

THE SNORKEL
GB 1958 90m bw

A man kills his wife with the aid of a snorkel, but is given away by his

stepdaughter.
Initially promising thriller which ultimately lacks the required skill to bring it off.

p: Michael Carreras for Hammer/Columbia
w: Jimmy Sangster, Peter Myers
story: Anthony Dawson
d: Guy Green
ph: Jack Asher
md: John Hollingsworth
ed: James Needs, Bill Lenny
ad: John Stoll

Peter Van Eyck, Betta St John, Mandy Miller, Gregoire Aslan, William Franklyn

SOMEONE AT THE DOOR
GB 1950 65m bw

Having inherited an apparently haunted house, a newsman and his sister make up the story of a killing - but it comes true.
Ho-hum re-working of a ho-hum play previously filmed in 1936 under the same title.

p: A. R. Rawlinson for Hammer/Exclusive.
play: Major Campbell Christie, Dorothy Christie
d: Francis Searle
ph: Walter Harvey
m: Frank Spencer
ed: John Ferris
ad: Denis Wreford

Yvonne Owen, Michael Medwin, Hugh Latimer, Danny Green, Gary Marsh

THE SONG OF FREEDOM
GB 1936 80m bw

A black dock worker becomes a singer and later discovers that he is the head of an African tribe.
Unusual blend of drama, music and globe-trotting, given stature by the presence of its star. Easily the best of Hammer's early productions.

p: J. Fraser Passmore for Hammer
w: Fenn Sherrie, Ingram D'Abbes, Michael Barringer, Philip Lindsay
d: J. Elder Wills
ph: Eric Cross

PAUL ROBESON, Elizabeth Welch, Esme Percy, George Mozart, Alf Goddard, Ambrose Manning, Sydney

Benson, Cornelia Smith, Robert
Adams

SPACEWAYS
GB 1952 76m bw

A scientist is accused of murdering
his wife and trying to hide the evidence in a space rocket.
The same old B thriller plot twists,
but this time given a science fiction
setting, with effects footage lifted
from Lippert's *Rocketship XM*.

p: Michael Carreras for Exclusive
w: Paul Tabori, Richard Landau
radio play: Charles Eric Maine
d: Terence Fisher
ph: Reg Wyer
m: Ivor Slaney
ed: Maurice Rootes
ad: J. Elder Wills

Howard Duff, Eva Bartok, Andrew
Osborn, Michael Medwin, Alan
Wheatley, Anthony Ireland

SPORTING LOVE
GB 1937 68m bw

Two stable owners attempt to kidnap
a horse and use the ransom money
to pay off their mortgage.
Mildly amusing comedy with music,
adapted from a stage success of the
time.

p: J. Fraser Passmore for Hammer
w: Fenn Sherie, Ingram D'Abbern
play: Stanley Lupino
d: J. Elder Wills
ph: Eric Cross

Stanley Lupino, Laddie Cliff, Henry
Carlisle, Eda Peel, Bobby Comber

STEEL BAYONET
GB 1957 85m bw Hammerscope

Wartime adventures of a platoon in
Tunis.
Standard wartime piece, rather typical of Hammer's various ventures in
this field.

p: Michael carreras for Hammer
w: Howard Clewes
d: Michael Carreras
ph: Jack Asher
m: Leonard Salzedo
md: John Hollingsworth
ed: Bill Lenny
ad: Ted Marshall

Leo Genn, Kieron Moore, Michael
Medwin, Michael Ripper, Bernard
Horsfall, Robert Brown

STOLEN FACE
GB 1952 72m bw

A plastic surgeon attempts to give a
scarred criminal the same face as the
girl he truly loves, with tragic results.
Silly but not intolerable second feature thriller with echoes of VERTIGO
to come.

p: Michael Carreas for
Hammer/Exclusive
w: Richard Landau, Martin Berkeley
story: Alexander Paal, Richard Landau
d: Terence Fisher
ph: Walter Harvey
m: Malcolm Arnold
ed: Maurice Rootes
ad: Wilfred Arnold
cos: Edith Head
sound: Bill Salter
make-up: Phil Leakey
ass d: Jimmy Sangster

Paul Henreid, Lizabeth Scott, Andre
Morell, Arnold Ridley, Susan Stephen,
John Wood, Mary Mackenzie

STOP ME BEFORE I KILL see THE
FULL TREATMENT

STRAIGHT ON TILL MORNING
GB 1972 96m Technicolor

A girl from Liverpool living in London
gradually comes to realise that her
boyfriend is psychotic.
Disappointing ragbag of tired situations in the familiar psycho-thriller
style. Also known as TILL DAWN US
DO PART.

p: Roy Skeggs for Hammer/EMI
exec p: Michael Carreras
w: Michael Peacock
d: Peter Collinson
ph: Brian Probyn
m: Roland Shaw
md: Philip Martell
ed: Alan Pattillo
ad: Scott MacGregor
cos: Laura Nightingale
sound: John Purchase

Rita Tushingham, Shane Briant, Tom
Bell, James Bolam, Katya Wyeth,
Annie Ross, Clare Kelly, Harold
Berens

THE STRANGER CAME HOME
GB 1954 80m bw

An amnesiac, missing for several
years, finds himself blamed for a
murder.
A standard second feature murder
plot is given standard second feature
treatment, and is notable only for the
surprising presnce of its star, one of
whose last films this proved to be.
Also known as THE UNHOLY FOUR.

p: Michael Carreras for Exclusive
w: Michael Carreras
novel: George Sanders
d: Terence Fisher
ph: James Harvey
m: Ivor Slaney
ed: Bill Lenney
ad: J. Elder Wills

Paulette Goddard, William Sylvester,
Paul Carpenter, Russell Napier, Alvys
Mahen, David King Wood

THE STRANGLERS OF BOMBAY *
GB 1960 80m bw Megascope

In 1826 India, a British officer investigates a series of Thugee related
killings.
Interesting for its theme rather than
for its presentation, this lurid and
sometimes quite violent historical
drama is not without its moments of
interest.

p: Anthony Hinds for
Hammer/Columbia
w: David Goodman
d: Terence Fisher
ph: Arthur Grant
m: James Bernard
md: John Hollingsworth
ed: James Needs, Alfred Cox
ad: Bernard Robinson
sound: Jock May

Guy Rolfe, Allan Cuthbertson, Marne
Maitland, Jan Holden, Andrew
Cruickshank, George Pastell, Paul
Stassino

THE SWEET SMELL OF DEATH
GB 1984 74m colour TVM

An American diplomat and his wife
rent a country house only to find
themselves being watched...
Tame and over-stretched tele-movie
from the HAMMER HOUSE OF MYS-
TERY AND SUSPENSE series (aka
FOX MYSTERY THEATRE).

p: Roy Skeggs for Hammer/Twentieth
Century Fox
w: Brian Clemens
d: Peter Sasdy
ph: John Mccabe
md: Philip Martell
ed: Bob Dearberg
ad: Carolyn Scott

Dean Stockwell, Shirley Knight,
Michael Gothard, Carmen du Sortoy,
Robert Lang, Alan Gifford, Toria
Fuller, Sturan Rodger

SWORD OF SHERWOOD FOREST
GB 1960 80m Technicolor
Megascope

Robin Hood and his men foil the
Sheriff of Nottingham's plans to murder the Archbishop.
Unimaginative big screen version of
the popular TV series.

p: Richard Greene, Sidney Cole for
Hammer/Columbia/Yeoman
w: Alan Hackney
d: Terence Fisher
ph: Ken Hodges
m: Alan Hoddinott
md: John Hollingsworth
ed: James Needs, Lee Doig
ad: John Stoll
sound: Alan Streeter

Richard Greene, Peter Cushing,
Richard Pasco, Nigel Green, Niall
MacGinnis, Sarah Branch, Jack
Gwyllim, Desmond Llewellyn, Dennis
Lotis, Vanda Godsell

TASTE OF FEAR **
GB 1961 82m bw

An heiress confined to a wheelchair
goes to visit the father she has not
seen for ten years at his Riviera
home, but when she gets there discovers that he has mysteriously disappeared...
Coiled-spring shocker, inspired by
LES DIABOLIQUES and somewhat
typical of Sangster's
they're-trying-to-drive-me-insane
thrillers for Hammer, other variations
being MANIAC, PARANOIAC,
CRESCENDO and FEAR IN THE
NIGHT. Stylishly done for all that, and
with enough twists and turns to keep
one watching. Also known as
SCREAM OF FEAR.

p: Jimmy Sangster for
Hammer/Columbia

w: JIMMY SANGSTER
d: SETH HOLT
ph: DOUGLAS SLOCOMBE
m: Clifton Parker
md: John Hollingsworth
ed: James Needs, Eric Boyd-Perkins
ad: Bernard Robinson
cos: Dora Lloyd
sound: Leslie Hammond, E. Mason,
Len Shilton

Susan Strasberg, Ann Todd, Ronald
Lewis, Christopher Lee, Leonard
Sachs

TASTE THE BLOOD OF DRACULA *
GB 1970 95m Technicolor

Three Victorian gentlemen in search
of excitement become involved in
black magic and the resurrection of
Count Dracula.
One of the studio's better Dracula
sequels, with everything grist to its
by now familiar mill and a stronger
cast than usual.

p: Aida Young for Hammer
w: John Elder (Anthony Hinds)
d: Peter Sasdy
ph: Arthur Grant
m: James Bernard
md: Philip Martell
ed: Chris Barnes
ad: Scott MacGregor
cos: Brian Owen Smith
sp: Brian Johncock
sound: Rod Barrod, Tony Lumkin

Christopher Lee, Geoffrey Keen,
Gwen Watford, Linda Hayden, Peter
Sallis, Isla Blair, Ralph Bates, Roy
Kinnear, John Carson, Martin Jarvis,
Madeleine Smith, Michael Ripper

TEN SECONDS TO HELL
GB 1959 93m bw

Members of a bomb disposal unit in
Berlin just after the end of World War
Two each bet on who will survive the
longest.
Uninvolving thriller, somewhat scup-
pered by an hilarious introductory nar-
ration, from which it never really
recovers. A long way after Michael
Powell's similar but superior SMALL
BACK ROOM.

p: Michael Carreras for
Hammer/UA/Seven Arts
w: Teddi Sherman, Robert Aldrich
novel: Lawrence Buchmann
d: Robert Aldrich

ph: Ernest Laszlo
m: Kenneth V. Jones
md: John Hollingsworth
ed: James Needs, Henry Richardson
pd: Ken Adam
cos Molly Arbuthnot
sound: Heinz Garbowski

Jack Palance, Jeff Chandler, Dave
Willock, Wesley Addy, Martine Carol,
Robert Cornthwaite

TENNIS COURT
GB 1984 74m colour TVM

An indoor tennis court affects the
new comers of a country house.
Lamentable nonsense which would
have failed to fill a TV half hour satis-
factorily. Part of the unfortunate
HAMMER HOUSE OF MYSTERY
AND SUSPENSE series (aka FOX
MYSTERY THEATRE).

p: Roy Skeggs for Hammer/Twentieth
Centruy Fox
w: Andrew Sinclair
d: Cyril Frankel
ph: Franks Watts
md: Philip Martell

Peter Graves, Hannah Gordon, Ralph
Arliss, Isla Blair, Annis Joslin, George
Little, Jonathan Newth, Peggy Sinclair

THE TERROR OF THE TONGS *
GB 1961 79m Technicolor

In 1910 Hong Kong, a merchant
avenges himself on those who killed
his daughter by using the services of
a secret sect.
Follow up of sorts to THE STRAN-
GLERS OF BOMBAY with similar
scenes of violence and torture, but
this time in colour.

p: Kenneth Hyman for
Hammer/Merlin/BLC
exec p: Michael Carreras
w: Jimmy Sangster
d: Anthony Bushell
ph: Arthur Grant
m: James Bernard
md: John Hollingsworth
ed: James Needs, Eric Boyd-Perkins
ad: Bernard Robinson, Thomas Goswell
associate p: Anthony Nelson-Keys

Geoffrey Toone, Christopher Lee,
Yvonne Molnaur, Richard Leech,
Brian Worth

TERROR STREET see 36 HOURS

THAT'S YOUR FUNERAL
GB 1973 82m Technicolor

Comic disasters behind the scenes at
a funeral directors.
Occasionally amusing low comedy
based on the popular sit-com.

p: Michael Carreras for Hammer
w: Peter Lewis from his series
d: John Robins
ph: David Holmes
md: Philip Martell
ed: Archie Ludski
ad: Scott MacGregor

Bill Fraser, Raymond Huntley, David
Battley, John Ronane, Dennis Price,
Sue Lloyd, Richard Wattis, Roy
Kinnear

THESE ARE THE DAMNED see THE
DAMNED

THIRD PARTY RISK
GB 1955 70m bw

An American songwriter finds himself
accused of murder in London.
Same-as-usual murder mystery plot
with a better cast than it deserves.

p: Robert Dunbar for Exclusive
w/d: Daniel Birt
novel: Robert Chapman
ph: Jimmy Harvey
m: Michael Krein
ed: James Needs
ad: J. Elder Wills

Lloyd Bridges, Finlay Currie, Maureen
Swanson, Ferdy Mayne, Simone
Silva, George Woodbridge, Roger
Delgardo, Peter Dyneley

36 HOURS
GB 1953 84m bw

An American airman on leave in
London discovers that his wife has
gone missing and is later arrested for
her murder.
Tedious low budget mystery, of no
outstanding interest, despite the
imported star. Also known as TER-
ROR STREET.

p: Anthony Hinds for Exclusive
w: Steve Fisher
d: Montgomery Tully
ph: Walter Harvey
m: Ivor Slaney
ed: James Needs
ad: J. Elder Wills

cos: no credit given
sound: Bill Salter
ass d: Jimmy Sangster

Dan Duryea, Elsy Albin, John
Chandos, Kenneth Griffith, Ann
Gudrun, Jane Carr, Michael Golden

THREE STOPS TO MURDER see
BLOOD ORANGE

TICKET TO HAPPINESS
GB 1959 10m Eastmancolor

Little seen travelogue short.

p: Michael Carreras for Hammer

TILL DAWN US DO PART see
STRAIGHT ON TILL MORNING

TO HAVE AND TO HOLD
GB 1950 61m bw

Learning that he is dying, a country
gentleman makes plans for the future
happiness of his wife.
Stiff upper lip romantic melodrama,
not quite so bad as it sounds.

p: Anthony Hinds for Exclusive
w: Reginald Long, Godfrey Grayson
play: Lionel Browne
d: Godfrey Grayson
ph: Walter Harvey
md: Frank Spencer
ed: James Needs
ad: no credit given
sound: Edgar Vetter
2nd unit d: Derek Greene

Avis Scott, Patrick Barr, Robert Ayres,
Ellen Pollack, Harry Fine, Richard
Warner, Eunice Gayson

TO THE DEVIL... A DAUGHTER *
GB/Ger 1976 93m Technicolor

An occult writer protects a young girl
from Satanists.
Engagingly silly horror hokum which
moves fast enough to disguise its
far-fetched plot. Surprisingly, one of
only three Dennis Wheatley novels
adapted for the screen by Hammer,
the other two being THE DEVIL
RIDES OUT and THE LOST CONTI-
NENT.

p: Roy Skeggs for Hammer/EMI/Terra
Filmkunst
w: Christopher Wicking, John
Peacock
novel: Dennis Wheatley

d: PETER SYKES
ph: David Watkin
m: Paul Glass
md: Philip Martell
ed: John Trumper
pd: Don Picton
cos: Laura Nightingle
sp: Les Bowie
sound: Dennis Whitlock

Richard Widmark, CHRISTOPHER
LEE, Denholm Elliott, Natassja Kinski,
Honor Blackman, Anthony Valentine,
Derek Francis, Michael Goodliffe

TWINS OF EVIL *
GB 1971 87m Eastmancolor

One of a beautiful pair of twins staying with their puritanical uncle is
turned into a vampire by the evil
Count Karnstein. But which one?
Tolerable vampire yarn, part of
Hammer's Karnstein trilogy, the other
episodes being THE VAMPIRE
LOVERS and LUST FOR A VAMPIRE.
Moments of atmosphere, but on the
whole more style and pace would
have helped.

p: Harry Fine, Michael Style for
Hammer
w: Tudor Gates
d: John Hough
ph: Dick Bush
m: Harry Robinson
md: Philip Martell
ed: Spencer Reeve
ad: Roy Stannard
cos: Rosemary Burrows
sp/2nd unit d: Jack Mills
sound: Ron Barron, Ken Barker

Peter Cushing, Madeleine Collinson,
Mary Collinson, Dennis Price,
Kathleen Byron, Isobel Black, Damien
Thomas

THE TWO FACES OF DR JEKYLL *
GB 1960 88m Technicolor
Megascope

Dr Jekyll experiments with a potion
which separates good from evil and
turns him into a handsome sadist.
Promising variation on the old, old
story, with an unusual emphasis on
sex. Let down, however, by dull han-
dling and the wide screen, though
interesting moments survive. Also
known as HOUSE OF FRIGHT and
JEKYLL'S INFERNO.

p: Michael Carreras for Hammer
w: Wolf Mankowitz
novel: Robert Louis Stevenson
d: Terence Fisher
ph: Jack Asher
m/songs: Monty Norman, David Heneker
md: John Hollingsworth
ed: James Needs, Eric Boyd-Perkins
ad: Bernard Robinson
cos: Mayo
sound: Jock May
make-up: Roy Ashton
ch: Julie Mendez
sound ed: Archue Ludski

Paul Massie, Dawn Addams, Christopher Lee, David Kossoff, Francis de Wolff, Oliver Reed

THE UGLY DUCKLING
GB 1959 84m bw

Young Henry Jekyll experiments with his famous relative's potion and turns into Teddy Hyde.
Mildly amusing comic take on the Robert Louis Stevenson story.

p: Michael Carreras for Hammer
w: Sid Colin, Jack Davies
story: Sid Colin
d: Lance Comfort
ph: Michael Reed
m: Douglas Gamley
md: John Hollingsworth
ed: James Needs, John Dunsford
ad: Bernard Robinson

Bernard Bresslaw, Reginald Beckwith, Jon Pertwee, Maudie Edwards

THE UNHOLY FOUR see THE STRANGER CAME HOME

UP THE CREEK *
GB 1958 83m bw Hammerscope

The crew of a run down shore establishment try to hide their black market activities from their new commander.
Mildly amusing naval comedy with bright spots along the way. It proved popular enough to provoke a sequel, FURTHER UP THE CREEK, which appeared later the same year.

p: Henry Halsted for Exclusive/Byron
w/d: Val Guest
ph: Arthur Grant
m: Tony Lowry
md: Tony Fones

ed: Helen Wiggins
ad: Elven Webb, Ward Richards
sound: George Adams
cam op: Moray Grant

David Tomlinson, Peter Sellers, Wilfred Hyde White, Lionel Jeffries, Vera Day, Tom Gill, Sam Kydd, Michael Goodliffe, Reginald Beckwith, Patrick Cargill, David Lodge, Frank Pentigell, Liliane Scottane

VAMPIRE CIRCUS *
GB 1971 87m Eastmancolor

A cursed village is visited first by the plague and then a circus of vampires. Perhaps the liveliest of Hammer's later vampire sagas, with a few neat directorial touches, a stronger cast than usual and an impressive twelve minute pre-credit sequence which is a film in itself.

p: Wilbur Stark for Hammer
w: Judson Kinberg
d: ROBERT YOUNG
ph: Moray Grant
m: DAVID WHITAKER
md: Philip Martell
ed: Peter Musgrave
ad: Scott MacGregor
cos: Brian Owen-Smith
sp: Les Bowie
sound: Claude Hitchcock

Adrienne Corri, Laurence Payne, Thorley Walters, John Moulder Brown, Lynn Frederick, Elizabeth Seal, Robert Tayman, Robin Hunter, Dave Prowse, Robin Sachs, Lala Ward

THE VAMPIRE LOVERS
GB 1970 91m Movielab

A beautiful vampire insinuates herself into a nobleman's household and feeds off his impressionable daughter.
Despite a promising start, this is a slow and rather dull variation on CAMILLA, with the studio's old style sadly lacking. Part of the Karnstein trilogy, also see LUST FOR A VAMPIRE and TWINS OF EVIL.

p: Harry Fine, Michael Style for Hammer/American International
w: Tudor Gates, Harry Fine, Michael Style
novel: J. Sheridan Le Fanu

d: Roy Ward Baker
ph: Moray Grant
m: Harry Robinson
md: Philip Martell
ed: James Needs
ad: Scott MacGregor
cos: Brian Cox
sound: Claude Hitchcock, Tony Lumkin, Dennis Whitlock

Ingrid Pitt, Peter Cushing, Pippa Steele, Madeleine Smith, George Cole, Kate O'Mara, Dawn Addams, Jon Finch, Ferdy Mayne, Douglas Wilmer, Janet Key, John Forbes-Robertson

THE VENGEANCE OF SHE
GB 1968 101m Technicolor

A young woman finds herself possessed by the spirit of the dead Queen Ayesha.
Creaky follow up to SHE, with shoddy production values and little in the way of inspiration. The solid supporting cast is totally wasted.

p: Aida Young for Hammer/Warner/Pathe
w: Peter O'Donnell
d: Cliff Owen
ph: Wolfgang Suschitzky
m: Mario Nascimbene
md: Philip Martell
ed: Raymopnd Poulton
ad: Lionel Couch
cos: Carl Toms
sound: Bill Rowe, A. W. Lumkin

Olinka Berova, John Richardson, Edward Judd, Colin Blakely, Derek Godfrey, Jill Melford, Andre Morell, Noel Willman

THE VIKING QUEEN
GB 1967 91m Technicolor

In Roman Britain, a Viking queen has an affair with a Roman officer.
Inept and lamely-scripted piece of nonsense whose dialogue is totally and hilariously inappropriate to its period. Keep an eye out for the wrist watch!

p: John Temple-Smith for Hammer/Warner
w: Clarke Reynolds
d: Don Chaffey
ph: Stephen Dade
m: Gary Hughes
ed: James Needs
pd: George Provis

Don Murray, Carita, Donald Houston, Andrew Keir, Patrick Troughton, Adrienne Corri, Niall MacGinnis, Wilfred Lawson, Nicola Pagett

VILLAGE OF BRAY
GB 1951 11m bw

Travelogue short displaying the charms of the village of Bray, home of Hammer Films, on which count it is of passing interest.

p: Exclusive
no other credits available

VISA TO CANTON
GB 1961 75m Technicolor

Attempts are made to get a group of refugees out of Communist China. Adequate Cold War action thriller. Also known as PASSPORT TO CHINA.

p: Michael Carreras for Hammer/Swallow
w: Gordon Wellesley
d: Michael Carreras
ph: Arthur Grant
m: Edwin Astley
md: John Hollingsworth
ed: James Needs, Alfred Cox
ad: Bernard Robinson, Thomas Goswell

Richard Basehart, Lisa Gastoni, Eric Pohlmann, Athene Seyler, Bernard Cribbins, Marne Maitland, Burt Kouk

WATCH IT, SAILOR!
GB 1961 81m bw

A sailor finds his plans to marry disrupted when he is issued with a paternity suit.
Tame domestic comedy, a follow up to the rather more hilarious SAILOR, BEWARE! (aka PANIC IN THE PARLOR), successfully filmed by Romulus in 1956.

p: Maurice Cowan for Hammer/Columbia/Cormorant
exec p: Michael Carreras
w: Falkland Cary, Phillip King from their play
d: Wolf Rilla
ph: Arthur Grant
m: Douglas Gamley
md: John Hollingsworth
ed: James Needs, Alfred Cox
ad: Bernard Robinson, Don Mingaye

Dennis Price, Marjorie Rhodes, Liz Fraser, Vera Day, Irene Handl, John Meillon, Cyril Smith, Graham Stark

WE DO BELIEVE IN GHOSTS
GB 1947 36m bw

Documentary featurette about haunted historic buildings, whose ghostly theme was a presage of things to come.

p: Exclusive
d: Walter West

A WEEKEND WITH LULU
GB 1961 89m bw

Misadventures on a weekend jaunt. Sometimes lively comedy for the local market. Little revived though, even on television.

p: Ted Lloyd for Hammer
exec p: Michael Carreras
w: Ted Lloyd
story: Ted Lloyd, Val Valentine
d: John Paddy Carstairs
ph: Ken Hodges
m: Trevor H. Stanford
md: John Hollingsworth
ed: James Needs, Tom Simpson
ad: John Howell

Bob Monkhouse, Leslie Phillips, Alfred Marks, Irene Handl, Shirley Eaton, Kenneth Connor, Sid James

WHAT THE BUTLER SAW
GB 1950 61m bw

Little seen comedy featurette about which little is known

p: Anthony Hinds for Hammer/Exclusive
w: A. R. Rawlinson, E. J. Mason
story: Roger Good, Donald Good
d: Godfrey Grayson

Edward Rigby, Mercy Haystead, Michael Ward, Peter Burton, Henry Mollison, Anne Valery

WHEN DINOSAURS RULED THE EARTH
GB 1970 100m Technicolor

A prehistoric girl escapes sacrifice and befriends a small dinosaur. Childish but occasionally lively prehistoric nonsense, let down by its low budget and some poorly integrated studio work

p: Aida Young for Hammer/Warner
treatment: J. G. Ballard
w/d: Val Guest
ph: Dick Bush
m: Mario Nascimebe
md: Philip Martel
ed: Peter Curran
ad: John Blezar
cos: Carl Toms
sp: Jim Danforth, Allan Bryce, Roger Dicken, Brian Johncock
sound: Kevin Sutton
2nd unit ph: Johnny Cabrera
narrator: Patrick Allen

Victoria Vetri, Patrick Allen, Robin Hawdon, Imogen Hassall, Patrick Holt, Sean Caffrey, Magda Konopka, Carol Hawkins, Drewe Henley

WHISPERING SMITH HITS LONDON
GB 1951 82m bw

An American detective investigating an apparent suicide is led to suspect it was murder.
Better than average programmer, a follow-up (minus star Alan Ladd) to Paramount's WHISPERING SMITH (1948). Also known as WHISPERING SMITH vs. SCOTLAND YARD.

p: Anthony Hinds for Exclusive
w: John Gilling
story: Frank Spearman
d: Francis Searle
ph: Walter Harvey
m: Frank Spencer
ed: James Needs

Richard Carlson, Greta Gynt, Herbert Lom, Dora Bryan, Rona Anderson, Reginald Beckwith, Alan Wheatley

WHISPERING SMITH vs SCOTLAND YARD see WHISPERING SMITH HITS LONDON

WHO KILLED VAN LOON?
GB 1948 48m bw

Little seen crime featurette about which little is known.

p: Exclusive

Raymond Lovell, Kay Bannerman, Robert Wyndham

WINGS OF DANGER
GB 1952 75m bw

When his buddy goes missing, a pilot

investigates and uncovers a smuggling ring.
Muddled lower berth thriller in the standard Exclusive manner, wasting a better cast than usual.

p: Anthony Hinds for Exclusive
w: John Gilling
novel: Elleston Trevor, Packham Webb
d: Terence Fisher
ph: Walter Harvey
m: Malcolm Arnold
ed: James Needs
ad: Andrew Mazzei
sound: Bill Salter
ass d: Jimmy Sangster
casting: Michael Carreras

Zachary Scott, Robert Beatty, Kay Kendall, Diane Cilento, Colin Tapley, Naomi Chance

THE WITCHES
GB 1966 91m Technicolor

Having been subjected to witchcraft in Africa, a schoolteacher retreats to a quiet English village - where she discovers more of the same.
Genteel horror story with little in the way of surprise, save that more wasn't made of the situations available. Also known as THE DEVIL'S OWN.

p: Anthony Nelson Keys for Hammer/Warner
w: Nigel Kneale
novel: Peter Curtis
d: Cyril Frankel
ph: Arthur Grant
m: Richard Rodney Bennett
md: Philip Martell
ed: James Needs, Chris Barnes
pd: Bernard Robinson
cos: Molly Arbuthnot
sound: Ken Rawkins
ch: Denys Palmer

Joan Fontaine, Kay Walsh, Alec McCowen, Gwen Ffrangcon Davies, Ingrid Brett, John Colin, Martin Stephens, Carmel McSharry, Leonard

Rossiter, Michele Dotrice
WOMEN WITHOUT MEN
GB 1956 68m bw

Life behind bars at a women's prison. Better than average support.

p: Anthony Hinds for Exclusive
w: Richard Landau
d: Elmo Williams
ph: Walter Harvey
m: Leonard Salzedo
md: John Hollingsworth
ed: James Needs
ad: no credit given
cos: Molly Arbuthnot
sound: Bill Sweeney
production manager: Jimmy Sangster

Beverley Michaels, Joan Rice, Thora Hird, Avril Angers, Paul Carpenter, Hermione Baddeley, Bill Shine, Gordon Jackson, David Lodge

X - THE UNKNOWN *
GB 1956 81m bw

Whilst on training exercises in Scotland, the army unearths a strange force which feeds off radioactive energy.
Overpadded variation on THE QUATERMASS EXPERIMENT, let down by poor effects work and a restricted budget. Sci-fi fans may enjoy the cliches.

p: Anthony Hinds for Hammer/Exclusive
w: Jimmy Sangster
d: Leslie Norman
ph: Gerald Gibbs
m: James Bernard
md: John Hollingsworth
ed: James Needs
ad: Bernard Robinson
cos: Molly Arbuthnot
sp: Jack Curtis, Les Bowie
sound: Jock May

Dean Jagger, Edward Chapman, Leo McKern, William Lucas, John Harvey, Peter Hammond, Michael Ripper,

Anthony Newley, Michael Brook, Marianne Brauns, Fraser Hines

YESTERDAY'S ENEMY
GB 1959 95m bw Megascope

Wartime drama involving the takeover of a Burmese village. Adequately made exploits in a familiar vein, with an element of mystery thown in for good measure.

p: T.S.Lyndon-Haynes for Hammer/Columbia
w: Peter R. Newman from his TV play
d: Van Guest
ph: Arthur Grant
m: none
ed: James Needs, Alfred Cox
ad: Bernard Robinson

Stanley Baker, Guy Rolfe, Leo McKern, Gordon Jackson, Philip Ahn, Percy Herbert, Bryan Forbes, David Lodge, David Oxley, Richard Passco, Russell Waters

YOGA AND THE AVERAGE MAN
GB 1951 26m bw

Second follow up to *Yoga and You* (also see *Keep Fit with Yoga*). That Exclusive were able to extract three films from this subject must surely indicate *something*.

p: Exclusive
no other credits available

YOGA AND YOU
GB 1950 26m bw

Documentary featurette, long unseen, on the art and benefits of yoga. The results must have been hilarious. It was followed the following year by *Keep Fit with Yoga* and *Yoga and the Average Man*.

p: Exclusive
no other credits available

hammer on tv

Forays into television by Hammer and about Hammer have been numerous over the years. The following is a chronological guide to the programmes available.

TALES OF FRANKENSTEIN
US 1958 1x50m bw

Aborted attempt by Screen Gems (a subsidiary of Columbia Pictures) to make a TV series based round the character of Baron Frankenstein. The pilot was made but deemed unsatisfactory by all concerned. Plans for the TV series were thus scrapped and the pilot episode never shown.

THE FACE IN THE TOMBSTONE MIRROR

Frankenstein transplants a brain from one of his patients into the creature he has been working on in his laboratory.

p: Curt Siodmak for Screen Gems/Hammer
w/d: Curt Siodmak

Anton Diffring, Don Megowan.

JOURNEY TO THE UNKNOWN *
GB 1968 17x50m colour

The aborted TALES OF FRANKEN-STEIN aside, this was Hammer's first official foray into television. A fairly smooth and professional collection of stories with either horror or supernatural elements, remembered chiefly for its opening title sequence, filmed at a deserted Battersea fun fair, accompanied by Harry Robinson's haunting theme music. It proved to be a good training ground for many of Hammer's future feature directors, Alan Gibson and Peter Sasdy among them. Sadly, it is too infrequently repeated.

p: Anthony Hinds for Hammer/ABC/TCF
exec p: Joan Harrison, Norman Lloyd
story ed: John Gould
theme m: Harry Robinson
md: Philip Martell

EVE

w: Michael Ashe, Paul Wheeler
story: John Collier
d: Robert Stevens

Carol Lynley, Dennis Waterman

THE NEW PEOPLE

Two new residents at an isolated village community discover themselves to be pawns in a deadly game.

w: Oscar Millard, John Gould
story: Charles Beaumont
d: Peter Sasdy
m: John Patrick Scott

Robert Reed, Jennifer Hilary, Patrick Allen, Milo O'Shea, Adrienne Corri, Melissa Stribling, Damien Thomas

JANE BROWN'S BODY

A sucide victim is brought back to life with a new wonder drug.

w: Anthony Skene
story: Cornell Woolrich
d: Alan Gibson
m: Bob Leaper

Stephanie Powers, David Buch, Alan MacNaughton, Sarah Lawson

INDIAN SPIRIT GUIDE

A private detecive attempts to exploit a woman trying to get in contact with her dead husband via a series of mediums.

w: Robert Bloch
d: Roy Ward Baker
m: Basil Kirchin

Julie Harris, Tom Adams, Tracy Reed, Catherine Lacey, Marne Maitland

MISS BELLE

w: Sarett Rudley
story: Charles Beaumont
d: Robert Stevens

George Maharis, Barbara Jeford

DO ME A FAVOUR - KILL ME

An alcoholic actor arranges for his agent to kill him so that his wife can collect on his life insurance - then changes his mind.

w: Stanley Miller
story: Frederick Rawlings
d: Gerry O'Hara
m: John Patrick Scott

Joseph Cotten, Judy Parfitt, Douglas Wilmer, Kenneth Haig, Joyce Blair

PAPER DOLLS

A schoolteacher discovers that one of his pupils is one of four identical brothers with deadly telepathic powers.
w: Oscar Millar
story: L. P. Davies
d: James Hill
m: David Lindup

Michael Tolan, Nanette Newman, Barnaby Shaw, John Welsh, Roderick Shaw

GIRL OF MY DREAMS

w: Robert Bloch, Michael J. Bird
story: Richard Matheson
d: Peter Sasdy

Michael Callan, Judy Lord

MATAKITAS IS COMING

A magazine writer finds herself transported back in time where she meets the serial killer whose life she has been researching.

w: Robert Heverley
d: Michael Lindsay-Hogg
m: Norman Kaye

Vera Miles, Gay Hamilton, Leon Lissek, Dermot Walsh

SOMEWHERE IN A CROWD

A train crash victim keeps seeing those who died in the accident, and comes to believe that their presence heralds another disaster.

w: Michael J. Bird
d: Alan Gibson
m: Harry Robinson

POOR BUTTERFLY

w: Jeremy Paul
story: William Abney
d: Alan Gibson

Chad Everett, Edward Fox

THE BECKONING FAIR ONE

A young man becomes obsessed with a portrait of a beautiful woman who was killed during the blitz.

w: William Woods, John Gould
story: Oliver Onions
d: Don Chaffey
m: Harry Robinson

Robert Lansing, Gabrielle Drake, John Fraser, Larry Noble, Gretchen Franklin

STRANGER IN THE FAMILY

The son of a radiation victim discovers that he has special powers, which several people attempt to exploit.

w: David Campton
d: Peter Duffel
m: David Lindup

Janice Rule, Maurice Kaufman, Anthony Corlan, Jane Hylton, Phil Brown

LAST VISITOR

Holidaying in a quiet seaside town, a young woman discovers her landlady to be a lunatic, obsessed by her dead husband.

w: Alfred Shaughnessey
d: Don Chaffey
m: David Lindup

Patty Duke, Kay Walsh, Geoffrey Bayldon, Joan Newell, Blake Butler

KILLING BOTTLE

Two brothers who love and hate animals with equal measure fall foul of eachother.

w: Julian Bond
story: L. P. Hartley
d: John Gibson
m: Bernard Ebbinghouse

Roddy McDowall, Ingrid Brett, Barry Evans, John Rudling, William Marlow

THE MADISON EQUATION

Husband and wife scientists find their lives in peril from the computer they have invented, which seems to have a mind of its own.

w: Michael J. Bird
d: Rex Firkin
m: Basil Kirchin, Jack Nathan

Barbara Bel Geddes, Allan Cuthbertson, Sue Lloyd, Paul Daneman, Jack Hedley

ONE ON AN ISLAND

w: Oscar Millard
d: Noel Howard

Brandon de Wilde, Suzanna Leigh

HAMMER HOUSE OF HORROR *
GB 1980 13x50m colour

Perhaps Hammer's best foray into television, this collection of horror stories made use of such themes as witchcraft, lycanthropy and possession to general good use and utilised a good deal of past Hammer talent, including Peter Cushing, James Bernard, Alan Gibson and Robert Young, etc.

p: Brian Lawrence, Roy Skeggs for Hammer/ATV
md: Philip Martell

Episode titles:

RUDE AWAKENING

A series of nightmares involving the murder of his wife and a mysterious country house haunt an estate agent.

w: Gerald Savory
d: Alan Gibson
m: Paul Patterson

Denholm Elliott, James Laurenson, Pat Heywood, Eleanor Summerfield

GROWING PAINS

After the death of their son, a scientist and his wife adopt another young boy, who becomes possessed by his predecessor.

w: Nicholas Palmer
d: Frances Megahy
m: John McCabe

Barbara Kellerman, Gary Bond, Norman Beaton, Tariq Yunus

SILENT SCREAM

Out of prison, an habitual criminal goes to work for his prisoner visitor only to find himself the captive of a lunatic ex-Nazi.

w: Francis Essex
d: Alan Gibson

m: Leonard Salzedo

Peter Cushing, Brian Cox, Elaine Donnelly, Robin Browne

THE HOUSE THAT BLED TO DEATH

Strange events lead a family to believe their new house to be haunted.

w: David Lloyd
d: Tom Clegg
m: James Bernard

Nicholas Ball, Rachel Davies, Milton Johns, Brian Croucher

CHARLIE BOY

A businessman uses an African fetish doll to extract revenge on those associates who have let him down, only to succumb to the doll's powers himself.

w: Bernie Cooper, Francis Megahy
d: Robert Young
m: David Lindup

Leigh Lawson, Angela Bruce, Marius Goring, David Healey

CHILDREN OF THE FULL MOON

Stranded travellers find refuge at an isolated house, one of whose inhabitants proves to be a werewolf.

w: Murray Smith
d: Tom Clegg
m: Paul Patterson

Diana Dors, Christopher Cazenove, Celia Gregory, Robert Urquhart, Jacob Witkin

THE CARPATHIAN EAGLE

A policeman invetigating a series of murders in which the victims' hearts have been torn out discovers them to have been the work of a schitzophreic authoress.

w: Bernie Cooper, Francis Megahy
d: Francis Megahy
m: Wilfred Josephs

Anthony Valentine, Suzanne Danielle, Sian Phillips, Jonathan Kent

THE 13TH REUNION

A lady journalist investigates a mysterious health farm and gets more than she bargained for when its members turn out to be cannibals

THE TWO FACES OF EVIL

A family's holiday turns into a nightmare when they pick up a hitchhiker.

GUARDIAN OF THE ABYSS

A lady antiques dealer buys a mirror only to discover it has evil powers.

WITCHING TIME

A seventeenth-century witch returns to the farmhouse where she was born and gives its present residents a hellish time.

VISITOR FROM THE GRAVE

A young woman goes to a seance to get in touch with her dead fiance, who was burned to death in a car accident.

THE MARK OF SATAN

A mortuary worker becomes convinced that he has been chosen to be a disciple of the Devil.

HAMMER HOUSE OF MYSTERY AND SUSPENSE
GB 1984 13x74m colour TVM

Disappointing - in fact frequently dismal - movie-length collection of twist-in-the-tail thrillers, produced by Hammer in association with Twentieth Century Fox. The material might have made a passable half-hour series, but is stretched beyond snapping point, whilst the production values are sub-standard at best, despite the involvement of such Hammer directors as Val Guest and Peter Sasdy. Also known as FOX MYSTERY THEATRE.

Episode titles (all of which can be found in the film guide index):

CZECH MATE
SWEET SCENT OF DEATH

A DISTANT SCREAM
THE LATE NANCY IRVING
IN POSSESSION
BLACK CARRION
LAST VIDEO AND TESTAMENT
MARK OF THE DEVIL
THE CORVINI INHERITANCE
PAINT ME A MURDER
CHILD'S PLAY
AND THE WALL CAME
TUMBLING DOWN
TENNIS COURT

THE STUDIO THAT DRIPPED
BLOOD *
GB 1987 1x50m colour

Fortieth anniversary tribute to
Hammer Films, featuring interviews with Hammer regulars and
clips from the films themselves.
Moments of interest, but much
more could have been made of the
opportunity available, fifty minutes
not being long enough to do justice to a forty year history.

p: Nick Jones, David Thompson
for BBC
narrator: Charles Gray

PETER CUSHING - ONE WAY
TICKET TO HOLLYWOOD *
GB 1989 74m colour

Lengthy, entertaining interview (by

Dick Vosbergh) with Peter
Cushing, interspersed with film
clips. Of obvious interest for his
Hammer work.

p: Gillian Garrow for Tyburn
exec p: Kevin Francis
d: Alan Bell
ph: Freddie Francis
m: James Bernard, Malcolm
Williamson
md: Philip Martell
ed: David Elliott
sound: John Murphy, Rupert
Scrivener

THE WORLD OF HAMMER *
GB 1990 26x25m colour

BEST OF BRITISH-style compilation series whose episodes concentrate on various aspects of
Hammer Films. Of occasional
interest, though some of the programmes are remarkably thin and
the title theme is on the naff side.
The programme didn't air in Britain
until 1994 when it appeared in a
late night slot on Channel Four.

p: Ashley Sidaway, Robert Sidaway
for Hammer/Best of British
exec p: John Thompson
theme m: Brian Bennett
ed: Ashley Sidaway
narrator: Oliver Reed

Episode titles:
THE WORLD OF HAMMER -
FORTY YEARS OF HAMMER
FILMS
FRANKENSTEIN
DRACULA AND THE UNDEAD
COSTUME ADVENTURE
HAMMER STARS -
PETER CUSHING
SCIENCE FICTION
WEREWOLVES, MUMMIES AND
ZOMBIES
WAR
HAMMER STARS 2 -
CHRISTOPHER LEE
LANDS BEFORE TIME -
PREHISTORIC ADVENTURE
COMEDY
THRILLERS
MONSTERS
HEROES
HEROINES
GOOD vs. EVIL - THE CHURCH IN
HAMMER FILMS
WICKED WOMEN
PURSUERS AND PURSUED -
CHASE AND DETECTION
RADIO AND TELEVISION
SPIN-OFFS
VAMP - CARMILLA AND OTHER
FEMALE VAMPIRES
IN THE FAMILY -
STUDIES OF FAMILY LIFE
THE OCCULT AND
DEMONOLOGY
MIND GAMES - PSYCHOLOGICAL

DRAMA
HAMMER IN THE FAR EAST
HENCHMEN
THE SUPERNATURAL

FLESH AND BLOOD - THE HAM-
MER HERITAGE OF HORROR *
US 1994 1x90m colour

Documentary on the history of
Hammer films, featuring a good
selection of clips and interviews
with many of Hammer's old guard,
let down by poor picture quality,
sound and too hurried a pace
(three one-hour programmes
would have done better justice to
the material). Nevertheless, plenty
of interest for devotees, particularly since it was the last thing Peter
Cushing worked in.

w/p/d: Ted Newsom
narrators: Christopher Lee, Peter
Cushing

Proposed television projects, never
realised, include:
THE HAUNTED HOUSE OF
HAMMER
MOULIN ROUGE
THE HAMMER MYSTERY
THEATRE
THE PROGRESS OF JULIUS
RAFFLES - GENTLEMAN CROOK
TOWER OF LONDON

index

Introductory Statement

The index is compiled on a word-by-word basis, eg *The Bank Messenger Mystery* precedes Bankhead, Tallulah. Location references in bold print refer to illustrations. Film and other titles are in italics. Unless there is a note in brackets, all titles are film titles.

Due to unavoidable restrictions on space, the index cannot cite every film or person mentioned in passing. Priority has been given to Hammer's productions and to those persons most directly involved with them. The index only covers the narrative section of the book, the rest being effectively self-indexing.

Subheadings are arranged chronologically rather than alphabetically to match the narrative structure of the book.